Proclaiming the Gospel to Zion

A Textbook on Jewish Evangelism

Mitch Triestman

LIFELINE PUBLICATIONS

9 Primrose Lane
Levittown, PA 19054
foibs@aol.com

215-945-3277

Unless otherwise noted, all Scripture references are taken from the King James version of the Bible.

Proclaiming the Gospel to Zion

Author: Mitch Triestman

Copyright © 2016 by Mitch Triestman

Printed in the United States of America for

Lifeline Publications
19 Primrose Lane
Levittown, PA 19054
215-945-3277

Printed by H.G. Publishing
Langhorne, Pennsylvania 19047

The views expressed in works published by
H.G. Publishing are those of the author.
The author is solely responsible for the contents.

Library of Congress Control Number: 2016949339

ISBN 978-0-997888-0-5

ACKNOWLEDGMENTS

God has given me the ability to teach His word to the believer and to proclaim it to the lost. I have learned, however, that just because you can speak publicly, that doesn't mean you are gifted in the area of writing. That was a painful lesson to learn, and the patient believers who taught me the lesson are the ones who worked long and hard hours bringing my ranting into a format that could be read and understood.

I want to express my sincerest gratitude to Carol Popkave, Linda Beauchamp and Tracy Higley, the faithful Christians who labored for the Lord in editing and correcting and rewording this manuscript. I thank God for their talents and for their willingness to serve the King.

FOREWORD

by Tom Huckle

Director, The Evangelization Society of Phila., Inc.
Hananeel House
Jewish Mission in Philadelphia since 1911

God told the Israelites that if they would ever worship "that which is not God" and in turn "move Him to jealousy" (Deu 32:21a), He promised that He would then "move them to jealousy" via "those which are not a people" (i.e. the Gentiles, Deu 32:21b). Paul very likely had this reference in mind when he wrote to the saints of Rome: "I say then, have they" [the Jewish people] "stumbled that they should fall? God forbid: but rather through their fall salvation is come unto the Gentiles, for to provoke them to jealousy" (Rom 11:11). God in a very special way desires to use Gentile believers to be effective witnesses to His people. By giving us the Messiah that rightly belongs to the Jewish people, God can use us as instruments to provoke them to jealousy. The questions that believers must ask themselves are: Am I effectively reaching Jewish people with the gospel? Am I a tool fitted for the master's use?

Since Jewish Evangelism is not an option, but a mandate for both the Jewish and Gentile Christian alike, then the answers to the questions must be "yes", and worthy of our time to find out how. There have been times when I found myself looking for an effective way to just get the entire gospel message out, let alone see fruitful results! Did you or do you presently ever find yourself in contact with Jewish people, and feel that you want to tell them about the Lord; but you just don't know how to get started? Perhaps you mustered up the courage once to say something about the Lord, but ended that conversation by saying: "that's a really good question -I'll have to get back to you with that later." The fact that I have been a volunteer, part-time and full-time missionary to Jewish people since 1976, makes me somewhat of an expert on mistakes you can make when witnessing to Jewish people. In nearly every church in which I have spoken, inevitably I meet believers who are looking for advice on how they might be able to effectively and sensitively present the gospel to a Jewish friend, neighbor, co-worker or relative.

The one person you would want to write a source book on any given subject would be the person most proficient in that field! As far as I am concerned, the author of this book, Mitch Triestman, is without a doubt, the best one-on-one missionary to Jewish people that I have ever met. Mitch presently serves as a missionary with Friends of Israel Gospel Ministries and he teaches a course in Jewish Evangelism at the Institute of Jewish Studies at Philadelphia College of Bible. My relationship with the author started in 1976 as his missionary trainee at Chosen People Ministries. I lived first hand some of the experiences that Mitch shares with you in this work. The Lord richly blessed me and you will be too as you learn what Mitch shares about understanding Jewish sensitivities. He'll give you some provocative answers to some of the most difficult objections to the gospel message that you'll ever encounter. Far more importantly however, I trust that as you read this book's contents you will have an encounter with the heart of this writer. Without ever having to verbalize it, Mitch has taught me by his example that the most important ingredient necessary in reaching Jewish people with the gospel is to love them. Knowing the best terminology to use when sharing the gospel with Jewish people is important, and being able to handle Jewish objections correctly is very helpful, but there is no substitute for a genuine love of Jewish people. They have no defense prepared for love! It's not something you can fake -it has to be real -and I can verify that this author's love for Jewish people is very real.

The first day that I started as a full-time missionary, Mitch Triestman drove me to a Jewish cemetery in Philadelphia. We got out of the car and walked up to the fence. I couldn't help but notice the many tombstones with common Jewish last names; many had the star of David on them. At that point Mitch asked me a question that I'll never forget! He said, "Tom, how many of these Jewish people do you think died without knowing the Lord?" It was if a magnet drew my eyes and now my heart with them back to gaze at the tombstones once again. I shuddered at the very thought of what his words meant. At the same time however, I suddenly found myself feeling very fortunate to be saved. Without even waiting for my answer (I was speechless anyhow), Mitch then turned to me and said, "Well, then I guess we still have a lot of work to do." Yes, we do Mitch!

TABLE OF CONTENTS

SECTION ONE
JEWISH EVANGELISM

INTRODUCTION

Gil Singer, a fellow missionary with Friends of Israel (F.O.I.) coined the verb "to mish." A Jewish missionary ought to know how to mish. After all, that's what a Jewish missionary does. The reason a new term has been employed is because the job of a missionary is complex. Bible colleges and seminaries don't teach you how to mish. Church leaders, therefore, don't know how to go about reaching the Jewish community. If you can't learn how to mish in church, Bible college, or seminary then where do you learn?

There are various methods of learning as you go -"OJT" (on the job training, for the civilians amongst us). I'm most familiar with two possibilities. The long way is to grow up in a Jewish home, get saved, and then learn evangelistic techniques in Bible college and seminary. Then you worship in a local church for twenty years and attempt to apply various programs of evangelism within that local church. After twenty years, if you haven't become totally frustrated, you will begin to learn what works and what doesn't, and you will know how to mish. The shorter method is simply to enroll in a course at The Institute of Jewish Studies (IJS) and we, by the grace of God, will teach you how.

This book has been designed to be the textbook for the course in Jewish evangelism at IJS. Everything in this book is designed for dual usage. First, that you might employ the information into your personal life, that you might become an effective evangel, by lip and by life to both Jew and Gentile, as God opens doors of witness to you. Second, that you might train others to do the work of evangelism, that wherever the Lord calls you to serve, you might be used of him to disciple others, that they might learn to mish.

ONE

The Biblical Mandate

The Biblical Basis for Jewish Evangelism

"For I am not ashamed of the gospel of Christ; for it is the power of God unto salvation to everyone that believeth; to the Jew first, and also to the Greek" (Romans 1:16).

Several members of an Evangelical Church developed a burden to reach out to the Jewish community, but I was astonished to discover that the pastor of that church, a very gracious and caring man, cared little for Jewish outreach. The pastor did not believe in the command of reaching the Jew first. His reluctance made it impossible for him and other church members to encourage the folks of that community.

We must realize that he is not alone in his beliefs. There are many godly leaders who hold positions distinct from ours in the area of Jewish evangelism. I suppose that in order to establish the requirement of reaching the Jew first, some would insist that we begin by substantiating Scriptures' requirement of any kind of evangelism. The pastors and churches we will be serving are already convinced of the Gospel call. We need only to establish two facts: (1) the Gospel is to the Jew also, and (2) the Scriptures do indeed give the instruction to reach the Jew first.

The Great Commission

Matthew 28:19-20 reads: "*Go ye therefore, and teach <u>all nations</u> [my emphasis], baptizing them in the name of the Father, and of the Son, and of the Holy Ghost: Teaching them to observe all things whatsoever I have commanded you: and, lo, I am with you alway, [even] unto the end of the world. Amen.*" Does not the term "all nations" include Israel? Certainly, all means all, and all includes Israel. And yet as I travel from church to church there are numerous evangelical ministries that have no outreach to Jewish people whatsoever.

Evangelical churches usually fall into two categories. The first category includes those who have chosen to take the responsibility of reaching the world. These churches frequently have very impressive missionary budgets, and even the smaller churches will often pride themselves on the percentage of their income that is committed to missions. I have, over the years, heard many a pastor say as he looks at his missionary board, "Not bad for a little church, eh?" I have been amazed at how frequently there is not a single Jewish ministry or missionary represented on that board. I usually ask about it, and often I'm not invited back. However, on occasion we have been used of the Lord to create a burden for Jewish outreach in that church.

The second category of evangelical churches care little for the world. They see their responsibility as reaching the community first, basing their methods on Acts 1:8, *But ye shall receive power, after that the Holy Ghost is come upon you: and ye shall be witnesses unto me both in Jerusalem, and in all Judaea, and in Samaria, and unto the uttermost part of the earth*. They see Jerusalem as symbolic for their community, and before they give or go or pray for world evangelism they emphasize reaching the neighborhood. These churches often have large bus ministries, Christian schools, and evangelical programs designed to reach the lost. But there are usually no programs designed to reach out to the Jewish people, who are often prevalent in their community. The norm is to ignore those Jews who are in their vicinity.

In Matthew chapter 10:1-15, the disciples were instructed to go to the Jew only. Jesus is very specific in his mandate. The disciples were to bring this message exclusively to the lost sheep of the house of Israel, and to no other. In the "Great Commission," the disciples are actually being recommissioned. They are given a new message, and now they are being sent to other nations also. The Gospel wasn't to include Israel as an afterthought, the Gospel was to include the other nations, as well as Israel.

The Great Commitment

In 2 Corinthians 5:19, we read how the Lord committed unto us the ministry of reconciliation. In Hightstown, New Jersey we were privileged to see forty-five Jewish people respond to the Gospel. This marvelous movement of the Spirit of God, however, was not appreciated by one local pastor. The Jewish community raised up a protest, saying that evangelism is a form of anti-Semitism. There was a great deal of opposition and modernist churches sided with and added to the rhetoric of the Rabbis. This one local pastor had no heart for the conflict. He preferred a peaceful path and chose not to cooperate with the Gospel. I heard him say things like, "It's unbecoming to single out the Jewish people for the purpose of evangelism. The Jewish people are decent enough, and they pray to the same God we do, why do we need to persist in converting them?" I was shocked to hear these things from a brother in Christ and a pastor. Over the years, I've grown accustomed to it. If you pursue Jewish missions you will hear more, and you will hear worse.

In 2 Corinthians 5:19, the word translated "committed" means he placed that ministry of reconciliation in us. Does that mean that the desire to reconcile men to God is in our souls? I don't know. But it seems to me that many of us have lost sight of both the commission and the commitment to the lost. Certainly that is true when it comes to our commitment to Israel.

There are those Christians who think that being Jewish assures one a place in heaven and that Jews are not in need of the Gospel. One noted evangelist has been quoted as saying "The Jewish people have a relationship to God through the law of God as given through Moses."[1] I've met many religious Jewish persons over the

---

[1] John Hague, *The Liberty Flame*, vol. 23 no 402

years. I have never found one who was not in need of reconciliation. I recently was speaking with a practicing orthodox man who admitted to me that when he spoke about believing in God, he meant that he believed in the intellectual possibility of God.

There is a great difference between the belief of religion and the faith of relationship. Years ago, we were conducting an outreach at Temple University. In those days Temple U was the quintessential, spiritually dead campus. Often we found ourselves resorting to drastic activities to stir up some spiritual interest. To advertise a multimedia presentation on life after death, we borrowed a coffin and brought it into the student activities center. It wasn't long before we noticed a distinction between the way Gentiles and Jews reacted to the presence of the coffin outside the cafeteria door. The Gentiles, for the most part, were rather unimpressed, but the Jewish students, by contrast, were very upset by the spectacle.

The Jewish students were visibly shaken by the coffin. Some were afraid of it, and all were disturbed by it. After observing the phenomenon repeat itself several times, we asked a Rabbinical student to stand by us to see if he also noticed the different way the various students responded to the reminder of death we had brought on the campus. It didn't take him long to recognize the same curious thing that we had perceived. We asked him if he had any explanation. He reflected for a moment and said, "The Yiddin* are afraid of death, the Goyim* are not." In the ensuing conversation, my friend said something that I will never forget. "The Goyim believe in Jesus and believe they are going to heaven. I, as religious as I am, have no hope." My friend never became a Rabbi. Today he is a dentist and is still a pious, practicing Jew. A pious, practicing, hopeless Jew. Jewish people are in need of the ministry of reconciliation, the ministry that God has committed unto us. *"For the love of Christ constraineth us; because we thus judge, that if one died for all, then were all dead"* -even the religious ones.

---

* see glossary of terms

14

Anti-Semitism is allowing pious people to go on unconverted and unchanged by the Gospel. People who are decent and who attempt to pray to the same God are in need of the ministry that God has placed in us, and that is why we are persisting to reach them.

The Biblical Imperative for Jewish Evangelism

When I first made application to a Jewish mission, I was asked what my position was on the phrase in Romans 1:16, "*to the Jew first*". At that time, I had just graduated from Bible college and probably felt like most Christians, that Romans was describing the historical progression of the Gospel. It seemed so illogical to prioritize a small minority before the vast billions of lost souls. God is no respecter of persons, and God is not willing that any should perish. I expected that my understanding of the verse would disqualify me from serving in Jewish missions, and was delighted to discover that the mission was big enough to tolerate my views and gracious enough to allow me to grow into the truth.

We spoke of an earlier commission in Matthew chapter ten: *And when he had called unto [him] his twelve disciples, he gave them power [against] unclean spirits, to cast them out, and to heal all manner of sickness and all manner of disease. Now the names of the twelve apostles are these; The first, Simon, who is called Peter, and Andrew his brother; James [the son] of Zebedee, and John his brother; Philip, and Bartholomew; Thomas, and Matthew the publican; James [the son] of Alphaeus, and Lebbaeus, whose surname was Thaddaeus; Simon the Canaanite, and Judas Iscariot, who also betrayed him. These twelve Jesus sent forth, and commanded them, saying, <u>Go not into the way of the Gentiles, and into [any] city of the Samaritans enter ye not: But go rather to the lost sheep of the house of Israel.</u> And as ye go, preach, saying, The kingdom of heaven is at hand. Heal the sick, cleanse the lepers, raise the dead, cast out devils: freely ye have received, freely give. Provide neither gold, nor silver, nor brass in your purses, Nor scrip for [your] journey, neither two coats, neither shoes, nor yet staves: for the workman is worthy of his meat. And into whatsoever city or town ye shall enter, enquire* *who in it is worthy; and there abide till ye go thence. And when ye come into an house, salute it. And if the house be worthy, let your peace come upon it: but if it be not worthy, let your peace return to you. And whosoever shall not receive you, nor hear your words, when ye depart out of that house or city, shake off the dust of your feet. Verily I say unto you, It shall be more tolerable for the land of Sodom and Gomorrha in the day of judgment, than for that city.*

If that commission were ours, we wouldn't be permitted to preach to anyone but the Jews. The message they were to proclaim is *"the kingdom of God is at hand."* That is not the message of today, and it has not been the message of Christendom since the time of Matthew 10. To attempt to squeeze the Gospel from that message both invalidates the *"kingdom of God "* and does disservice to the message of eternal life.

If Matthew chapter ten is not our commission, then how are we to know if Matthew 28 belongs to us? I suppose that there would be those among us who really don't want to know. At least some of us behave that way. Being sent out by Jesus is a great honor. Being sent out with this task is also a great responsibility. In Matthew 10, the scriptures limit the commission with the words *"these twelve Jesus sent forth."* In Matthew 28, no such limitation occurs. The commission here is directly linked to the power that Jesus has with the phrase *"all authority is given unto me."* In Acts 1:8, the Scripture again relates the witness to the power *"But ye shall receive power, after that the Holy Ghost is come upon you: and ye shall be witnesses unto me both in Jerusalem, and in all Judaea, and in Samaria, and unto the uttermost part of the earth."* The word for power in Acts is referring to the Holy Spirit. The Lord has empowered believers to proclaim the Gospel. We still see believers being empowered today. Where the power of the Holy Spirit is, that is where the witness is. When we see the witness, we know that the empowered witness was commissioned by the Lord.

In Matthew 28, Jesus concludes the commission with the encouragement of *"Lo, I am with you alway, [even] unto the end of the world."* The end of the world means to the end of the age. This commission of power is to all believers throughout this age. The commission is extended to the end of the age. That resolves any doubts about the commission being temporary or partial.

The message has changed from Matthew chapter ten, and the recipients of the message have changed, as well. From being an exclusively Jewish message, Jesus now sends the disciples to declare the new proclamation to the Gentiles, as well as the Jews. We can conclude from Matthew 28 that the Scriptures do teach evangelism for today, and that evangelism includes all nations, and all nations includes the Jews. "The Jews are still God's Chosen People," Deuteronomy 7:6, and "God still loves Israel."[2]

The motivation we have to reach the Jewish people is not based on personal experience. We believe that reaching the Jews is a Biblical Command -a command that has been largely ignored by the Church, to great detriment. In Romans 1:16, we read, *"For I am not ashamed of the gospel of Christ: for it is the power of God unto salvation to every one that believeth; to the Jew first, and also to the Greek."*

16 Ου γαρ επαισχυνομαι το ευαγγελιον, δυναμι γαρ θεου εστιν εισ σωτηριαν παντι τω πιστευοντι, Ιουδαιω τε πρωτον και Ελληνι (NA26)

Most would say that Paul is simply stating the historical progression of the Gospel. In its course it went first to the Jew, then to the Greek. If that were the case, then are we to understand that the Gospel is no longer to go to the Jew? Some behave that way. I was out on a church visitation program that was proceeding door to door. Several houses were deliberately being skipped. These houses were the ones that had a mezuzah* on the door, identifying them as a Jewish home. The Jewish homes were regularly passed by. The church leaders felt that visiting there would be time consuming at best, certainly be unproductive, and in some cases result in a confrontation and cause harsh feelings. When you see that kind of thinking, you get to the place where you would settle for

---

[2] *Speak Tenderly to Jerusalem* Friends of Isarael
* see glossary of terms

"to the Jew also." "God commands us to evangelize all people, including the Jew."[3]

There are three clauses that are in the predicate in Romans 1:16. All three clauses are controlled by the same verb "estin" εστιν, the verb "to be." The three clauses all function as predicate adjectives, describing the subject. The subject is the Gospel. The Gospel is, according to Paul, the power of God to salvation. The Gospel is also to everyone that believes. The third clause is that the Gospel is to the Jew first. All Evangelicals would agree that the Gospel is, and continues to be, the power of God to salvation. All evangelicals would agree that the Gospel is, and continues to be, to everyone that believes. How is it that somehow many, if not most, believe that the Gospel is not, and does not continue to be, to the Jew first? The word "estin" is in the present tense and has the idea of continuous action. All three clauses are controlled by the same verb.

Logically and grammatically, we expect that all should agree that the Gospel according to Paul is, and continues to be, to the Jew first. And yet somehow, either by faith or by practice, Evangelicals seem to interject that the Gospel was, but no longer is, to the Jew first.

The Biblical Example of Jewish Evangelism

Paul's Practice

Acts 13:5 ***And when they were at Salamis, they preached the word of God in the synagogues of the Jews: and they had also John to their minister.***

Acts 13:14 ***But when they departed from Perga, they came to Antioch in Pisidia, and went into the synagogue on the Sabbath day, and sat down.***

From the history that Luke records for us, we can learn about the practice that Paul used as he journeyed from city to city. At each location, Paul proceeded to go first to the synagogue to practice what he preached, to bring the Gospel to the Jew first.

---

[3] IBID

Paul's Procedure

Acts 13:46 *Then Paul and Barnabas waxed bold, and said, It was necessary that the word of God should first have been spoken to you: but seeing ye put it from you, and judge yourselves unworthy of everlasting life, lo, we turn to the Gentiles.*

In Acts 13:46, we read a very telling account. The Jews of that city rejected the message. The apostles declare that although they had shown themselves to be unworthy of eternal life, it was still necessary that the word of God should first be declared to the Jews. Once those Jewish people had rejected the word, the apostles proceeded to bring the message to the Gentiles. Notice, however, what we read in Acts 14:1. *And it came to pass in Iconium, that they went both together into the synagogue of the Jews, and so spake, that a great multitude both of the Jews and also of the Greeks believed.*

From these passages we can see how the Gospel was brought to the Jew first, and then when the Jewish people rejected the message the word was then preached to the Gentile. However, in the next city the procedure is repeated over again. In each city or location, they went to the Jew first, then to the Greek. Notice in Iconium, the Jews believed the message, and the result was that many Greeks responded as well. Isn't that what Romans 11:12 teaches us to expect? Romans 11:12 *Now if the fall of them be the riches of the world, and the diminishing of them the riches of the Gentiles; how much more their fulness?* We can only imagine the multitude of blessings modern missions have missed because they have broken with the pattern that was established by the early Church.

One possible reason for Paul's example is his priorities. Romans 9:1-3, *I say the truth in Christ, I lie not, my conscience also bearing me witness in he Holy Ghost, That I have great heaviness and continual sorrow in my heart. For I could wish that myself were accursed from Christ for my brethren, my kinsmen according to the flesh:* We can see from the Scriptures how strongly Paul felt about the Jewish people. Some would conclude that the practice of reaching the Jewish community first was an outgrowth of that strong emotional tie he had to his own nation. We can see that Paul did have much ethnic pride.

Philippians 3:4-7 *Though I might also have confidence in the flesh. If any other man thinketh that he hath whereof he might trust in the flesh, I more: Circumcised the eighth day, of the stock of Israel, of the tribe of Benjamin, an Hebrew of the Hebrews; as touching the law, a Pharisee; Concerning zeal, persecuting the church; touching the righteousness which is in the law, blameless. But what things were gain to me, those I counted loss for Christ.*

Paul, however, relegates that pride beneath the integrity of Christian service. His ministry was not based on his background, nor his wishes, but rather his ministry was built on Christ. The most reasonable explanation of Paul going to the Jew first is rooted not in the flesh, but in the leading of the Spirit, the will of God.

However, some would say that perhaps Paul's position influenced him to go to the Jew first. The position Paul had in the body is not without significance. Romans 11:13 *For I speak to you Gentiles, inasmuch as I am the apostle of the Gentiles, I magnify mine office:* Paul is the apostle to the Gentiles. Yet to reach the Gentiles, Paul begins each missionary endeavor by bringing the Gospel to the Synagogue. The conclusion is exactly what we quoted in Romans 11:12. Jewish people believing in Jesus will result in Gentiles believing in Jesus.

The phenomenon of Jewish people increasing evangelism in the community can actually begin before the first Jewish person even comes to faith. I've seen Jewish people who were lost being used of God to bring the Gospel to an unbelieving Gentile. One Jewish shop keeper loved to set up situations were I would be forced into a confrontation with a Catholic priest. Whenever possible, he would get us together and then bring up the topic. He would love to see us hurling Scripture at each other. The public impromptu debate often attracted a crowd of witnesses. To my Jewish friend it was an intellectual exercise, but to me it was a grand opportunity to publicly declare the Gospel.

20

Once saved, a Jewish believer can often become a dynamic witness, and the testimony of a Jewish believer will frequently create a curiosity in unbelieving Gentiles.

Practical benefits of Jewish Evangelism

The Lord's enabling

Deuteronomy 8:17-18 *And thou say in thine heart, My power and the might of mine hand hath gotten me this wealth. 18 But thou shalt remember the LORD thy God: for it is he that giveth thee power to get wealth, that he may establish his covenant which he sware unto thy fathers, as it is this day.*

A few years ago a church conducted a "Thank God for Israel" weekend. On Saturday night after Shabbes*, they invited the entire Jewish community to dinner at a local restaurant. The cost to the church was significant, but it was a gracious act of love that will be long remembered by scores of Jewish folks. Following the weekend, two Jewish ladies visited the church and asked the pastor if the church had any charitable needs that they could contribute to. The pastor mentioned how the congregation needed a new organ. The ladies gladly gave the church three thousand dollars for the purchase of the organ. The pastor called me that day, commending the work of Jewish evangelism, and quipped, "There's gold in them thar hills."

The pastor was only joking, but it is true that Jewish people have been enabled by the Lord to survive and prosper in the Gentile nations. Often a Jewish person has some affluence which can be an asset to the church. Obviously, we would deplore that as a motive to proclaim the Gospel; it is, however, a very real and practical blessing.

The Lord's Scattering James 1:1

Even as early as the writing of the epistle of James, the Jewish people had already been "**scattered abroad**." I once read of a mission's dilemma[4] that took place in one of the third world na-

---

* see glossary of terms
[4] *Evangelical Missions Quarterly*

tions in North Africa. The nation was predominately Muslim, and missionary teams, who were trained in Islamic evangelism, discovered several hundred thousand persons of the Hindu faith after numerous months of service.

These folks had migrated to this nation from Asia centuries ago. The mission board then sent over some personnel who were schooled in reaching the Asian Hindu for Christ. After starting Bible studies and making some progress into the community, the missionary discovered that these folks were splintered into several hundred tribes or sects. The tribes were so separated that a convert to the Gospel in one tribe would only have an effective testimony to members of his own sect. Once the missionary had begun his work with the people, the door to any of the other tribes was closed to him. To reach them all, it seemed that the mission board would need to send over one missionary for each tribe. The cost of sending over several hundred missionaries was preposterous. The thought of leaving several hundred thousand people remain in darkness is unthinkable.

The solution seems overly simplistic, but it is true. Reach the Jew first. In the early 1950's, when these nations first began to become developed, it was discovered that they frequently wore no shoes. An Italian firm was invited to market and distribute shoes to these people, but when they discovered that the people first needed to be educated in the concept of wearing shoes, the Italians became discouraged and were about to leave. An Israeli heard of the situation, and volunteered to take the shoes off the Italians' hands. Rather then ship them all back to Italy, they were delighted to sell the entire lot at a great discount.

The Israeli firm then began the task of educating the nation on the advantages of footwear. Today there are less then a hundred Jews in that nation. However, they are all in the shoe business. Today, if you need a pair of shoes in that nation, you need to do business with a Jew. The Islamic people buy their shoes from the Jews; the Hindu people buy their shoes from a Jew. Reach the Jews first, and let them place Gospel literature in every shoe box. Even if the Jewish shoe salesman doesn't get saved, he still may become a terrific ally in the preaching of the Gospel. If not, you are no worse off then before, and you have the encouragement of knowing that you tried to do things God's way.

The Lord's Blessing

In Genesis 12:3 we read *And I will bless them that bless thee, and him that curseth thee will I curse: and in thee shall all the families of the earth be blessed.* (ASV) There is a midrash* on the passage that I have always found to be a bit winsome. The Rabbis ask why is it that when it comes to blessing, God chooses to act first? He knows who is about to bless Israel, and before they can begin that blessing, God blesses that Gentile nation. However, in the cursing, the process is reversed. Here the Lord does not act until after the Gentile nation has completed its anti-Semitic activity, and then the Lord curses it. The Rabbis' answer is that a nation that will bless the Jews should have an abundance so that they might be able to amply bless his chosen people.

Conversely, it is not fitting that those who curse Israel should know about suffering. Let them curse in ignorance, not being fully aware of all that misery and suffering can bear. Then, when they have completed their meager and insignificant curse, God can unleash His fury upon them for their behavior towards His own.

There can be no greater blessing then the privilege of walking with the Lord. To extend that blessing to the Jewish people is to bless them. Proclaiming the Gospel to the Jewish people is a work that will not go unnoticed or unrewarded. "God will bless those who carry the Gospel to the Jew."[5] Conversely, to withhold the Gospel from God's ancient people is an act of cursing. The engagement in that activity would not go unnoticed. If the Rabbinical understanding of the literalness of the text is correct, then before we even begin the ministry, we should expect to see the provision and the freedom of the Lord in His blessing that work. As well, after we have made our decision to withhold the Gospel from the Jewish people, we might expect to see some dire effects of that decision.

---

* see glossary of terms
5 *Speak Tenderly to Jerusalem*

In the past twenty years, I've seen this phenomenon repeat itself many times. There was one church that was located in the middle of a predominant Jewish community. The congregants were for the most part elderly Germanic people. The pastor had a heart for reaching the community, but as it turned out it was his burden, and not that of the church. We addressed the elders concerning the ministry, and at that time tried to communicate a bit of the costs. We described the opposition they would face, and the kind of hostility they might encounter. We also spoke of the Biblical mandate with great encouragement and enthusiasm, a mistake I will try not to repeat. Apparently, I didn't leave them a gracious way to say, "No." After my presentation, anyone who wasn't eager to plunge ahead would have appeared to be unspiritual at best, and anti-Semitic at worst.

The training began, the meetings followed, and the ministry progressed wonderfully. Many Jewish people were baptized into the Church. A score had found the Lord, and were worshipping there at our weekly meetings. The pastor was a great encouragement to our ministry, and the Church was growing beyond the capacity of the building.

The opposition was there as was predicted. Jewish people would show up outside the church on Sunday mornings to hand out flyers and to disrupt the services. The pastor handled all of it in a godly manner, but all was not as bright as it appeared. The old guard resented the new families coming in and dominating the church service. The addition of Jewish songs, Hebrew liturgies, and contemporary choruses was uncomfortable for them. A rift developed between the Jewish believers and the Gentiles. They argued over everything: leaving food in the church refrigerator, cleaning the kitchen, and leaving the lights on in the men's room.

The pastor wouldn't allow the church to split, and he wouldn't allow the Jewish ministry to diminish. So the only solution that was possible, other then prayerfully working together, was to ask the pastor for his resignation. Once he left, the Jewish ministry was greatly restricted. The Jewish believers now knew they were not welcome. They left the church, some to roam, some to Messianic Congregations, and over the church it looked like you could write

"Icabod." Today the church can barely support its own physical plant. The once two hundred plus size service is down to around thirty people.

In the past twenty years, I have seen ministries both rise and fall. I'm certain that there are many factors at work that I'm not aware of. I'm not suggesting that the only rule for success in Christian service is to bless the Jews. Spirit led ministries tend to do several spiritual things in a godly way, and will then be blessed. Fleshly ministries tend to do fleshly things in ungodly ways, and will reap the results. I have, however, noticed that the principles of Genesis 12:3 are outworking in ministries, as well as in nations. Churches that endeavor to bless the Jews through evangelism will themselves be blessed. Giving towards, praying for, and working in Jewish evangelism will not go unnoticed.

TWO

The Biblical Messenger

Cultural Background of the Messenger

Gentile Christians

Romans 11:11 *I say then, Have they stumbled that they should fall? God forbid: but rather through their fall salvation is come unto the Gentiles, for to provoke them to jealousy.* Contrary to popular belief, God's primary means of reaching the Jewish people is through the Gentile.

Gentile Christians trying to reach Jewish people with the Gospel do have some advantages, one of which is their testimony. Often times, Jewish people think in a we/they manner. We Jews, those Gentiles. This is especially true of the older Jewish people. As well, they often confuse the terms Gentile and Christian. For the most part, they assume that the terms are synonymous, hence all Gentiles are Christians. This confusion once arose as I was speaking with a dear, elderly Jewish lady. She was troubled by the treatment of her family by some unsavory Gentiles she knew. Her bitterness was evident as she related the tale to me. She would constantly refer to the adversaries as "those Christians." I would attempt to correct her by adding, "Excuse me, Mollie, you mean, 'those Gentiles.' You see, Mollie, Gentiles are not the same as Christians. Technically, Christians are those who believe in Israel's Messiah, and therefore, you would expect them to have a high regard for the Jewish people." She would continue as if I hadn't said a word.

As she went on with her story she would inevitably refer to "those Christians." I would again interject a correction, and she would pass on with, "Yeah, yeah, whatever." This repeated itself several times until after one of my corrective interruptions she shouted, "You've told me that twenty times now!" I replied, "And you haven't gotten it right yet!" I don't know if it was twenty times, but I do know she never got it right. To her, and to most elderly Jewish people, it is, "Yeah, yeah, whatever."

That phrase says volumes about their attitude. There are some minuscule distinctions amongst the Goyim, but why split hairs. Gentiles, Smentiles, Christians, Catholics, whatever, they sure "ain't" Jews. Here is where the Gentile testimony can be so dynamic. "I was once a Gentile, and I wasn't a Christian." You might ask, "Mitch aren't Gentiles still Gentiles after they come to Christ?" I'm not so sure. The reading of Ephesians 2:11 ***Wherefore remember, that ye being in time past Gentiles in the flesh,*** seems to indicate that what we were before Christ is insignificant to what we become in Christ.

I have seen the Lord use the dynamic testimony of the Gentile repeatedly with the Jewish people. It is almost humorous as they listen to Gentiles explain how they became Christians. The Jewish person is thinking "I was born a Jew. I'm a Jew. You were born Gentile/ Christian. You're Christian." The believers are explaining how they were changed, and how they became Christians. The Jewish person scrunches up his face as he tries to assimilate the new information. The Gentile testimony doesn't seem to fit any of his preconceived ideas.

The Gentile testimony explodes myths and forces the Jewish person to rethink his preconceived ideas. First, if a person has to change to become a Christian, then all Gentiles can't be Christians. That means the Jew had the wrong definition of Christians and Christendom. Second, if a person has to change to become a

Christian, that means people can change, and perhaps Jews need to change, too.

Another advantage a Gentile Christian has is love. Many Jewish people tend to associate all Gentiles as Christians, and by carrying this mistake in logic one step further, they assume all anti-Semites are also Christians. Some Jews do not trust Christians because they think they are anti-Semitic. When a Gentile presents himself as being enthusiastic about Judaica, it destroys the Jews' stereotypical thinking and forces the Jewish person to consider the changes that have occurred and to consider the facts of the life-changing Gospel.

But there are disadvantages for the Gentile Christian. Friends of Israel has a tool called "Speak Tenderly to Jerusalem." In this booklet, one of the sections is entitled "Witnessing to Your Jewish Friends." I love asking folks what is the single largest obstacle to reaching Jewish friends? I get various responses, but the answer is both simple and obvious. The only real obstacle to reaching Jewish friends is, we don't have any. We don't cultivate social relationships with Jewish people.

Barriers between Jews and Gentiles exist. The walls are tumbling down a bit, but the barriers still exist, and they need to be hurdled. Gentiles and Jews live near and around each other, but they really don't live together; they don't play together; they don't socialize. In Yarmouth, Nova Scotia, there is a Jewish shop keeper. Most of the Christians in town have frequented his store throughout the past twenty years. I was the first person to ever give him a piece of Christian literature. The reason he took the literature was because I was the first Christian to ever invite him to go to lunch. The reason we felt comfortable going to lunch was because we had already developed a friendship.

In a few short moments, the Lord opened the door to befriend this lonely man. The amazing thing is not that he could be reached so quickly, but that no other Christian had done so! If we are going to reach Jewish friends, we have to have Jewish friends. If we are going to have Jewish friends, we have to be more friendly.

I know two Gentile laymen who have, through love, effectively brought many Jewish people to the Lord. Both are, by coincidence, named Bill. I'm going to assume that it's not the common name that has made them great soul winners, but I'm looking for their qualities that we might be able to develop in our own lives that could be used of the Lord in us in our outreach to our Jewish contacts.

Although only one of them is very talkative, both men are honest, objective about their respective faults, and quick to admit when they are wrong. Both readily recognize the gifts and talents of others, and enjoy discussing the strengths of other people. Those might not be the secret ingredients to winning souls, but they probably will do more for you in reaching Jewish people than changing your name to Bill.

Many of us have a God-given burden for the Jewish people, but have yet to develop a personal relationship with any of the Jewish contacts in our lives. The Scriptures teach us that the Lord strategically placed Israel in the midst of the nations to be a testimony for Him in the world. I believe that as Israel was, each Christian is now strategically placed in the world as a witness. Our task is to reach those around us with the Gospel, and I believe that should be to the Jew first.

Some would say that there are no Jewish people in their town. Well, it's admittedly tough to begin a program of befriending Jewish people from long distance. However, I wonder if we have prayerfully examined the community. The Lord has done an amazingly good job of scattering the Jewish people. I marvel at where we have been able to locate our people in our travels. I have always found that where there is a burden in a believer's heart to reach the Jews, there are also Jewish people to be reached nearby.

The first steps I ask folks to take are to PRAY and look. That's simple enough isn't it? Yet it's amazing what we discover under our very noses when we are prayerful. Ask the Lord to make you aware of those Jewish folks in your sphere of influence. Ask Him to bring Jewish people across your path, then watch and see what the Lord can do. We've had the privilege of sharing the faith with Jewish folks in places where no one would expect to find them. In one little town in Florida, we asked a group of concerned believers to pray about the Jewish people in their community. The believers were certain that there were none. However, as an answer to prayer, a Christian gal showed up in church, and her husband was Jewish. She knew of another Jewish person in town, and today, to my knowledge, the entire Jewish population of that little Florida fishing town is saved (both of them).

Often, we have contacts with Jewish friends, but we are not properly prepared to witness to them. While teaching a Jewish evangelism seminar in a local church, the pastor confessed to me that he never had an opportunity to speak with a Jewish person about the Lord. After brief conversation, it became apparent that this pastor was not prepared to talk with the Jews. He was a dynamic Christian leader, but very insensitive to the Jewish people and not competent enough in the Old Testament to bring a person to faith through the Jewish Scriptures.

Three days after the seminar I received an exciting phone call. This pastor could hardly contain himself. He not only had his first real opening to speak with a Jewish person about the Lord, but he also had the sensational experience of bringing that Jewish man to faith in the Messiah.

So along with PRAYER there's PREPARATION. It's possible we haven't had much contact with the Jewish community because we haven't been equipped properly to reach them. I have found that once we receive adequate training, the Lord will begin to bring Jewish people across our paths.

There is no substitute for PRAYER and PREPARATION when it comes to breaking down barriers. But to PRAYER and PREPARATION, add PERSONABLENESS. I'm not talking about personality, nor the techniques that Dale Carnegie popularized in *How to Win Friends & Influence People*, although it does seem to be true that everyone appreciates being appreciated. When we use the term PERSONABLENESS, we mean love.

It's not phony to learn to recognize God-given talents in others and to acknowledge them. We can give glory to God and make friends at the same time. In Colossians 4:3 *Praying also for us, that God would open unto us a door of utterance, to speak the mystery of Christ, for which I am also in bonds*: Paul makes an interesting prayer request. He asks that he might have an open door of utterance. He requests prayer for a way through the barrier. I've found that the answer to that request is often an opportunity to demonstrate love by taking an interest in the things that interest others, by identifying with their difficulties or sorrows, by being complimentary, and by being quick to help out in any way possible.

Al and Deirdre managed a grocery store. Actually Al ran the store; Deirdre ran Al. Deirdre seemed to be there only around the lunch hour. She was a dear Jewish lady who was very easy to speak with. Al was surly, and it seemed to me that the better Deirdre and I got along, the worse I fared with him. One day Deirdre was hospitalized. I asked Al for permission to visit her. He barely grunted an affirmative reply. When I arrived she was as pleasant as ever, but she was noticeably concerned. Her worry was about who would help Al during the noon rush. I never noticed before that there were several office buildings and a factory nearby the shop. At noon, Al would have to make scores of sandwiches for lunches. People would be on the run, and he couldn't work the cash register and make sandwiches at the same time. So Deirdre would stop down every day around noon just to take care of the grocery customers while Al worked the sandwich bar. Deirdre's concern was how would Al get through the noon hour without her.

At 11:45 AM, I walked into the store, and Al never even looked up. I found Deirdre's apron right where she said it would be hanging, and put it on without saying a word. Al looked over at me and said, "I won't pay a cent." I said, "I'm not here for your money. I'm here to help." Al responded, "I don't need your help." I knew he needed it; he just didn't want it. I said, "I'm not here to help you, I'm here to help Deirdre." Al said, "I give you five dollars an hour." I said, "I'll take a sandwich and a soda when we're done." I didn't know the prices on the first day, and the rest of our conversation was restricted to how much for a gallon of milk or a loaf of bread. When the rush was over, Al made us both a sandwich, and we ate together in silence. After lunch he asked me two questions. Question number one was, "Are you really Jewish?," and question number two was, "Will you be back tomorrow?"

Now I realize that few folks have the time or luxury to be able to pitch in like I do. However, I'm certain that most of us could do a great deal more in establishing friendships and in breaking down barriers. In South Carolina, the Christians are attending Friday night services at the synagogue, and some even traveled to Israel with the Temple to establish friendships and break down barriers.

In Brighton Beach, a pastor is playing chess with the Russian speaking Jewish people. Christians have attended fairs and flea markets at the Temple. Frequenting Jewish shops, taking Hebrew and Yiddish classes under the Rabbi, attending meetings, concerts, Jewish cooking seminars, you name it, Christians have done it to break down barriers.

The Gentile Christian will also face misconceptions. I am always surprised about how wrong I can be. After all these years of experience, I still tend to stereotype. I'm inclined to think that all Jewish people are like my family and friends. Jewish people are really quite diverse. Most assume that all Jews are similar in appearance. The descriptions of a Jew are certain to include "references to a large nose, short stature, and curly black hair. The truth is not all Jews have big noses. Not all Jews are short. Not all Jews have curly black hair. Stereotypes are just not always true."[6] "If asked to describe the behavioral characteristics of the Jewish people, the words stingy or bookish might come to mind."[7] It is quite possible that some of the thinking behind these stereotypes might be rooted in the peculiar history of the Jewish people. In many European lands, and in different centuries, the Jewish people were forbidden to own land or apprentice in a trade. The only occupations open to them were to become merchants or money lenders.

The church forbade the loaning of money but did permit one to borrow. Therefore, since no Catholic could do the lending, the task fell to the Jew. The return of the loan, however, could be negotiated. Often a gift to the church could exonerate one from his commitment to the pagan Christ-killer. So to recoup his losses, a Jewish businessman would frequently set the usury at a high rate.

---

[6] *Our Jewish Friends*, Louis Goldberg, Louazeaux Brothers, Neptune, NJ
[7] *You Bring the Bagels, I'll Bring the Gospel*, Barry Rubin, Fleming Revel

The traveling Jew would buy things where they were made cheap, travel to where the price was higher, and sell to eke out a living. Subject to robbers and to periodic church or State sanctioned confiscations of the wares he carried, the Jewish people soon grew to appreciate the things that couldn't be taken. They began to stress learning and literature and gravitated to the professions and education.

The history of the harsh treatment of the Jewish people did shape the lives of many. However, there are many misconceptions about the Jews. On all too many occasions someone has told me of their Jewish friend who was actually very giving and thoughtful. The story was related as if I should have been surprised. I mean, can you imagine a Jew who isn't cheap? Well, I suppose we do realize that all Jews aren't cheap, but many actually do think that the Jews have all the money.

"That all wealth is controlled by Jews is a well-worn cliché... In answer, we must examine this claim more closely and get down to specifics. Of America's ten wealthiest families... not one of them is Jewish! Of America's four hundred wealthiest families, less then ten percent are Jewish!... The largest banks in this country have very few Jewish people on their boards of directors. In light of such facts, we can see that the Jewish people are not generally the monied people.[8]"

In Luke 12:19 we read *And I will say to my soul, Soul, thou hast much goods laid up for many years; take thine ease, eat, drink, and be merry.* It's not a surprise to find that people who don't believe in eternity live very materialistic lives. Because this life is all there is, flaunting wealth becomes a national obsession. Call it "the rat race," or "keeping up with the Jones, it amounts to the same thing, but it certainly isn't a strictly Jewish trait, nor is it true of all Jewish people.

Jewish people don't all look alike, spend alike, and they certainly don't believe or behave religiously alike. "Perhaps you always assumed that all Jewish people share the same theology. Nothing could be further from the truth. Along with varying degrees of Bible knowledge and differing Messianic expectations,

---

[8] *Our Jewish Friends*

you will find that Jewish people hold extremely diverse opinions about God, the after life, Israel, and most other subjects"[9] The most common concept of a Jewish person is that of the kosher* keeping, yarmulkeh* wearing, observant Orthodox. Many Jewish ministries target the Orthodox, not realizing that the Orthodox represent less than 9% of the Jewish population.

The reason for the misconception is that originally all Jewish people were Orthodox. Either you were practicing your faith, or you were cut off from your people. As any religion, Judaism has gone through phases of change. Throughout the Middle Ages, Judaism was influenced both by Islam and Christianity. However, until the 18th century, Rabbinic authority had remained intact. At that time, Jews in Europe came in contact with a modernizing society. It was inevitable that the tension between the ancient faith, the new ideas in philosophy, the European modes of living, and the new discoveries in the scientific community would influence reform.

Reform Judaism became institutionalized in Germany in the 1840's. Reform Judaism never really had any great success in Europe. When millions of Jews migrated to the United States in the 1880's, they brought Reform Judaism with them, and in the fertile soil of a new land the movement flourished. By 1880, most of the synagogues in the United States were Reform and were members of the Union of American Hebrew Congregations which was formed in 1873.[10]

In response, Orthodox Judaism became very critical of its budding new brother. The two factions polarized. Reform Judaism grew more liberal, and the Orthodox retreated back further into ancient traditions and rabbinic rule. The majority of the Jewish people found themselves ideologically somewhere in between the two extremes. It was in this environment that the Conservative movement, which had been stumbling since its inception in the 1840's, began to prosper. Conservative Judaism soon surpassed Reform as being the largest of the Jewish groups.

---

[9] *You Bring the Bagels, I'll Bring the Gospel*
* see glossary of terms

[10] *Compton Encyclopedia*, "Judaism"

Conservative Judaism is very varied, however. They run the entire gamut from Reform to Orthodox. Sabbath services in one Synagogue can last four hours, while another will be finished in less then two. In one synagogue, there is no driving on the Sabbath. The next will have a huge parking lot. This diversification in service and practice and beliefs in the Conservative movement gave birth to the fourth branch of Judaism called Reconstructionalist which began in the 1920's.[11] The Reconstructionalist used to boast that the Conservative of today will be the Reconstructionalist of tomorrow. However, at this time that boast remains just a boast. The movement has never seemed to expand as expected.

Perhaps the most recognizable of the Jewish people are those that belong to the Chassidic sect. Stemming from their roots in 17th century Poland, the group maintains its strict European and Orthodox traits. They originally began as a reaction to dead religious orthodoxy. Due to the many demands of working life, it was easier for the wealthiest to keep the Jewish traditions. Our traditions required and demanded a study schedule that the working man couldn't keep. The wealthy began to dominate the faith. The wealthy grew aloof, and the religion grew stale.

Into this picture there arose a Rabbi named Israel Ben Eliezer. He became known as the master of the good name, or as it is said in Hebrew, the Baal Shem Tov. He, according to the legend, had the knowledge of the Holy name of the Lord. To keep people from ever taking the name of the Lord in vain, the sacred name is never pronounced and never written with the proper vowel points, so it is kept in mystery. Those who have the knowledge of the name are believed to have the power to work miracles.

Rabbi Eliezer brought the religion back to the common man. He introduced a charismatic movement into the ancient faith. They stressed a religion of experience and emotion that boasted of power and wonders. Today the Chassidic Jew is very visible. He wears the traditional uniform of a white shirt buttoned up to the collar. He wears no tie and sports a black hat. Beneath his hat is the traditional head covering. As well, the Chassid is dressed with the fringes under his garment, and he has a beard and the side

---

[11] Ibid.

36

burns that are symbolic of the law that no razor has come to his head. The Chassidim are really a sub-set of the Orthodox. Their distinctives are that they live in a community that is loyal to one Rabbi, and they follow and teach the Kaballah.*

As we mentioned before, only 9% of the Jewish people are Orthodox. 17% of the Jewish people are Reform, and 27% are Conservative. That accounts for 53% of the Jewish people. An additional 54% of the Jewish people are not affiliated with any Synagogue at all. That adds up to 107%. We got em all! What happens is that when you take a survey, people say that they are affiliated with a certain synagogue; however, when you ask the Rabbi, the truth is that they aren't members and never attend. So in reality 7% lied about what they were. I'm not sure how to accurately reduce the percentages of Orthodox, Conservative, and Reform Jewish people. But we can affirm that the majority of the Jewish people are secular, non-practicing Jewish people, who are Jewish in name more then in religion.

A sixteen-year-old boy found the Lord through a Bible study in Freehold, NJ. He soon was prohibited from attending the meetings by his parents. I volunteered to speak with his folks, and my suggestion was greeted with pure terror. "You don't know my mother," he said. Everyone nodded their heads to show their agreement with the statement. They all began talking at once, describing this pious, impossible Orthodox Jewish woman and warning me not to go any further with her. I envisioned a cross between the wicked witch and a Yiddish mamma. They had me convinced and, admittedly, a bit frightened by the prospect of having to deal with her. When I reached the peak of dread of ever meeting this woman, the conversation began to change. People started saying things like, "I think Mitch can handle her. Sure Mitch will be fine." Before I knew what was happening, I was in the middle of a parade down the street to confront what was certain to be the Jewish Medusa.

When we arrived at the door, I was compelled to the front of the line. I knocked at the door, and opening it was the fearsome mother. She took one look at the assembly, and instantly knew

---

* see glossary of terms

37

who we were and what the purpose of our call was. She shouted what was apparently her war cry, "THIS IS AN ORTHODOX JEWISH HOME!" Everyone coward back. I responded with, "Hi, I'm Mitch." She seemed startled that any one was talking to her. It was obvious that in the past her initial yell was all that was needed to scatter the troops. I was as surprised as she was when I asked if I could come in. I wondered for a second, "Did I say that?" She seemed as surprised as I was when she stepped back from the door, allowing us to enter. I think she was asking herself, "Did I let them in?"

The instant we were in the house, I began to suspect their orthodoxy. Further conversation proved my misgivings. She proudly proclaimed their Jewish pedigree by way of a question, "Did you know that Dennis' great grandfather was one of the chief Orthodox rabbis in Poland?" Marvelous. On the basis of, not her religion, nor her parent's, but that of her grandfather's, she has intimidated an entire Christian community. The bold claim of, "This is an Orthodox Jewish home," should be interpreted to mean that we were orthodox. Right now we aren't practicing Judaism. But our heritage is an orthodox one: our roots are orthodox. The ironic thing is that everyone's roots are orthodox. We can grow so fearful, and can be so easily discouraged. Here, this delightful family kept everyone at bay because of the misconceptions we Christians often have.

Jewish Believers

Acts 17:10 *And the brethren immediately sent away Paul and Silas by night unto Berea: who coming thither went into the synagogue of the Jews.*

Jewish believers, of course, have some advantages in their witness that Gentiles do not. They have a familiarity the Gentile does not have. Yes, no two people are alike. Yes, everyone is different, but being a Jew helps in your witness because you are familiar with the Jewish people. Knowing the customs, the religion, the language, and the behavior is a big asset. I love our people. They are just like everyone else, only more so. I remember showing a Gospel film in a hotel in Longbranch, New Jersey. Several

Jewish unbelievers were in attendance, many of them "first-timers." In the midst of the film, an argument broke out between a mother and her daughter. I found the distraction to be humorous. A Gentile friend accompanied me to the program, and he was obviously discomfited by the cultural shock. Admittedly, I took some delight in his uneasiness. The loud arguments and cutting remarks were distressing to my gentle Gentile friend.

When a Gentile screams, "I never want to see you again," it is usually serious business. With a Jew, that shouting threat may last the whole night. Over the years I have seen many gentle Gentiles taken by surprise when they were in the midst of the Jewish people. Gentiles can be shocked and embarrassed by the candor and the bluntness of the Jewish people. Most of us know better than to get upset by the decibel level. It is usually just so much noise and you don't take it personally.

There is more than noise levels to make a Gentile uncomfortable. What do you do at a wedding, funeral, or Bar Mitzvah? What gifts are appropriate? What do you wear? How do you act? Do you wish someone a happy Yom Kippur*? Do you send a Christmas card? Do you have to eat Gefilte fish*? Does anybody really eat Gefilte fish?

Jewish believers also have more opportunities. When I came to the Lord in 1969, I had a circle of close friends in North Jersey. All were Jewish. My family are all Jews. It was not a problem finding Jewish people to speak with. I had a small mission field open to me. Most Jewish believers have close personal friends who are Jewish; all have family who are Jewish, and there will be open doors.

But there are disadvantages for the Jewish believer. He or she will face hostility.

When we first met, I picked him up hitchhiking. I invited him out to the coffeehouse, where I had only recently found the Lord myself. I was very surprised and delighted when he showed up. We met again at Temple University, and over the years, our friendship grew. He finished school and became a professor of political science. I became a missionary. He joined the Jewish de-

---

* see glossary of terms

fense league. Our friendship grew, and he came to the place where he openly stated that, for him, Christianity was the only cogent faith. However, that was the good news. The bad news was that he had no faith and was a confessed atheist.

Yet even that much interest in Christianity was a danger for a leader of the Jewish defense league. He later was encouraged to resign, but before he did, he had mentioned my name to several people in the organization. His intent was to open doors of communication; he never intended to do me any disservice. However, as a direct result of that communication there was a religious trial conducted in Philadelphia. They called it a "Din." Twenty individuals across the country were ex-communicated from Judaism. I was number fourteen. I had hoped to make the top ten, but considering the other names on the list, I was honored to even be considered. Men like Daniel Fuchs, Marv Rosenthal, and Moishe Rosen were mentioned, to name a few.

There hadn't been any action of this nature taken since Bernard Spinoza. We all were found guilty of the crime of destroying Jewish souls through proselytizing. The decision was five fold: 1. No Jewish person is to dine with us or associate with us in any social way. 2. No Jewish person is to employ us or to be involved with us in any business contract. None are to be benefited by us or are allowed to benefit us. 3. At no time are we to be allowed to take part in any religious service or to be included in a minyon*, and we are not permitted to be buried in Jewish soil. 4. We are forbidden to enter the land of Israel under the law of return. 5. Because there is no existing system of capital punishment available for religious crimes at this time, they are calling down the Holy judgment of God upon us that He might take our lives.

Admittedly, the Din has had little effect on my ministry. Most are unaware of it and would not care much if they knew. To those who know, the result has only been positive. For a brief time I was a bit of a celebrity, well, more correctly, an item of curiosity, and that opened doors.

However, Jewish believers in Jesus can face some distinct disadvantages. Friends and family can perceive their faith as an act of

---

* see glossary of terms

traitorism. "You have abandoned us." While a Gentile is allowed to speak of Jesus, even expected to, a Jew who does so is a traitor or, as they refer to us, a Meshumad.*

A Jewish believer will also face a certain reluctance. Anticipating that rejection can cause a Jewish believer to be reluctant to witness with his loved ones, it would be a humorous scenario if it wasn't of such a serious nature. The new Jewish believer is reluctant to tell his family about his or her faith, even resorting to hiding it. However, he is convicted that he should be telling others about the changes in his live. Those changes are evident, but the family has no idea what has happened. The lack of communication and the changes in lifestyle are interpreted that something is wrong.

Meanwhile, as the believer turns down opportunity after opportunity out of fear, the conviction to witness grows ever stronger. Finally, when the guilt overtakes the fear, the believer forces a confrontation, and the ensuing argument is almost always painful and defeating. Accusations are leveled in both directions and doors, both physical and metaphysical, are slammed shut. To prevent this crisis, a new believer should begin communicating early and honestly. Talking to your family about Jesus is like a lot of things in life; the longer you let it go, the harder it is to do. Conversely, it is better to start early and honestly.

Young people should to explain to their parents that they are investigating the Jewish Scriptures, and invite them to enter into the search. This says, "Mom and Dad, I respect your opinion, and I'm not ashamed of my beliefs." We can never totally eliminate the confrontation, but this method is a great deal better than coming home six months after you have believed and saying, "Mom, Dad, guess what I just did ?" No Jewish parents ever raised their children to become Christians, and the sudden realization that they have is never received as good news.

There are distinct disadvantages that a Jewish person has when trying to tell Jewish people about Jesus. Beyond the fear of disenfranchising family and friends, there is also the problem of personal guilt. Jews who believe in Jesus feel like they let their people and their heritage down. That often results in an attempt to misrepresent themselves in front of other Jewish people as being more Jewish than ever.

The Messenger Must Be Committed

Whether or not the witness is Jewish or Gentile, the witness should be a committed Christian. In Philadelphia there was a preacher known as the "walking Bible." One fall night I was called to share my testimony, and the "walking Bible" brought the sermon. I was deeply honored to be ministering alongside of a man of that stature. He, true to his reputation, preached his entire sermon from memory, quoting every verse and referring to specific words in their respective verses without a note or a Bible opened for him to read.

After the sermon that night, people were complimenting him on his vast knowledge of the Scriptures. The so called "walking Bible" then related the most interesting story. He spoke of a man in Philadelphia who lived on the street, a drunk, who boasted that he could match anyone on his Bible knowledge. Eventually the "walking Bible" was introduced to the boastful drunk. To the delight of those who had gathered for the occasion, the two combatants went at it. Furiously, they recited passages, naming chapter and verse. One would begin a text, and the other would as quickly conclude it, all from memory. It became obvious that there would be no winner; both were equally matched. The question that was begging to be asked was finally voiced by one of the spectators. The street person was the one addressed, "How is it that you know the Scriptures so well, and you're still a drunk living on the street?"

All grew quiet, embarrassed that the question had been asked, but relieved as well, since they all in their minds had already asked the same thing. The drunk said sadly as he walked away, "He's called the 'Walking Bible'; I'm just a 'Talking Bible.'" Being a witness may mean that you are the only Bible some people will ever read. There is something very sad about a talking witness who is not a walking witness.

The first year I was saved, I saw four hundred people pray to receive Christ. I started in good faith, equipped each morning with the "Four Spiritual Laws" booklet. After seeing some success, folks began to heap praise upon me for my evangelistic efforts. This went to my head, and my pride took over. I decided to become the most effective witness ever. I began keeping statistics in an effort to break records. I chased one guy down a train platform, insisting he pray the sinner's prayer as he was trying to board the commuter train as it was pulling out of the station. I think our biggest day was nine decisions, and the best weekend was seventeen. When I realized that the four hundred mark was an attainable goal, I began setting quotas. I wouldn't quit witnessing until I reached the needed total of the day. I think you could say I had grown to become a bit overbearing and obnoxious.

Upon arriving at the goal number, I couldn't wait to begin bragging. I asked my wife how many people had she led to the Lord that year. She thought that the whole subject was unbecoming and was averse to answering me. However, since I was so insistent, she said she'd let me know tomorrow. "Tomorrow!" I shouted, "Why not today?" Her answer floored me. "Tomorrow we'll go to church, and I'll look around and count the folks that are there."

The next day she went up to the balcony and spotted three gals whom she had dealt with during the past year. All three were in church that Sunday morning. I might mention that some of my four hundred were absent. In fact, none of them were in our church service that morning. I jokingly added that they were absent due to weather. We don't know whether or not they were really saved at all. The three gals that my wife had dealt with were not only saved, but they were growing because they were discipled by a committed Christian. It seems that too often, the folks who have the least to say speak the loudest and talk the most. We need to realize that those who are defeated by sin will be impressed when they see someone living a victorious life. That observable, committed life is more important than everything that we say.

Spirit filled

John 16:8 *And when he is come, he will reprove the world of sin, and of righteousness, and of judgment:* Before people get saved, they first must realize they are lost. The Holy Spirit of God is the agent of the Godhead who convicts people of that fact. It is logical then, that to be an effective witness one must be filled with the Spirit.

Ephesians 5:18 *And be not drunk with wine, wherein is excess; but be filled with the Spirit;* I once heard a message on the filling of the Spirit, where the pastor tried to illustrate Ephesians 5:18 with a glass of water. The Spirit is like air, he said, and as long as the glass was filled with water it could not be filled with air. He then poured out the water from the glass, emptying it of its contents and allowing the glass to be filled with air.

The pastor went on to teach that in order to be filled with the Spirit we must first empty ourselves of self. The illustration was admittedly lost on me. I couldn't understand how I was expected to empty myself of self. I couldn't just stand on my head and wait for self to pour out my ear could I? I am self. How do I go about being not being? It seemed ludicrous.

Following the command to be filled with the Spirit, we see four present active participles and one passive participle. These seem to express the result of the Spirit-filled life: *speaking to yourselves in psalms, and hymns, and spiritual songs, singing and making melody in your heart to the Lord, giving thanks always for all things unto God and the Father in the name of our Lord Jesus Christ, and submitting yourselves one to another in the fear of God,* Eph. 5:19.

In Colossians 3:16-18, we read *Let the word of Christ dwell in you richly in all wisdom; teaching and admonishing one another in psalms and hymns and spiritual songs, singing with grace in your hearts to the Lord. And whatsoever ye do in word or deed, do all in the name of the Lord Jesus, giving thanks to God and the Father by him. Wives, submit yourselves unto your own Husbands, as it is fit in the Lord.* The Colossians passage also contains four present active participles: **Teaching, admonishing, singing** and **giving thanks**.

In Ephesians, one participle is speaking, while in Colossians, it was teaching and admonishing. In Ephesians, we read of singing and making melody, while Colossians only says singing. Both passages include the giving of thanks, and both make mention of psalms, hymns, and spiritual songs. The Ephesians passage goes on to speak of submission one to another, and then specifically of the husband and wife relationship, while Colossians mentions only the wife submitting to the husband. There are distinctions between the two passages; however, the two texts are also remarkably similar.

Both passages result in joyous instruction through song, submitted behavior, and thankfulness. In mathematics, things that equal the same thing are equal to each other. I don't know if that holds true for Scripture, but if two activities result in similar manners of comportment, then can we conclude that the two activities are themselves related? It makes sense that the filling of the Spirit would be related to the Word of God. After all, the Holy Spirit is the ultimate author of the Scriptures. The filling of the Spirit is consistent with obedience to the Word. Hebrews 4:12 *For the word of God is quick, and powerful, and sharper than any two edged sword, piercing even to the dividing asunder of soul and spirit, and of the joints and marrow, and is a discerner of the thoughts and intents of the heart.*

The effective witness needs to be certain that the Spirit is in control when Jewish people are present. The evidence of the Spirit controlled life is an undeniable testimony to the power and the truth of God. The overwhelming number of Jewish believers I know have been provoked to jealousy by observing the power of the Lord, revealed through the fruit of the Spirit, visible in the lives of believers.

Sensitive

It is astonishing to observe just how obnoxious we believers can be. It is true that we never stop being a witness; however, there are times when we ought to stop talking. 1 Peter 3:1 *Likewise, ye wives, be in subjection to your own husbands; that, if any obey not the word, they also may without the word be won by the conversation of the wives;*

We were visiting a woman who lost her husband of thirty-five years. My newly saved comrade could not contain himself and immediately jumped in, warning this woman not to repeat the error of her husband and tragically follow him into the tortures of an eternity separated from God. Yes, he spoke the truth, but we are admonished in Ephesians 4:29 to *Let no corrupt communication proceed out of your mouth, but that which is good to the use of edifying, that it may minister grace unto the hearers.* Now I realize that my friend spoke the truth, but I doubt that his witness was edifying to the grieving widow. In 2 Corinthians 5:20, we read how *we are ambassadors for Christ.* If that is true of all believers, then we are the representatives of God in this foreign nation. My experience has been that people do not respond to the threat of justice. They seem too proud to admit to fear. However, they can be reached through a message of love. They will respond to a God of mercy. We represent that God, and people must see that tenderness and caring in us.

At the time of bereavement, it is difficult to know what to say. There may not be a right thing to say. I usually try something like, "We leave our loved ones in the hands of a tender God who cares more for them than we do. God has provided everything needed for them to be saved, and He desires that none should perish. We never really know what a person will decide in the quietness of their own hearts as they face eternity. We do know the Judge of all the earth shall do right."

Believers, intent on being a witness, have barged into peoples lives without any thought or taking any notice of what things people might be experiencing or what needs they might have. We have to be more sensitive, far more sensitive, to be effective. If people are too busy then we wait. If people are amongst friends and are embarrassed by our presence, then we respect that. Prayer is a tremendous resource. We pray God will allow us to be more concerned with the feelings of others, that we will listen and focus on others, and that we will sense where the need is so that we can immediately minister to them.

Sound

In our desire to be sensitive, we can err in the other direction by trying too hard not to offend. There is a tendency to deny the bad news. We cannot compromise on the truth. We must be clarions of the truth. As we read in John 8:32 *And ye shall know the truth, and the truth shall make you free*. The truth is what frees men from the bondage they are under. Of course, before one can proclaim the truth, one must know the truth. The most effective evangelicals are ones who know the Word. God's Word contains wisdom for every aspect of life. As we give consistently wise and sound council, those under bondage will be impressed with the character of the Word of God. When that same Word declares them to be lost, they will have to come to grips with the supernatural integrity of the message because of the soundness of its witness. John 17:17 *Sanctify them through thy truth: thy word is truth*. The soundness of our witness also relates to the stability of our lives. If we are to be provoking people to jealousy, then there ought to be something provocative about us. If we are unstable then few will desire to follow. If we, through obedience to the Word, are living on top of the details of life, then others will see our stability and give credence to our message.

The Messenger Must Be Consecrated

Our lives belong to God and we must live accordingly to highlight His testimony to its greatest level. Not too long ago, a shop keeper I visit on a regular basis was opening up when I arrived at the store. He held the door open for me, and immediately two youths armed with a pistol forced their way in. The store has a front area where the customers frequent and a back security area behind two corrugated steel doors and bullet proof glass. The back area is where the cash is, where the shop keeper works, and where the alarm can be shut off. As soon as the front door is ajar, the shop keeper has a few minutes to open the security doors to enter

47

the back section and to type in the security code so that the alarm will be dismissed. If this isn't done in the allotted time, the alarm signal will begin to blast and within a few hours the police will arrive. It's a joke that the police come within minutes.

The "would-be" thieves were not expecting more then one person to be there and were a bit flustered by my presence. But they were not as flustered as I was with their presence, however. They yelled at me to get on the floor. I refused to move. I'm not brave; I serve the living God and take my instructions from Him. I had no unction to do anything, so I stood still. They insisted all the more, and so the shop keeper began to get on the floor. They yelled, "Not you, you shut the alarm." He started to get up, and they yelled, "Put your hands behind your head." It was almost like an Abbott and Costello skit, as the shop keeper began to put his hands behind his head, they yelled, "Not you, you shut the alarm!" He walked over to the security door, and as the gun-wielding youths were concentrating on me, he locked the door behind himself. They soon realized that they had blundered by allowing him to escape to safety. However, they still had a hostage in me. They vowed to shoot me if he didn't shut the alarm, but he didn't budge. Although I have a special relationship with the people I witness to, the shopkeeper wasn't going to allow that closeness to coerce him into giving in to the demands of the gunmen. They yelled that they would kill me, but he remained unmoved. The alarm continued to buzz, and we all knew it would be only seconds before it would begin to ring out in earnest. One youth turned to the other and said, "Let's get out of here." They ran out the front door, and I calmly closed the door behind them.

I told the shopkeeper that they had gone and all was secure. He had two questions for me. First, did they get anything? And second, was I alright? I didn't relate that story to gain any credit for myself. I'm not brave or macho. I have heard one shopkeeper tell another what had happened that morning, and I could tell that the way the story was told, that they had respect for the courage that faith produces.

At no time during the scenario did I ever feel threatened or frightened. You see, our lives are hid in Christ; we are not our own. Our God is always in control, and His will is always best. So with the songwriter we should sing, "Take my life, and let it be consecrated Lord to Thee." The opportunities to witness by tongue grow more splendid and more frequent when the witness is evidenced by a consecrated life.

Power of Prayer

We have mentioned the power of prayer at other times, and we will mention it again. Several years ago, I received a letter from Harrisburg, PA. A Gentile believer was married to an unsaved Jewish man. She thought that her husband was open to the Gospel, and if he could meet with a Jewish believer, her husband would get saved. She mentioned in conclusion, "Please don't tell him I mailed you this letter." I was living 120 miles from them at the time, and I had a lot of reservations about visiting him. There were, of course, the obvious complaints of not enough time, too far away, bad stewardship, someone else must be closer who has more time, etc.

The real difficulty I was having was fear. Two fears rose to my mind. Both were fears of failure. The first was how would I get in? I couldn't very well say, "Hi! Your wife never mailed me a letter." I was used to knocking on doors, but it was always within the vicinity of where we were having meetings. I felt comfortable going up to a stranger's house and inviting them out to services or to a Bible study nearby. I didn't feel confident in driving 120 miles and inviting them back to our meetings in Philadelphia.

The second was that she thought that he would get saved. What if he didn't? This occurred during the time I was serving at Temple University. As I mentioned before, the school was a very difficult place to minister. We always faced opposition and hostility. The expectations were low, and the most modest of accomplishments were viewed as major victories.

However, this was a "no-win" situation. She expected him to get saved, and there was a chance I might not even get in the door. If he did get saved, then we only met up to her expectations, and anything less, even if we were a great witness, would be a disappointment. When I reflect on those days, I'm amazed at how gracious our God is in using the likes of us to represent Him.

Because of my discomfort with the letter, I shuffled it to the bottom of the pile of mail. Every time it surfaced to the top I replaced it at the bottom. My supervisor at the time knew of the correspondence and after a week or so asked me of my intentions. I said I'd get around to it some day. He immediately began to arrange the day. He was scheduled to drive out to Harrisburg for a missionary conference that week, so we could ride out together. When I asked how I would get back, he handed me a bus ticket.

So my trip to Harrisburg was all planned out. I began to voice all kinds of complaints about why it wasn't the best stewardship of time and money for me to make this trip, none of which represented my real hesitations of how I would get in and the fear of failure. For the entire trip out there, I was trying to engage my boss in the argument. He just turned up the Christian radio and drove on. As we arrived in town, we stopped for a meal and discovered that the water pump on his car wasn't functioning. We pushed the car into a garage next door to the restaurant, and I left my boss in a phone booth trying to arrange a last minute ride to the church. I had my bus ticket, money for a cab to the bus station, and directions to the house, which was within walking distance of where we were.

As I began walking to the house, the same fears began to work in my mind. How would I get in? What would I say? I could never say, "Hi! your wife never mailed me a letter," could I? Then I began to think, "Why don't I just call a cab and take the bus back to Philly?" What would I tell my boss? Well, I could go to the house and quietly, very quietly, I mean very quietly knock on the door. When no one answered, I would just return home and say, "Well I tried." I asked myself, "Is that all you think of the high calling of God? Is that what you would allow your ministry to become, tapping and booking?"

In the midst of this little debate, it started to drizzle. So I decided to put out a little fleece. Did you ever notice how we only employ "fleece-ology" when we are convinced of the right behavior, but we don't want to obey, so we look for a second opinion or option or direction from the Lord? I asked the Lord to stop the drizzle. Mind you I looked around, and the sky looked like there would be "drizzle weather" for the next few hours. I thought, if it stops drizzling, I'll do the job and believe I was called to it. If it continues to drizzle, I'm tapping and booking, and it is now in God's hands. With that, the heavens opened up in this torrential downpour. I was instantly drenched from head to foot. The first thought that came to my mind was, this sure ain't no drizzle.

When I had asked the Lord to stop the drizzle, in my mind the rain would stop, the sun would come out, the sky would turn blue, and a little bird would lead me right to the doorstep. Regardless, I had to admit that the drizzle had indeed stopped. So I began running. Now my greatest concern was getting in out of the deluge. Finding their house, I ran up to the door and began loudly banging on it. The man who answered was about 6 feet, 4 inches tall, and sported a fiery red beard. He was the largest, most ominous Jewish man I had ever seen. I was most comfortable witnessing to college students, preferably shorter than I, and always younger and less educated. He was none of these things. As soon as he saw how wet and cold I was, he pulled me into the house. I did the normal shaking and wiping motions people do when coming in out of the rain. Then he turned to me without a word, but his body language said, "Okay, who are you? What do you want? What are you doing here?"

Before I could think of a proper response, I noticed a copy of our monthly magazine on the shelf. I picked it up and treated it like an old familiar friend. My first words were, "I see you get our magazine." His response was, "That's not mine. I don't fool with it, that belongs to my wife." I answered, "You know, I've got an article in that very issue about the Spirit of God working in South Jersey." He said that he didn't believe in the Spirit of God. "You don't! Do you have the Jewish Scriptures?"

He quickly returned with his Bar Mitzvah* Bible. I then showed him the Holy Spirit in the Scriptures, and in the ensuing forty-five minutes, we read Scriptures together as God the Holy Spirit convicted him of his sin and need of salvation. We knelt be-

---

* see glossary of terms

51

side his couch together as he expressed his thankfulness to God for sending his Son to be his Savior. It started to grow late, and I needed to catch that last bus out of Harrisburg, so I asked if I could use his phone to call a cab. He insisted on driving me himself, and so we packed the children into the car and went off to the bus station. As I was wiping the steam off the inside of the bus window, my new believing friend waved goodbye to me from the car. It was then that I first realized that we never even exchanged names. I never had to worry about how I was going to introduce myself. I never had to tell him that his wife never mailed me a letter. We just started talking about the Scriptures and we never stopped until it was time to leave.

The following morning, I was awakened by a phone call. One of the elderly ladies at our church wanted to know what kind of a night I had. The night before was Wednesday. Wednesday is the normal weekly prayer meeting at our church, and these ladies were led to pray for me. Specifically, they prayed that I would have an open door. Colossians 4:3-4 *Withal praying also for us, that God would open unto us a door of utterance, to speak the mystery of Christ, for which I am also in bonds: 4 That I may make it manifest, as I ought to speak.*

Today, the Harrisburg work has grown to become a congregation of Jewish people who are serving the Lord. From that work, missionaries have been raised up, and sent out to serve the Lord in Jewish missions in the United States, in Israel, and in the Soviet Union. Jewish families and individuals are being changed by the power of the Gospel. The blessings of the Lord are multitude in the work that continues there. People look at the results and think that I'm a great missionary. However, we all know that I was tapping and booking. The rewards belong to the faithful servants of God who attended prayer meeting that night. As I was looking for an excuse to go home, they were praying down thunder and storms to get me to run to my appointed task.

Bathe every work, every decision, every ministry, every time, and every day in prayer. Start in prayer, stop to pray, continue in prayer, and when your done, conclude in prayer, follow up with prayer, and then thank the Lord in prayer. If we learn that, we will not fail.

Purity of Motive

Matthew 6:24 ***No man can serve two masters: for either he will hate the one, and love the other; or else he will hold to the one, and despise the other. Ye cannot serve God and mammon.*** Every so often in my life, I start thinking that I need more income. It is never true. God has always miraculously provided for our family over the years. We invariably have more then we need and plenty of toys and gadgets that we don't need. An accountant would never be able to understand how we get by, but we do. However, that doesn't stop us from thinking we need to add to our income from time to time. In the past, we have worked nights as a janitor, mowed lawns, delivered for fast food restaurants, worked as a landscaper, cleaned houses, cut down trees, delivered phone books, moved furniture, and worked in various shops and stores to earn a few extra dollars.

The one thing I have never done is sales. I have only one thing to promote in my life, and that is Christ. I don't do any multi-level marketing, insurance, or any products, gimmicks, or gadgets. I have seen others who have tried to do both, and it always looked a bit awkward to me. Ministers who promoted faith, plus some great company, product line, or financial opportunity invariably got their motives mixed up and forgot just what their primary purpose was.

Years ago, there was a store on South Street called Hymans. It was directly across from Krass Bros. men's store. Krass Bros. is pretty well known because of the commercials they run on a local television station. However, to me it looked like Hymans did more volume. I had dropped some tracts off at Hymans over a period of months and had some brief conversations with one of the salesmen, a Jewish fellow named Larry. For months I hadn't met the owner who, for some reason, was named Moishe. One day, I met Moishe, and he is one very memorable character.

Moishe dressed a bit like Pinky Lee or Lou Costello -striped pants and dotted jackets. For a fine men's clothing store, he was the least likely candidate. To me he looked like an unmade bed, and given my mismatched reputation, that is quite a testimonial. Moishe stood all of 5 feet, 6 inches, and probably tipped the scale at about 200 lbs., at least five of which was an ever present cigar that appeared to be surgically attached to his upper lip. He was the quintessential Jewish salesman. I would enjoy watching him work, and he knew it, and he used to love to perform.

One time, he began bragging that he would make a great missionary, that he could make a living telling Jewish people about Jesus. In fact, he could sell any thing to anybody. I protested, and to prove himself, he boasted that he would sell a suit to the next man he saw walking down the street. Larry objected, but Moishe insisted it was a matter of honor, and so out onto the street we went.

Admittedly, he didn't sell the first person. He let several pass by before he went into his act. "Excuse me," he said, as he stepped in front of a slow walking pedestrian. "May I ask your name?" The man replied, if I remember correctly, "Roger." "May I call you Roger?" he asked. "Roger, I sell only tailor made designer suits. I just had a beautiful garment made for a guy, and wouldn't you know it, he up and drops dead on me. Now I'm stuck with the stinking $25 deposit and a suit made for a guy who's dead. His cheap wife wouldn't even agree to bury him in the suit, and so I'm stuck with the goods. You say, what does that have to do with you? Well, I'll tell you. You should live and be well; I saw the guy in the box this morning, and you're a spitting image of him. Now, I could be wrong, but I got an eye for size and style, and if I'm right, this is your lucky day! Larry go get your tape."

Larry then proceeds to get his tape measure, and while he is measuring the guy right out on the street, Moishe is talking non-stop. He babbles on about how the material is like butter, how he cut his finger taking the label out of the lapel that morning because he can't sell the suits with the designer labels for less then $400. While Moishe is rambling on, Larry gets Roger's measurements, and then goes back into the store. He pulls a pair of pants off of one rack, and then gets a jacket off of another. He has the guy's size, so he can put together a suit off the hangers with ease.

He then puts a plastic cover over the suit and comes back outside. Moishe squeals with glee as he pulls the cover off the suit and offers it to Roger to try on. The jacket naturally fits him, and they begin to talk price. It is a forgone conclusion that Roger will buy the suit; the only question is, how much will he pay.

Moishe offers to sell the suit for $65, and if Roger returns on Thursday with an additional thirty-five bucks, Moishe will throw in another pair of pants and a vest. Roger, thinking he has pulled a fast one, grabs the chance to take the suit for $65. Once he is out of ear shot Moishe gloats, "Half the suckers come back with the $35 in two days."

The tragedy is that Moishe thinks that Jewish missions is just like that, a dog and pony show, a hustle. He has dealt with enough Christians who have had an ulterior motive, and a con man can recognize a con. Moishe has heard enough television evangelists and radio preachers crying for funds and imploring the populace to keep those cards and letters coming. We have to be pure in motive. We should never deliver Spiritual things with one eye on physical benefits. That does not mean we can not receive benefits. The workman is worthy; we only have to be certain of our own hearts. One volunteer refused to take her $17.10 reimbursement check. I tried to explain that serving to get the check is wrong, taking the check is fine.

THREE

The Personal Testimony

While speaking with a group of believers, an interesting subject came up. How often, if ever, in your life, has someone approached you and asked you, "Why are you different?" There were five of us in the discussion, all of us believers, 45 to 55 in age. I was the spiritual baby, having a testimony that goes back only twenty-five years, and my wife, Jackie, was the senior Christian, walking with the Lord some forty-five years. Of course, this is far from scientific, but two of us had never been approached. One of us on infrequent occasions, and two of us had fairly frequent opportunities opened to us, opportunities where unbelievers have approached us and asked us basically what is it that makes us different. Few of us have made this a matter of prayer, and few of us are genuinely prepared for the opening when it arrives. My suggestion is that we first ask God to bring people across our paths, and second that we prepare ourselves sufficiently, so that if and when the door does open, we don't waste the opportunity stammering around searching for the right words to say.

<u>What it should be</u>

Shared as soon as possible

Every time I walk into a shop where the proprietor is Jewish, I instantly sense a rapport developing. I try to be congenial, and the shop keeper usually recognizes me as a fellow Jew, so it isn't unusual for us to cultivate some kind of comradeship. I know that the moment I tell my shop keeper that I'm a believer in Jesus, our relationship is going to radically change. The longer I allow the relationship to continue to grow without telling him, the more difficult it will be. Even if I only allow it to go on for a few brief days, the shop keeper will react as if I had deliberately deceived him. Often they think that I had permitted the friendship to grow under false pretenses.

Many unbelievers employ ribald language, and speak on topics which are unbecoming for the children of God. Once I inform people of my faith, they are uncomfortable with that kind of speech in my presence. Believe me, I'm not being a prude, and I have done nothing to encourage that kind of behavior. Folks just know the difference between right and wrong, and I think the Holy Spirit within us is convicting them. If I don't tell them right away, they will eventually say or do something that will make them feel uncomfortable with me around. They won't know why they feel strange, but they do. When I tell them who I am, and what I believe, they frequently are embarrassed by something they have said or done while I was present. After that, it is seems like no matter how much I try to reassure them, that discomfort prevails throughout our entire relationship.

That is why there is no such thing as telling your personal testimony too soon. Once they know who you represent, they will behave accordingly, and they won't embarrass themselves. The relationship can grow comfortably. Everything that you do, and all that you say, is now done in Jesus' name. No one will think that you happen to be a nice person. As well, when people know you are a believer they expect a certain modicum of behavior from you. It influences the way we behave and makes us very conscious of the things we say and the words we use. Plus, there is no chance of being accused of deception. There will be no misunderstanding when we tell them up front and immediately that we have been changed by the power of the Creator, that we are believers in Jesus the Messiah.

The personal testimony must be brief

This is not the testimony that you share at a church service; this is the testimony you share while waiting in line at the supermarket. It is going to be difficult enough to say what you have to say. There is no reason to prolong the agony. Keep it to under a minute. I was once looking for a religious book store in Lakewood, NJ. I had been there before, and I knew it was downstairs on a side street. I kept driving around the block, unable to spot it. At a traffic light I noticed a Chassidic man in the car next to mine. I motioned for him to roll down the window, and I asked him if he knew where the store was located. He looked at me and a perplexed look developed on his face. I instantly realized what his question must be. He was probably thinking, why would someone who is without a beard and without a skull cap* be looking for a store that caters to the needs of the Orthodox? The only answer I could think of was to share my brief testimony. I was able to tell him about my faith and even get directions before the light turned green. Don't try that in Pennsylvania; the traffic lights are much quicker there.

The personal testimony must be good news

We are forgiven. We are on the way to heaven. We are adopted sons of God, joint heirs with Jesus. We can not be moping around complaining about the unimportant things of planet earth. After all, this world is not our home. We are heavenly citizens, and we are only passing through. This testimony should focus on the positive change that has been wrought in our life. It should be a hook that would make a person want to listen to our message and want to watch our lives.

The personal testimony has to be easy to listen to

Often when I have the chance to share my testimony, I grow very nervous, very quickly. However, just because I'm agonizing, that is no reason to cause the poor, unsaved person that I'm speaking with to suffer also. Work at making your testimony flow.

---

* see glossary of terms

59

Share it among friends, get their opinions, improve it, and make it crisp. It takes practice to sound spontaneous.

The personal testimony should show change

What did happen to you? What makes you different? Share the change in feelings or the change of behavior that the Lord has brought to your life. Here is where the personal testimony is personal. Tell how the ancient story, which has changed millions, has changed you. Here is where we can show a little vulnerability through our honesty. People will feel that they can open up to us. They will feel safe with us, once we have been open and genuine with them.

What it should not be

The personal testimony is not a platform to brag

The purpose of a testimony is not to draw attention to ourselves; the purpose of a testimony is to draw attention to the Lord. I have deliberately omitted from my testimony any reference to anything that might be construed as an accomplishment on my part. It is natural that we want to be respected, and it is tempting to insert personal details to encourage this respect from others that may cause us to share our testimonies for the wrong reasons. We could be tempted to share our testimonies at the wrong time or place just to glorify ourselves. We need to be as certain as possible when we share our testimony, that we are doing so in the Lord's time and in His service. As well, if in our testimony we mention some great accomplishment on our part, the person we are dealing with might draw the wrong conclusion. He might think that he has to be accomplished to inherit eternal life. He may feel he is not that good or that successful, and is therefore not worthy of God's love.

The personal testimony is not rehearsing personal sacrifice

The personal testimony should rehearse the sacrifice of Jesus, not the sacrifice of self. Many people have given up lucrative careers for Jesus. Others have lost relationships with family or friends. The sacrifices on behalf of His kingdom may have been courageous and commendable, but they are not part of the personal testimony.

Years ago, a good friend of ours was being installed as a pastor in a church in Debuque, Iowa. I was honored to be part of the ceremony. That involved taking a train from Philadelphia to Chicago and a bus to Debuque, involving a four hour wait in Chicago. That opened a rare opportunity for me to visit a congregation of Jewish believers in Chicago. I dropped in for their services unannounced. Somehow, I forgot the time change between Chicago and Philadelphia, and so instead of arriving at what I thought was a half hour early for services, I actually arrived a half hour late. The service was already in progress, and the pastor was just beginning the sermon when I slipped in. In his message, he made reference to a Jewish believer who had been declared dead by his family. He shared how this young man had considered the great costs and decided to forsake all and follow Jesus. The details of the testimony were quite specific, and I soon realized that he was speaking about me. I was red-faced and embarrassed. Once I was certain that he was speaking about me, I slipped out the way I snuck in, as quickly and as quietly as possible. Although the things he shared were true, it really did not happen the way he said it did. I gave up nothing for Jesus; He gave up His life for me. I sacrificed nothing for Him; He sacrificed for me. I lost nothing; I had nothing to lose. I gained everything in Christ. That unusual coincidence has served me well. It was good for me to hear how my testimony sounds when it mentions the sacrifices that I seemingly made. Relating those details might serve as a descent sermon example, but those facts do little to glorify the Lord, and for that reason, they have no place in the personal testimony.

The personal testimony should not be sensational

In many Christian churches, there is a desire to hear extraordinary and electrifying life stories. It seems that the greater the depravity is, the higher the interest is. Some of you may happen to have a past life that was filled with debauchery. Some of you may have committed crimes that have raised you to a level of infamy. I'm not suggesting that such folks lie to make their testimony more acceptable. In such cases, use some selectivity. You can't mention everything, anyway, and some things need not be mentioned at all.

In a church service, we might want to mention the details of past sins for several reasons. We may desire to bring greater glory to God, by showing how even in dire circumstances, in the midst of great depravity, He can bring victory. We may want to encourage others in their witness. If someone as vile as I can be saved, then perhaps there is hope for the loved one you are praying for. As well, we might want to list the horrible wages of sin as a warning to others to choose a path of righteousness.

However, in the personal testimony on the street, our purpose is simply to identify ourselves in our relationship with the Creator. A remarkable story that can be appropriate in a church service may not be suitable in a personal testimony. We don't want our unsaved friend to say to himself, "Well, I'm not that bad." We don't want him thinking to himself that only the truly desperate need to get saved. A sensational testimony can serve to reinforce the thinking that religion is a crutch, and some crippled people are in need of a crutch. The sensational story simply presents us as being severely crippled.

First impressions have lasting effects. If I share the criminal aspects of my unchristian life, people tend to see me in that light. Most unbelievers think of themselves as moral people. The moral unbeliever can grow uncomfortable with a person once he has heard a sensational testimony. That discomfort can lead to a lack of trust, which can greatly hinder the witness.

The personal testimony should never be guessed

If people have noticed that there is something different about us, then we should inform them what the difference is. Once they start guessing in ignorance, they can draw some pretty bizarre conclusions. When we later share the truth, we may hear responses like: "Oh, so that's what it is. I knew there was something weird about you." If our personal testimony is shared at the proper time, we can prevent our friends from drawing wrong conclusions.

When I first got saved, I was afraid of what my parents would think, so rather than tell them up front, I tried avoiding the inevitable confrontation. At the time, I was living in an apartment downstairs in the same building where they lived. I starting going to services each Sunday, and my folks would ask me where I was because they noticed that my car wasn't in the parking lot. Too afraid to say I was in church, I said that I went to wash my car. Each Sunday I would drive to church and then get my car washed on the way home, so I could tell my family where I had been. The sneaking around, the half truths, and the deception continued for a time, but it couldn't go on forever. Sooner or later, family and friends are going to see that something has changed, and they are going to ask you, point blank, for an explanation. When my folks did, I was relieved when I finally had to testify. However, they had already drawn their own conclusions. They based those conclusions on what they knew. They knew that whatever it was that had happened to me, it was something that I was ashamed of. They knew it was something I was trying to hide. The Gospel deserves better.

As we mentioned earlier, Friends of Israel does not allow parents to guess at what is going on. Now having learned from our mistakes, we send dependent children home to explain to their parents what they are thinking about. Over the years this has proven to be far more effective than, "Mom, Dad -guess what I just did?" It matters little whether one is contemplating telling a loved one or a casual acquaintance. The personal testimony should never be guessed.

The personal testimony should not use "Christianese"

There are a number of theological terms that communicate to those who are Biblically educated. Terms like "saved" or "born again" are familiar to Christians, but these terms have little meaning to most of the lost. If our testimony is going to be effective, it has to communicate. If we want our testimony to communicate, we need to use only those terms and phrases that have meaning to the hearers. If we do use Biblical terms, we need to explain them. We also need to be careful to use unoffensive language, which is especially true when speaking to Jewish people.

When Benjamin finally agreed to be baptized, he was eighty-four years old. The reason he waited so long was that he had a great discomfort with the large wooden cross in the front of the church. When Benjamin was eight years old, he was playing along the side of the lane in a puddle of water in front of his home in a small village in Kiev. He remembers vividly how the priest was dressed as he marched out of the Ukrainian Orthodox Church. Ben remembers the macabre scene all too well. He remembers how the mob followed the priest down the lane. He remembers how they wielded the torches and shovels menacingly. He remembers how they methodically chanted in their own language "Kill the Christ killers. Kill the Christ killers." He remembers how his mother frantically ran across their path trying to rescue him, but she never made it. His mother was trampled before his very eyes. Ben was sent to England to stay with family, and he eventually came to America. Ben remembers the hatred and the horror. Ben also remembers the large brass cross carried by the priest, the cross that was carried by the priest that led the mob that trampled his mother to her death.

The cross to a Christian might be a symbol of love and sacrifice, but to a Jewish person, that cross can symbolize hatred and horror. We have concocted the phrase "four offending C's" to refer to frequently used words in witnessing that can be offensive or fail to communicate to Jewish people. These terms are: Cross, Christ/ Christian, Crucified, and Convert. We suggest replacing Cross with tree, Christ with Messiah, Crucified with sacrificed, and Convert with repent.

In place of Christ, we try to say Messiah. Most Jewish people have no idea what Christ means. For that matter, many Christians do not know what Christ means. I was once at an ordination council, and I asked the candidate that very question. What does Christ mean? The candidate replied that it means Lord, or something. If Christian leaders do not always know what Christ means, how can we expect unsaved Jewish people to know? Christ is a transliteration of a Greek term which translates the Hebrew word

Messiah. Both Christos and Messiah mean anointed one. Old Testament Prophets, Priests, and Kings were all anointed.

The Jewish people may not have any understanding of the term Christ, but they do recognize the word Messiah. Most are familiar with the term, and many are waiting for the Messiah, the anointed of God, to set up the Davidic Kingdom, and to usher in world peace. To use the term Christ will only identify you as a Christian. At best, the term Christian, to a Jewish person, can simply mean non-Jew; at worst, it can mean anti-Semite. By referring to the Messiah, your Jewish friend will know you believe the promises of the God of Abraham, you believe in the Old Testament, and you believe in the God of the Old Testament. Instead of saying Christian, say Bible believer; after all, that is what we are - we are the people who believe the Book.

Instead of saying crucified, we suggest saying sacrificed. There are Jewish people who are painfully aware that Christ was crucified. The reason for their acute awareness is that they have been blamed for that crucifixion. Jewish people who have been accused of killing Christ associate the term crucifixion with that painful accusation. The term sacrifice brings to mind Old Testament concepts and places the death of the Messiah in the realm of the Levitical system. It is also Biblically correct, as Jesus was the final sacrifice.

Some Jewish people are aware of forced conversions. They have heard of brave Jewish people who gave up their lives and did not forsake their rich heritage. The term conversion, although it is a sound Biblical concept, can conjure up thoughts of being a traitor to the Jewish people. Repentance is turning from self to God. The Hebrew term for repentance is Teshuva[*] and it is a well known term among the Orthodox. We suggest using the verb "to repent" rather than the verb "to convert."

Now that we have described the perfect personal testimony, let me share what I have been memorizing, improving, adding to, reducing, altering, editing, rewording, and sharing through stammering and stuttering, both in private and in public, on the line, and in rehearsal for a quarter of a century now:

---

[*] see glossary of terms

I was born and raised in a conservative Jewish home. When I was twenty-two years old, I became convinced that the Messiah of Israel had already come. I became convinced that Jesus was an incontrovertible fact of history. I was going to Synagogue, and I felt good about myself at services, and I felt clean. However, there were things in my life that proved that I really wasn't close to the Creator, that I really wasn't a righteous person. I met several Bible believers who told me that the things I was experiencing were what the Jewish Scriptures call sin. They showed me how the Scriptures teach that Jesus is the solution to the sin problem. He was the Kipporah* for my sins, the sacrifice that the Creator had provided. I placed my faith in that sacrifice, and I instantly knew that there is a big difference between feeling clean and being cleansed, between feeling good and being declared righteous.

A family outing to the shoe store is a modern day version of a torture chamber for many of us. I'm usually disgruntled by the incredible prices assigned to brand name sneakers. I never seem to properly prepare myself for the culture shock. My children have to suffer through the same old story of how my first car was cheaper then their basketball shoes. I'm looking for bargains, which they affectionately refer to as BOBO's (non brand name seconds). The teens are thinking style. My wife is trying to keep the budget and the peace, which is seemingly impossible. At the height of one of these wonderful nights of family torment, I struck up a conversation with a salesman at the other end of the store. My wife had just paid the extravagant bill and was looking forward to getting home. She said with a bit of impatience in her voice, "Where is your father?" Our daughter, the youngest, replied, "Oh, he's telling that man his life story again." It provided a break in the tension and gave us all a chance to smile. Daddy is telling his life story again. I like that. I like it because it essentially is my life story. Without Jesus there is no life. John 14:6 *Jesus saith unto him, I am... the life."*

---

* see glossary of terms

FOUR

The Message

The Preamble

Before presenting the message, it is a good idea to start with a "hook." In the "Four Spiritual Laws," a booklet published by Campus Crusade For Christ, the first law is "God loves you and has a wonderful plan for your life." This law serves as a hook to give the listener a reason to listen. The message of God's love, the idea of a Divine plan, should whet some appetites. You can hardly go through the day without seeing or hearing an ad for a psychic reader; the promise of fortune and romance lures people in to spend their hard earned money on foolishness.

The Gospel is good news. It is the good news that people really need. Jesus states that one of the reasons He came was to bring an abundant life. John 10:10 *The thief cometh not, but for to steal, and to kill, and to destroy: I am come that they might have life, and that they might have [it] more abundantly*. Most people aren't ready to consider eternity. They want temporal blessings. We need to show them practical, earthly reasons for considering the validity of the Gospel.

We can use verses that speak of the blessings that belong to those who belong to the Lord, like Psalms 1:1, 1:3, 23:6, 30:11,

32:1, 34:8, 84:12, 144:15, 1436:5, Proverbs 30:11-12, or Jeremiah 17:7-8. We could use verses that speak of the protection and care that the Lord has for His own, like Genesis 12:2, Leviticus 26:5-6, Deuteronomy 7:13, 10:15, Isaiah 1:18, Jeremiah 31:8, or Zechariah 2:8. We could share a verse that shows God's guidance or the benefits of His direction, like Psalms 16:11, 23:1, 23:6, 30:11, 37:4, 79:13, Proverbs 3:5-6, or Isaiah 2:2. There are numerous verses that we could recommend. However, we can only suggest a verse or an idea. The verse that you share to provide a hook should be a personal one. It should be one that has had genuine meaning in your life.

The message we preach is not a canned presentation. Our method involves one person telling another person about the marvelous good news. Then the new believer will tell others. We read in Romans 10:9-17 *That if thou shalt confess with thy mouth the Lord Jesus, and shalt believe in thine heart that God hath raised him from the dead, thou shalt be saved. 10 For with the heart man believeth unto righteousness; and with the mouth confession is made unto salvation. 11 For the scripture saith, Whosoever believeth on him shall not be ashamed. 12 For there is no difference between the Jew and the Greek: for the same Lord over all is rich unto all that call upon him. 13 For whosoever shall call upon the name of the Lord shall be saved. 14 How then shall they call on him in whom they have not believed? and how shall they believe in him of whom they have not heard? and how shall they hear without a preacher? 15 And how shall they preach, except they be sent? as it is written, How beautiful are the feet of them that preach the gospel of peace, and bring glad tidings of good things! 16 But they have not all obeyed the gospel. For Esaias saith, Lord, who hath believed our report? 17 So then faith [cometh] by hearing, and hearing by the word of God.*

Paul explains for us that people need to believe to be saved. He teaches how saving faith comes from hearing the word. The English word, "word" usually translates the Greek word *logos*. It is interesting that in Romans 10:17, Paul uses the word *rhema*. The difference between the Greek words *rhema* and *logos* is that *logos* means a written word, while *rhema* means the spoken word. That should effect our methodology. Those who don't see a distinction between the two Greek words will concentrate their ministry on tract distribution. Distributing portions of Scripture can be of great value. We have from time to time involved ourselves in that kind of outreach. However, people are saved by faith, and faith comes from hearing the spoken word. Jesus didn't call twelve printers, he called twelve disciples.

Paul writes in 2 Timothy 2:2, *And the things that thou hast heard of me among many witnesses, the same commit thou to faithful men, who shall be able to teach others also.* We can see the process that continued for four generations: Paul was the first generation, Timothy, the person to whom Paul was addressing the charge, was the second generation. The faithful men and women that Timothy was to commit these things unto was the third generation. The fourth generation are the others that these people are also enabled to teach. Teaching implies that someone is learning. If someone is learning, it means he is listening. The preamble and the personal testimony work together to bring a person to the place where he or she will be ready to listen to the message in the Word.

The Scriptures

It is important to use the Jewish Scriptures to communicate the Gospel to the Jewish people.

Once I counseled a Jewish wife and a Catholic husband. They had given up on secular psychologists and agreed that they needed clerical help to save their marriage. He wanted a priest, she wanted a Rabbi. They got me. When I arrived without a clergyman's collar, Mike asked me if I were a priest. I said, "Me! No, I'm Jewish!" On the basis of that statement, Mike assumed that I was going to be prejudiced on her side. He stormed out of the room, and he refused to listen to another word I had to say.

Left with Shelly, I tried to begin by explaining the roles of husbands and wives in the book of Ephesians. She immediately protested, and insisted that I show it to her in her Bible. The most specific passage of Old Testament Scriptures relating to the role of wives that I could think of was Proverbs chapter 31. The high level of commitment and submission called for in that passage seemed to be a little too challenging for Shelly. I knew the real problem was sin, and so rather than deal with marriage, we went right into the message.

The question is, why did she insist on hearing it from her Bible? Most would say, "Well, that's simple, she believes in her Bible and she doesn't believe the New Testament." Jesus taught that the Old Testament spoke of Him, John 5:46 *For had ye believed Moses, ye would have believed me: for he wrote of me.* In that phrase, Jesus also taught that those who believe the Torah will also believe in Him. The negative of that is also true. If you don't believe in Jesus, you don't believe the Torah. I realize that is quite an indictment. However, I have come to that conclusion on the basis of John 5:46. It is astonishing to think that if they don't believe in Jesus, none of the Rabbis, none of the practicing Orthodox, and none of the pious Chassidim actually believe the Torah. They may give some intellectual assent to the Scriptures. But what they are really trusting in is tradition, oral commentary, and their own logic and feelings. Since that is the case, why wouldn't we just share the "Roman's road"? Because they don't always know that they don't believe. Many think that their beliefs are based on the Scriptures, and most know that they are supposed to believe the Jewish Scriptures. Because they know that they are supposed to believe the Jewish Scriptures, Jewish people might listen to us more carefully when we proclaim the Old Testament.

Jews think the New Testament is for the Gentiles. They are quite certain that the Gospel can't be found in anything that is truly Jewish. So when we show the Gospel to them in the Jewish Scriptures, they are surprised to discover the truths that are there. When they say, "Show it to me in my Bible," we will be only too happy to oblige. We must be prepared to bring the word that Jewish people will respectfully listen to so they will find faith from the Scriptures.

The Bad News

Several years ago we were enjoying a family day at the beach. My three boys and I were hanging onto a Styrofoam raft in the shallow water. Ben was probably six years old that summer, Dan was four, and Josh would have been three. I was old enough to know better. Somehow I foolishly allowed the raft to drift out into deeper waters where I could no longer stand. I became a bit frightened, and I told the boys the situation. "Daddy is in over his head." We needed to aim the raft towards the shore and kick for all we were worth. Ben the oldest understood the gravity of the situation and immediately got in position with great sobriety. Josh, the youngest, sensed how serious his brother Ben had grown and followed suit. Dan, however, didn't seem to understand. He continued to play and was trying to dunk me, just like he did when we were close to the shore.

Danny represents many of the Jewish people we are trying to reach. He couldn't care less about being saved; he had no idea that he was in need of salvation. To the expression "Jesus saves," the Jewish people have a whimsical response; they say, "Moses invests." They don't know what we are talking about when we speak of salvation. They don't know that they are lost. They don't see the need.

It is on this point that Judaism and Christianity are in sharp distinction. Milton Steinberg succinctly expressed the Jewish position. *"Between God and man stands no one, not God-man, not angel, not advocate. Nor is intercession or intervention required. As nothing comes between soul and body, father and child, potter and vessel, so nothing separates man from God, Soul of his soul, his Father and Fashioner.*

To be sure , out of their obtuseness or bewilderment, men may fail to perceive how close He is to them. Through their sins they may make themselves unworthy of His presence and come to feel alienated from Him. But no one can push Him away or estrange Him altogether. And if a need arise for a rediscovery of God or a return to Him, then each man must accomplish this on his own account. Is he blind? He must learn to see for himself, since no one can see on his behalf. Is he lost? He must find his own way home.

71

Other men may help him. They may give him courage, guid-ance, instruction; they may blaze trails and set examples. But in the end, sight is not sight if it is vicarious. Companionship, whether with God or anyone else, must be immediate or it is not companionship.

In sum there is and can be no vicarious salvation. Each man must redeem his own soul. "[12]

The reason man can redeem himself, in Jewish thinking, is their belief in man's nature. In Judaism man is basically neutral; he has both an evil inclination and a good inclination. Sin in Judaism is missing the mark, or stepping over the line. It doesn't refer to depravity. The Jewish Scriptures, however, teach us something rather different.

Man's Nature

Genesis 6:5 tells us how God sees us. *And GOD saw that the wickedness of man was great in the earth, and that every imagi-nation of the thoughts of his heart was only evil continually.* Something happened in the garden of Eden, and only Christianity deals with it. The Christian faith accepts the way the Scriptures describe fallen man. The Bible says that our wickedness was great, that every thought was only evil, and continually evil.

Scripture also tells us what we are internally. Jeremiah 17:9, *The heart [is] deceitful above all [things], and desperately wicked: who can know it?* The Hebrew word for deceitful is translated "polluted" in Hosea 6:8. Judaism is a religion of cleanli-ness. There are numerous washing and purifying rituals in the Jewish religion. As ceremoniously sanitary as one's household might be, however, the heart stays polluted.

Many Jewish people pride themselves on how kosher (clean) they keep their homes. They can hardly wait to mention that they keep strictly kosher in their diet as well. There are varying degrees of keeping kosher. There is an expression called "Glatt" kosher. In order for an animal to be clean for eating, it first must be one of the animals the Bible declares to be clean. Then the animal must be slain in a manner that is in accordance with rabbinical regula-tions. Still, there is always the possibility of contamination. Any food we eat could somewhere along the line come in casual contact with a product from an unclean animal and thereby be contaminated. To be strictly kosher, an animal must be not only Biblically kosher and slain according to ritual, but also free from any possible contamination with an unclean animal or any product from an unclean animal all of its life. Glatt kosher assures that all of the above is true, not only for the particular animal, but for all of its ancestors as far back as can be traced.

After we are certain that we are eating only the cleanest of food, we must also consider our plates and utensils as well. The pious Jew must separate the dishes. Those utensils and dishes used for meat are to be kept apart from those that are used for dairy products. Then there are always those dishes which are kosher for Passover. They must be kept free from any contact with leaven. In a Jewish home, one grows familiar with the Yiddish terms of Pesedic,* milchik,* and flaishik.* Some families have four sets of dishes, two for Passover and two for the rest of the year. There is so very much involved in keeping kosher.

One Chassidic friend of mine is exceedingly proud of the great lengths he goes to keep his kitchen perfect. He preens with delight because his Rabbi will eat at his house, but he will not eat at his Rabbi's house because his standards for following the Kosher laws are stricter than his rabbi's standards. As clean as he keeps his kitchen, as careful as he is in buying only the choicest of Kosher meats, as perfect as he might be in guarding his dishes and utensils, however, his heart is still polluted.

Externally, our natures are also sinful. Isaiah 64:6, **But we are all as an unclean [thing], and all our righteousnesses [are] as filthy rags; and we all do fade as a leaf; and our iniquities, like the wind, have taken us away.** Judaism, like all religions, is oriented to works. The Hebrew word for righteousness in Isaiah 64 is "tzedawkaw." The more popular term that the Jewish people use is the word mitzvah.* Technically mitzvah means commandment. However, it has the connotation of any good work; any good deed, any act of righteousness is a mitzvah. Hence, to do tzedawkaw is a mitzvah.

---

* see glossary of terms

73

If there is a concept or phrase that is central to Judaism, it would be the concept of doing mitzvahs. Where Jesus is chief to the Christian faith, doing mitzvahs has become dominant to the Jewish religion. It is commonly held that if we do mitzvahs, we will receive blessings. This connection between doing good works and receiving good benefits has knitted the two concepts firmly together. A Jewish person will think of both the good deed as a mitzvah and any blessing received in life as a mitzvah, too. So, if someone gives a great deal of money to charity, that would be a mitzvah. If you stop and help a neighbor fix a flat, that would also be a mitzvah; and if one day your single, thirty-five year old daughter comes home engaged to a doctor, that would be a mitzvah, too. Both the good things we do, and the good things that happen to us are looked upon as mitzvahs.

The things we are proud of, the things that we are anxious to share with our loved ones, these are the mitzvahs of our lives. However, the Scriptures indicate that these things are filthy rags in the sight of God. The word for filthy rag is a ceremoniously unclean garment. It is something polluted and despicable. The same word is used in the Mishnah* to describe an Arab's underwear after three days journey in the desert. There is no mention of what the things we are ashamed of look like. There doesn't have to be. If the things we are proud of are despicable, one can only imagine what our sins look like before God if our righteousness is filthy rags.

Man's condition

Isaiah 59:1-2 *Behold, the LORD'S hand is not shortened, that it cannot save; neither his ear heavy, that it cannot hear: 2 But your iniquities have separated between you and your God, and your sins have hid his face from you, that he will not hear*.

In bringing the bad news, Isaiah 59:1-2 are probably the principal verses. Over the years, we have observed the most unusual phenomenon. Frequently, when we share these verses with our Jewish friends, they start asking questions. However, the questions they ask are usually far removed from the theme of the verses.

---
* see glossary of terms

Often they will ask questions about the incredible aspect of miracles or about evolution. When I'm asked a question, I feel compelled to answer it. What I discovered is that it is just like the lyrics of the old silly song about the bear that went over the mountain. "And what do you think he saw? He saw another mountain." Just like the bear who continues to find mountains without end, after every answer, no matter how brilliant and insightful it might be, I find another question. The realization we have come to is this: The word of God has exposed the old sin nature for what it is, separated from God and in need of redemption. Once exposed on the authority of the Word of God, the only recourse left to the sin nature is to attempt to undermine the authority of the Scriptures. These questions that are asked are not sincere inquiries, but are, instead, attempts to raise doubts in the Word.

When we expect to have an opportunity to share the Gospel in the Jewish Scriptures, we usually carry a pad and pencil. When we arrive at Isaiah 59 and start getting all the stalling questions, we jot the questions down instead of spending the entire evening discussing empty objections. We even suggest a few questions that they might not have thought of, "Did you ever think about where Cain got his wife?"

We could have been waiting several years for this occasion; it would be a mistake to waste the evening. So we suggest saying something like "Jake, how long have we been trying to get together to discuss the Scriptures? Listen, let's focus our attention on what the Scriptures have to say about us and our relationship with the Creator. We can always look at these questions later, Jake, but tonight I think we should concentrate on what the Tenach* teaches." Then with his permission, we press on. You see, we have discovered that only two things can happen. Jake could get saved. If Jake comes to faith in his Messiah, guess what! There will be no real questions. If Jake doesn't come to faith that night, there will be no real answers.

Isaiah 59 shows clearly man's condition. It shows that we are both sinful and separated from God. It also shows that a Holy God will not hear our prayers. Up until now, all we really established is

---

* see glossary of terms

75

that nobody is perfect. In Jeremiah 17:9 and in Isaiah 64:6, the Scriptures teach universal depravity, but all the unsaved person really hears is nobody is perfect. The religious person hears that, and thinks, "Fine, I agree, and on Yom Kippur,* 'the Day of Atonement,' I'll fast and pray for forgiveness. Isaiah 59 changes all that.

I remember the High Holidays* as being pretty glum times. The religious observances were particularly oppressive for children, and I would have actually preferred going to school. The seriousness of the high holidays are in accordance with the religious teaching. In a Guide to Jewish Religious Practice, we read, "In accord with the solemnity of Yom Kippur, it used to be customary for people to stay in the synagogue for additional prayers and meditations. Some even spent the night in the synagogue... The air of solemnity and awe should be maintained even after the services, not only in the synagogue, but also at home."[12]

When we returned to school or work after the Holidays, we were always greeted by Gentile friends chiding us for how lucky we were. They always thought we were fortunate because we got to get off from school. Most of us Jewish kids would have rather been anywhere else than in services. After services we had to fast all day; we had to wear suits; and we were forbidden to watch television. We couldn't play all day, nor could we use the telephone, and for a teenager, that was as pleasant as a trip to the dentist.

The day of atonement was given to the Jewish people in the Torah. Leviticus 16:29-30 *And [this] shall be a statute for ever unto you: [that] in the seventh month, on the tenth [day] of the month, ye shall afflict your souls, and do no work at all, [whether it be] one of your own country, or a stranger that sojourneth among you: 30 For on that day shall [the priest] make an atonement for you, to cleanse you, [that] ye may be clean from all your sins before the LORD.*

Leviticus 23:27-29 *Also on the tenth [day] of this seventh month [there shall be] a day of atonement: it shall be an holy*

* see glossary of terms
[12] *A Guide to Jewish Religious Practice,* Isaac Klein, KTAV House inc. p. 217

convocation unto you; and ye shall afflict your souls, and offer an offering made by fire unto the LORD. 28 And ye shall do no work in that same day: for it [is] a day of atonement, to make an atonement for you before the LORD your God. 29 For whatsoever soul [it be] that shall not be afflicted in that same day, he shall be cut off from among his people.

The admonition to afflict the soul is observed by the Jewish people today. The warning about being cut off from the people is taken seriously. However, the Biblical day included the atoning work of the ordained high priest. Leviticus 16:31-33 *It [shall be] a Sabbath of rest unto you, and ye shall afflict your souls, by a statute for ever. 32 And the priest, whom he shall anoint, and whom he shall consecrate to minister in the priest's office in his father's stead, shall make the atonement, and shall put on the linen clothes, [even] the holy garments: 33 And he shall make an atonement for the holy sanctuary, and he shall make an atonement for the tabernacle of the congregation, and for the altar, and he shall make an atonement for the priests.*

Notice the language of Leviticus 16:32; the anointed priest is consecrated to minister in his father's stead. We believe that anointed son, that consecrated priest, is Jesus. In Leviticus, an offering was made by blood. The priest would make atonement for the holy sanctuary, for the altar, and for the tabernacle. Today there is no offering, there is no altar, there is no sanctuary, and there is no tabernacle.

How are we to keep the perpetual celebration without an altar, without an offering, without a priest, without a sanctuary, and without a tabernacle? The rabbinic solution is prayer. But then we return to Isaiah 59. The rabbinic solution is impossible. The soul that is truly searching for peace with God will see the dilemma. My heart is wicked -Jeremiah 17:9. I am incapable of good work - Isaiah 64:6. I am separated from God, and I can not pray for forgiveness -Isaiah 59:2. That is the bad news. It is taught in the Jewish scriptures, and it is very bad news indeed.

The Good News

The Sacrifice Predicted

Leviticus 17:10-11 *And whatsoever man [there be] of the house of Israel, or of the strangers that sojourn among you, that eateth any manner of blood; I will even set my face against that soul that eateth blood, and will cut him off from among his people. 11 For the life of the flesh [is] in the blood: and I have given it to you upon the altar to make an atonement for your souls: for it [is] the blood [that] maketh an atonement for the soul.* These two verses teach three facts. First, they teach us the prohibition against the eating of blood. The Jewish religion, as mentioned earlier, stresses kosher rules. In this verse the rabbis see the prohibition against eating blood and develop a method of slaying animals so that the blood will be properly drained.

The second thing that is taught is that the life of the flesh is in the blood. This may not be of great religious significance, but it is a biological fact. The Scriptures knew the truth regarding the physical nature of man thousands of years before these things were discovered by the scientific community. The medical profession, with all of its grand wisdom, was practicing blood letting as recently as a century or so ago. The first president of the Untied States was bled to death by his own physicians. I jokingly say that if George Washington's doctors would have believed the Bible, he would still be alive today.

The third fact taught in this verse is the lesson on atonement. The verse establishes the role that blood plays in the sacrifice system. There are offerings that were acceptable in the Scriptures that did not include blood. However, as we read in Hebrews 9:22 *And almost all things are by the law purged with blood; and without shedding of blood is no remission.* The altar upon which the sacrifices were offered was sanctified by blood. All of the lesser sacrifices were contingent upon the ultimate sacrifice offered on the day of atonement. The soul that was not afflicted on that day was cut off from the nation of Israel. All other offerings were dependent upon a blood offering and the altar itself was cleansed with blood; therefore all offerings, even the ones without blood, required blood. Blood is necessary for the atonement of the soul.

Both Judaism and Christianity see Leviticus 17:11 as an important verse. However, both emphasize different aspects. Neither Judaism nor Christianity seem to care much about the biological wisdom of the verse, nor does either care much about the polemical value of that wisdom. The Jewish people emphasize the dietary aspects of the verse. In the New Testament, Jesus set aside the dietary restrictions. Mark 7:19 *Because it entereth not into his heart, but into the belly, and goeth out into the draught, purging all meats?* The expression purging all meats has been understood by most Christians to mean that the dietary rules are no longer important. Therefore Christians do not see the dietary instruction as being of much significance. Rather, Christianity stresses the phrase: "The blood atones for the soul." Now which of the two do you think has discovered the really important teaching: Judaism with the dietary emphasis, or Christianity with its stress on the blood atonement for the eternal soul?

The good news is that although we are sinful and separated from God, we can see that God has made provision for our condition. The provision of God is the sacrifice system. Notice how in the phrase, "The blood maketh atonement for the soul," the subject is the word "blood." The soul is the indirect object. The soul doesn't do the action. The soul receives the benefit of the activity of the subject. It shows the truth of the faith system; works are not in view here.

The Sacrifice Provided

Psalm 22:1, *My God, my God, why hast thou forsaken me?* While on the cross, Jesus cried out the opening phrase of this psalm. The Lord was not casually quoting the Scriptures at that moment. He was living the Psalm. The experience of the Lord is unique. In John 1:1, we read how Jesus had always enjoyed fellowship with the Father. *In the beginning was the Word, and the Word was with God, and the Word was God.* The phrase "Was with God," reads pros ton Theon in the Greek language. The preposition pros, translated with the accusative case, can be rendered "face to face with." Throughout all eternity, Jesus was in complete fellowship with the Father, face to face. The man Jesus was the only one to be born in a perfect harmonious relationship with the Creator. Then when Jesus became sin for us, He was ripped out of fellowship from His heavenly Father. God is too holy to allow sin in His presence, and Jesus, who became sin, screams in anguish, *"My God, my God, why hast thou forsaken me?"*

The words of Jesus direct us to the 22nd Psalm. The Psalm pre-pictures the cross 1,000 years before crucifixion became a method of capital punishment. In this Psalm there are several references to the events of the cross that were fulfilled in the New Testament. The Psalm predicts they would mock him and shake their heads in disgust at him 22:7 *All they that see me laugh me to scorn: they shoot out the lip, they shake the head.* In Luke 23:35, we see the rulers holding Him in derision *And the people stood beholding. And the rulers also with them derided him*, and in Matthew 27:39 we read of how they shook their head in revilement *And they that passed by reviled him, wagging their heads.*

The following verse predicts that He would be made the object of ridicule, 22: 8 *He trusted on the LORD [that] he would deliver him: let him deliver him, seeing he delighted in him.* Either knowingly or unknowingly, His mockers said those exact words in Matthew 27:43 *He trusted in God; let him deliver him now, if he will have him: for he said, I am the Son of God.*

In verse 15, we see the grueling exhaustion of the cross and a reference to Jesus' thirst. *My strength is dried up like a potsherd; and my tongue cleaveth to my jaws; and thou hast brought me into the dust of death.* One of the final sayings that Jesus spoke was *I thirst* in John 19:28. In verse 16, we read *they pierced my hands and my feet.* There is some question on how to best translate the Hebrew word we render "pierced." We, of course, have the advantage of the further revelation of the New Testament to assist us. However, there is no question about the mention of hands and feet. The Jewish translations will read "they are like a lion at my hands and feet."[13] The fact of the piercing is also taught in other Scriptures like Zechariah 12:10 *they shall look upon me whom they have pierced, and they shall mourn for him, as one mourneth for his only son.* No matter how you translate verse 16,

---

[13] *The Holy Scriptures* Hebrew Publishing Company Harkavy translation Psalm 22:16

there is still plenty of language in Psalm 22 to pinpoint the fulfillment of the Psalm at Mount Calvary. In verse 2 *O my God, I cry in the daytime, but thou hearest not; and in the night season, and am not silent*, there is mention of both daylight and darkness. We know from the New Testament that there was an unusual darkness, perhaps an eclipse or something supernatural, for three hours in the afternoon. Matthew 27:45 *Now from the sixth hour there was darkness over all the land unto the ninth hour.*

Some of the predictions might be a little vague; two very clear prophecies, however, cannot be denied. Perhaps the clearest of these is the gambling for his cloak. In verse 18 we read *They part my garments among them, and cast lots upon my vesture.* The fulfillment of that can be found in Matthew 27:35 *And they crucified him, and parted his garments, casting lots: that it might be fulfilled which was spoken by the prophet, They parted my garments among them, and upon my vesture did they cast lots.*

The second has to do with the death of the Messiah. In both verse 14 and in verse 17, we read the phrase *all my bones* which agrees with Exodus 12:46 *In one house shall it be eaten; thou shalt not carry forth ought of the flesh abroad out of the house; neither shall ye break a bone thereof* where we read how the Passover lamb was not to have any of its bones broken. That thought is repeated in Numbers 9:12 *They shall leave none of it unto the morning, nor break any bone of it: according to all the ordinances of the Passover they shall keep.* In Psalm 34:20, the idea that bones are not to be broken is transferred from the lamb to a Messianic prophecy *He keepeth all his bones: not one of them is broken.* There are three references to the unbroken bones in the Old Testament besides what we read in Psalm 22. At a casual glance, unbroken bones seem to be insignificant. If it were so unimportant why would the Jewish Scriptures repeat the prophecy so frequently?

We can read about the fulfillment in John 19:32-33 *Then came the soldiers, and brake the legs of the first, and of the other which was crucified with him. 33 But when they came to Jesus, and saw that he was dead already, they brake not his legs:* When the Roman soldiers came by to remove the men from the cross, they broke their legs. The reason the legs were broken was to insure a quick death. With broken legs you can not push yourself up. Those being crucified would soon be unable to breathe, and they would drown in their own fluids. What the soldiers discovered, and what the unbroken bones testify to, is that Jesus was already dead. Nobody killed Jesus! Jesus told us in John 10:17-18 that no one could take His life, *Therefore doth my Father love me, because I lay down my life, that I might take it again. 18 No man taketh it from me, but I lay it down of myself. I have power to lay it down, and I have power to take it again. This commandment have I received of my Father.* The crucifixion did not kill Jesus; an atom bomb could not kill Jesus. Jesus voluntarily dismissed His life with dignity, nobility, and majesty. Luke 23:46 *And when Jesus had cried with a loud voice, he said, Father, into thy hands I commend my spirit: and having said thus, he gave up the ghost.* The sacrifice that was predicted was completely voluntary, given freely, but at a great cost. The sacrifice was provided for us because the good shepherd loves us and gave himself for us.

When I first met Richard he was a teenager. A Christian family was witnessing to him, and they thought that Richard had been saved. I felt that he had acquired a head knowledge, but that he really was not trusting for salvation. After the initial contact I did not see Richard again for almost twenty years. When we met again he was the insurance agent for a business man in our church. At first, we did not realize that we had previously known each other. Richard said that he had been a believer since he was a youth. But Richard did not believe in the deity of Jesus.

It was a strange ministry that we had. We spent about three weeks trying to convince him that he was lost. Richard was coming to Sunday school classes, attending weekly Bible studies and services, and he was being taught weekly by the assistant pastor. He was under a lot of Bible instruction, but he never seemed to respond positively to the Word.

During breakfast one morning, we were deeply involved in Biblical discussion. Richard wanted to be shown the evidence for the deity of Jesus in the Old Testament. With every verse I showed him, he would try to argue against the teaching. I accused him of being closed minded, but he assured me that he was genuinely searching. I asked, "If you are really searching for the truth, why can't we look at the evidence in the New Testament?" Richard had to admit that he did not have an answer to that question, so we turned to the first chapter of John. There we read together how the Word was God. At that moment, I was blessed to observe the most amazing transformation. As Richard was thinking out loud he began to appropriate the information. The word became flesh -the Word is Jesus. The word was God -Jesus is God. Jesus died for my sins -my God died for me.

Here was a Jewish man who had heard the Gospel for over twenty years. Richard had been under some pretty good and some pretty intense Bible teaching, but Richard remained unaffected and unimpressed until he realized that God died for him. Richard instantly recognized the magnitude of the sacrifice. He also realized that it had to have been voluntary because, who could force God to do anything, who could kill God? Christian hymns like "And Can it Be" and "Amazing Love" touch on the concept that is being taught and emphasized by the prophecies regarding the unbroken bones.

Why was this sacrifice provided? The 53rd chapter of Isaiah speaks so clearly of the sacrifice of Jesus that I have yet to find a Jewish person who did not recognize it. I used to hand out a booklet at Temple University with the text of Isaiah 53. After distributing the passage to everyone in the lounge, I would return and ask each student who was reading the booklet if he knew who it was talking about. Most would say, "Jesus, but I don't believe the New Testament. I'm Jewish."

The license plate on my car reads IZAYA 53. It was a gift of a Jewish business man, and now a close friend in the Messiah. I am amazed at how many Christians do not realize what it says, and I am even more surprised by how many Jewish people do. On more than one occasion, a Jewish person has stopped and asked me if I was a Jew for Jesus. When I asked them what made them think that, they would motion to my plate. I then would ask them, "O so you think Isaiah 53 is talking about Jesus?" They would quickly deny it saying, "I don't think any such thing." One Bible teacher has discovered 53 reasons why Isaiah 53 is talking about Jesus. I have not found quite that many. There are many that we have found; however, here we are only focusing on those that relate specifically to the Gospel.

Isaiah 53:3-6,8-12 *(3) He is despised and rejected of men; a man of sorrows, and acquainted with grief: and we hid as it were [our] faces from him; he was despised, and we esteemed him not. (4) Surely he hath borne our griefs, and carried our sorrows: yet we did esteem him stricken, smitten of God, and afflicted. (5) But he [was] wounded for our transgressions, [he was] bruised for our iniquities: the chastisement of our peace [was] upon him; and with his stripes we are healed. (6) All we like sheep have gone astray; we have turned every one to his own way; and the LORD hath laid on him the iniquity of us all. (8) He was taken from prison and from judgment: and who shall declare his generation? for he was cut off out of the land of the living: for the transgression of my people was he stricken. (9) And he made his grave with the wicked, and with the rich in his death; because he had done no violence, neither [was any] deceit in his mouth. (10) Yet it pleased the LORD to bruise him; he hath put [him] to grief: when thou shalt make his soul an offering for sin, he shall see [his] seed, he shall prolong [his] days, and the pleasure of the LORD shall prosper in his hand. (11) He shall see of the travail of his soul, [and] shall be satisfied: by his knowledge shall my righteous servant justify many; for he shall bear their iniquities. (12) Therefore will I divide him [a portion] with the great, and he shall divide the spoil with the strong; because he hath poured out his soul unto death: and he was numbered with the transgressors; and he bare the sin of many, and made intercession for the transgressors.*

The Hebrew noun that is translated *grief* is used twenty two times in the Scriptures. It is most frequently translated as sickness, sometimes a sickness unto death, and in every usage you could make the case that it is a sickness, or injury, that is directly related to sin.

When I was four years old, we had a cookie jar that sat on the top of the refrigerator in our kitchen. In order for a four year old to reach the cookie jar, he would have to pull a stool over to the refrigerator. In order to mount the stool, he would have to pull a kitchen chair up to the stool. In order to reach the elusive cookies, he would have to put two phone books on the stool. From the chair he could climb up to the stool, and then onto the top phone book, and from there he could reach the cookie jar. Now I know how to get to the cookie jar because I have made the treacherous climb on a number of occasions. You might wonder why they wouldn't leave the cookie jar on the counter top, or kitchen table, or some other easily accessible spot. Between meals, invasion of the cookie jar was forbidden.

Details like the cookie jar and how to reach it are the kinds of trivia from my childhood that I would normally forget, and I probably would have forgotten all about it had it not been for one eventful afternoon. My mom was supposed to be across the street for a minute. My twelve-year-old brother was supposed to be watching me. I assembled the furniture and began my climb. We have all heard of getting caught with your hand in the cookie jar. I thought this expression was named because of my experience. At the summit of my climb, as I was about to claim my prize, mom walked into the room. I don't know where she came from, but the question at that moment seemed to be more in relation to where I was, as opposed to where she was. I felt ashamed. I felt my face grow warm and flush as I was probably blushing with embarrassment. I remember the sick feeling of dread; I would call it grief. I also lost my balance and fell to the floor. I wrenched my knee and screamed in anguish. My knee hurt, but not that much. I was hoping that the injury might distract the inevitable justice, and maybe I could work up some mercy; none was forthcoming.

The hurt knee was grief. The embarrassment of being caught was grief. Grief can be the direct judgment of God for sin, or it could be reaping what you have sown. The shame could be grief; the injury could be grief. The word could refer to either or both. I shared that little incident from my youth because it was my earliest remembrance of an experience with grief. There have been many since. All of us know about grief. We have all been in the wrong place at the wrong time, and our sin has found us out. The reason we all are acquainted with grief is because we are all sinners.

The Hebrew verb translated *acquainted* in Isaiah 53:3 is a passive participle. The person being discussed in Isaiah 53 was not familiar with grief. He had to be passively introduced to grief. We know grief because we are sinners. He did not know grief because he was sinless. In verse four we read how he carried our griefs. The sickness that was ours, the shame that belongs to us, he took upon himself.

In verse nine we read how he made his grave with the rich in his death. The English Bibles do not reflect it, but the Hebrew word for death is in the plural. That concept is a bit difficult to render in the English language. It is also a bit difficult to understand. How does one die more than once? Part of the answer is given in the verse. In the next phrase we read *because he had done no violence , neither [was any] deceit in his mouth*. We are all born spiritually dead. That fact is evidenced by our deceitful speech and our violent nature. The man of Isaiah 53 did not show those human traits. He was not spiritually dead. He was spiritually alive.

We recognize that death in the Scriptures refers to separation. Physical death is the separation of the immaterial part of man from the body. Spiritual death is separation of the immaterial part of man from a relationship with God. Conversely spiritual life would be enjoying a relationship, a union with God. Now we understand how Jesus fulfills this prophetic statement. He was born in a right relationship with God, then he bore our griefs, he became sin for us, and the human Jesus was separated from his heavenly father. That was death one. He then dismissed his physical life, death two, and made his grave with the rich.

It is difficult to understand the plural death concept, but there is no other explanation that makes as much sense of the Scripture. In revelation 20 we read about the second death. The second death is not a plural death. Resurrected persons can die again. The man of Isaiah 53 died twice at the same incident, two kinds of death simultaneously. There is no other possible fulfillment for the plural death. Jesus is the only one who could die more than once because he is the only one who was born spiritually alive. Everyone else that is spiritually alive is made alive in Him, and that is eternal life, which lasts forever.

In verse eight we see the reason why the servant had to die. *for he was cut off out of the land of the living: for the transgression of my people was he stricken.* He died for the transgressions of my people. The word "cut off" is a violent death, an assassination. This violent death is, according to Isaiah, a sacrificial one. The Jewish religion does not recognize substitutionary atonement because the Jewish religion does not teach depravity. Both of these truths are taught in the 53rd chapter of Isaiah.

There are in this chapter references to other great truths in the area of soteriology. Truths that are normally thought of as New Testament doctrines are referenced in this passage of the Old Testament:

One of these truths is that of references to universal depravity. *All we like sheep have gone astray; we have turned every one to his own way;... the iniquity of us all.*

There are references to substitutionary atonement. *Surely he hath borne our griefs, and carried our sorrows:... But he [was] wounded for our transgressions, [he was] bruised for our iniquities: the chastisement of our peace [was] upon him; and with his stripes we are healed... the LORD hath laid on him the iniquity of us all... for the transgression of my people was he stricken.*

There are references to imputation. *For he shall bear their iniquities... he was numbered with the transgressors; and he bare the sin of many*, to Propitiation, *53:11 [and] shall be satisfied,* and to justification, *by his knowledge shall my righteous servant justify many.*

I am frequently asked, "What do Jewish people think when they see Isaiah 53?" First, very few ever get to see it. There are Scripture readings in the services each week. The first five books of the Bible, the Torah,* is read through in its entirety throughout the year. In addition a portion of the rest of the Scriptures (Haftorah*) is assigned to the weekly Torah selection, and read along with the Torah. The Haftorah readings are selected to com-

---

* see glossary of terms

87

pliment the Torah portion. The readings from the Haftorah go up
to Isaiah 52, skip the 53rd chapter, and then continue in Isaiah
chapter 54. Rabbis say that there is nothing in Isaiah 53 that
compliments any of the Torah readings. That of course is very
subjective. If you wanted to find a Torah reading that was com-
plimented by Isaiah 53 I am sure you could find several candi-
dates. Perhaps Genesis 15:6 could relate to Isaiah 53:1 or the
whole chapter could be a comment on the prophecy predicted in
Deuteronomy 18:15. Of course if you desired to keep Isaiah 53
hidden you would not find a suitable time to read it.

In ancient times the Rabbinic commentaries used to say that
the chapter was Messianic. However today the standard Rabbinic
position on Isaiah 53 is that the passage is referring to the nation of
Israel. At one Bible study in Eatontown, NJ, there was an individual who had met an Israeli who only spoke conversational Hebrew.
I know a little Biblical Hebrew, which is very far removed from
the modern Hebrew which he spoke, so we had a very challenging
conversation. I would show him a verse of Scripture in the Hebrew
Bible and then he would point to another in the way of response.
When we arrived at Isaiah 53, he said "Eratz Yisrael, Am Yisrael," which means in English, "The land of Israel, the people
of Israel." That much I could recognize, and it was exactly the
response that I had become accustomed to. It was obvious from
his quick reaction that he was familiar with the text, and was
expecting me to turn there. He was ready with the traditional
Rabbinic interpretation.

I directed him to verse eight. *He was taken from prison and*
from judgment: and who shall declare his generation? For he
was cut off out of the land of the living: for the transgression of
my people was he stricken. This verse clearly sets Israel apart
from the person that the passage is discussing. Israel is *my people*.
He died for my people. He can not also be my people. He can not
be Israel. I tried my best to communicate that train of logic in the
Hebrew language. He understood me because he said "good
point." I heard that, and continued on struggling with Hebrew. I
started to try to translate the phrase "good point," and then realized
that I was going in the wrong direction. " Wait a minute, if I'm

translating into Hebrew, you must have spoken in English!, and you used vernacular English." He laughed; he wondered how long it would take me to discover that he spoke English fluently. So he made a fool of me. That's alright, because in the end, it was a good point. It is still a good point. The Rabbinic interpretation does not hold up to scrutiny.

As we mentioned earlier, Jewish people usually will have no trouble recognizing Jesus in Isaiah 53. The passage has more to say beyond Messianic prophecy. In Isaiah 53 we can clearly see New testament truths, as they relate to the Gospel, taught in the Old Testament, truths either ignored or denied by the Jewish religion, but clearly taught in the Jewish Scriptures. We listed the references in Isaiah 53 to universal depravity, substitutionary atonement, imputation, propitiation, and justification. Beyond the aspects of Isaiah 53 that relate specifically to the Gospel, there are many more facts that point to Jesus. Allow me to list a few here.

1. vs. 2 root out of dry ground
2. vs. 3 acquainted with grief
3. vs. 3 rejected
4. vs. 4 bore our griefs
5. vs. 5 wounded for us
6. vs. 7 submitted without protest
7. vs. 8 dies for Israel
8. vs. 9 violent death
9. vs. 9 plural death
10. vs. 9 rich man's grave
11. vs. 9 innocent
12. vs. 10 resurrection
13. vs. an offering

When would this sacrifice be provided? Daniel 9:24-26 *Seventy weeks are determined upon thy people and upon thy holy city, to finish the transgression, and to make an end of sins, and to make reconciliation for iniquity, and to bring in everlasting righteousness, and to seal up the vision and prophecy, and to anoint the most Holy. 25 Know therefore and understand, [that] from the going forth of the commandment to restore and to build Jerusalem unto the Messiah the Prince [shall be] seven weeks, and threescore and two weeks: the street shall be built again, and the wall, even in troublous times. 26 And after threescore and two weeks shall Messiah be cut off, but not for himself: and the people of the prince that shall come shall destroy the city and the sanctuary; and the end thereof [shall be] with a flood, and unto the end of the war desolations are determined.*

The prophecy of Daniel chapter nine is complex. However, it does, when unraveled, clearly pinpoint the time of the Messiah. The passage begins with the words *know therefore and understand*; from that expression you would conclude that as difficult as it might seem, the understanding is knowable. The prophecy has a distinct starting point. Everything begins with the commandment to restore and to rebuild Jerusalem.

There are three different possible starting dates where decrees to return and rebuild are issued. Dr. Alva J. McClain discusses these different possibilities. " 'This commandment,' by a large number of interpreters, has been identified with the decrees issued by Cyrus, Darius, and Artaxerxes, recorded in the book of Ezra. But theses decrees without exception have to do with the rebuilding of the Temple, not the city. Let the student read carefully Ezra 1:1-2; 4:1-5,11-24; 6:1-5, 14-15; 7:11, 20,27, and notice that in every case the decree concerns the 'house of the Lord' but there is no authorization for the rebuilding of the city... There is only one decree in Old Testament history which, apart from all expedients of interpretation, can by any possibility be identified as the 'commandment' referred to in Daniel's prophecy. That decree is found in the book of Nehemiah."[14]

Nehemiah 2:1 *And it came to pass in the month Nisan, in the twentieth year of Artaxerxes the king, [that] wine [was] before him: and I took up the wine, and gave [it] unto the king. Now I had not been [beforetime] sad in his presence.* Nehemiah 2:8 *And a letter unto Asaph the keeper of the king's forest, that he may give me timber to make beams for the gates of the palace which [appertained] to the house, and for the wall of the city, and for the house that I shall enter into. And the king granted me, according to the good hand of my God upon me.* The first thing to notice in the Nehemiah decree is that there is a clear starting date. The second thing to single out in the Nehemiah decree is the reference to the condition of the wall, and the emphasis on the rebuilding the wall during difficult conditions. Nehemiah 2:17 *Then said*

---

[14] *Daniel's Prophecy of the Seventy Weeks* Dr. Alva J. Mclain Zondervan 1940 p. 17-18

I unto them, Ye see the distress that we [are] in, how Jerusalem [lieth] waste, and the gates thereof are burned with fire: come, and let us build up the wall of Jerusalem, that we be no more a reproach.

The prophecy in Daniel specifically mentioned the wall being built in **troublous times**. Because of the clear starting date, the mention of the wall, and the decree for rebuilding the city, we can confidently begin our calculations on the starting date of the twentieth year of Artaxerxes. Artaxerxes began his reign in 465 B.C.E.[15] The twentieth year of Artaxerxes then would be the year 445 B.C.E. From there we count seven weeks. The Hebrew word translated "week" is שָׁבֻעַ (shevua). It means a group of seven. It can refer to seven days, as we commonly use the expression, as in Daniel 10:3, or it can refer to seven years, like the Levitical Sabbatical year, as in Genesis 29:27 *Fulfil her week, and we will give thee this also for the service which thou shalt serve with me yet seven other years.*

In this context the seven year usage is more probable. That means we count from 445 B.C.E. 49 yrs. It is possible that the length of time it took to totally complete the securing of the walls, and to secure and reinstate the sacrifice system, was 49 years. The Old testament canon is closed, and so the prophecy is sealed in the first 49 years. From there we count an additional three score and two weeks or 434 years (62 * 7).

Daniel says that after the three score and two weeks, after the total of 483 years, the Messiah will be cut off. The rabbis insist that the messiah referred to here should be translated as a messiah, not "The Messiah." If that were the case why would he be referred to in the text as the Messiah nagid, Messiah the prince? The terminology points to the anointed of God, the Messiah.

To determine when the Messiah would be cut off, we need to do further calculations. The prophecy is given in terms of Lunar years. We measure time in solar years. The lunar year contains 360 days. The total number of days in the prophecy is 360 multiplied by the total number of years, 483. This is a total of 173,880 days.

---

[15] *Encyclopedia Britannica*

In order to convert that into solar years, we now need to divide our total number of days by 365. The number of solar years in the prophecy is 476.3. Since the starting date was 445 years B.C.E., and the total number of years in the prophecy is 476 years, we move forward on our time line to the year 31 CE. After the 31st year of the common era, the Messiah will be cut off.

$$7 \times 7 = 49, 62 \times 7 = 434$$
$$49 + 434 = 483$$
$$483 \times 360 = 173,880$$
$$173,880 / 365 = 476.38$$
$$476 - 445 = 31$$

Dr. McClain has included into his calculations both the lunar and solar leap years, and begins his calculations on the first of the month of Nissan. His date of completion is the 6th of April, 32 CE.[16] the day that Messiah Jesus made His triumphant entry into the city of Jerusalem. The above calculations ignore the leap years, and I never know what to do with the year zero. I have a zero on my time line between -1 B.C.E. and +1 CE, but in reality there was a year that year. There was no zero year. It was the ninth year of Tiberias or somebody. Therefore the above calculations are off by a few weeks. The Jewish people, however, have missed it by twenty centuries. So being off by a month or so is not a big deal. We do not have to be mathematical geniuses. We are not trying to calculate the vector of reentry for the Apollo 13. We have only to establish that there is a marvelous prediction of the time frame for Israel's Messiah, and that time frame points us in a superb way to the days of Jesus.

Who would be the sacrifice? In Daniel 9:26 we read that *after three score and two weeks the Messiah will be cut off.* As we mentioned earlier the traditional Jewish position is that the Messiah mentioned here is simply an anointed one, and not the Messiah. However, as we pointed out, the anointed one of Daniel is the Messiah the prince, and that points to the Messiah the son of David. The reason for the controversy is that the term in Daniel does not have the definite article. The word Messiah, that means

---

[16] *Daniel's Prophecy of the Seventy Weeks* p. 19

anointed one, occurs 38 times in the Massoretic text.[*] In only three places is it used with the definite article, all of them in Leviticus chapter 4 verses 3, 5, and 16. In each of these occasions it is used with the word priest, הַכֹּהֵן הַמָּשִׁיחַ. That transliterates to *"Ha Cohen Ha Mashiach."* The phrase translates in English to "the priest the anointed." In every other usage of the term Messiah, it appears as an anarthrous noun, even when it is obviously definite.

In Habakkuk 3:13 the word Messiah follows the sign of the object. In Hebrew the sign of the object is only used when the object is definite. Therefore in the opinion of the Massorites the term Messiah is definite. However, although the word Messiah is definite, it does not use the definite article. In every use of Messiah in the Scriptures it seemed like it was a definite usage. I think the word Messiah is by its nature a definite concept. Because it is always definite, it does not seem to require the definite article. The lack of the definite article in Daniel nine does not mean that we should translate the term as "a Messiah," especially since he is Messiah "Nagid," Messiah Prince.

The Sacrifice Applied

Isaiah 1:18 gives us God's invitation. *Come now, and let us reason together, saith the LORD: though your sins be as scarlet, they shall be as white as snow; though they be red like crimson, they shall be as wool.*

In Genesis 15:6 we read man's response. *And he believed in the LORD; and he counted it to him for righteousness.* The Scriptures teach us that Abraham, the Patriarch of the Jewish people, established his relationship with God by faith. Like all religions, Judaism is works oriented. Only Biblical Christianity recognizes the concept of salvation by grace through faith. Ephesians 2:8-9 *For by grace are ye saved through faith; and that not of yourselves: [it is] the gift of God: 9 Not of works, lest any man should boast.*

In apologetics, we deal with the argument of works. In Evangelism, we need to explain the concept of faith to our Jewish friends. Both the Hebrew and Greek languages have verbs for

---

[*] see glossary of terms

93

faith. One difficulty in explaining the Gospel is that in the English language, we do not have a verb for faith. To translate the Hebrew and Greek verbs, we use the English word "believe." The problem with believe is that believing is an act of the intellect. Often Jewish people say "I wish I could believe the way you do." They think that before they can believe in Jesus, they have to be intellectually convinced of all the facts, no wavering, and no doubts. However, faith, although it does not contradict the intellect, is not based on the intellect.

Another word that is close to faith is trust. The word trust in our culture always seems to have limitations. Faith is a non-intellectual trust that is without limitations. I place my trust in Jesus without reservation forever. Faith is an act of the volition; it is a matter of choice. We choose to believe, we choose to exercise our faith in Jesus.

Abraham heard the word of God and believed it. That is, he chose to place his faith in the word of God. The Hebrew word translated "belief" is simply the word "amen." Abraham said amen to God; and God declared Abraham righteous. What Abraham experienced is exactly what Jesus the Messiah explained in John 5:24. *Verily, verily, I say unto you, He that heareth my word, and believeth on him that sent me, hath everlasting life, and shall not come into condemnation; but is passed from death unto life*.

After we have completed the presentation of the Gospel, we tend to begin the struggle of trying to coerce our Jewish friends into praying the "sinner's prayer." We have all heard the expression "praying to receive Christ." The Bible says nothing about a sinner's prayer. I know that in Romans 10:13 we read *For whosoever shall call upon the name of the Lord shall be saved*, but that verse does not teach that a person can be saved by prayer. Romans 10:9-10 says *That if thou shalt confess with thy mouth the Lord Jesus, and shalt believe in thine heart that God hath raised him from the dead, thou shalt be saved. 10 For with the heart man believeth unto righteousness; and with the mouth confession is made unto salvation*. Jesus teaches in Matthew 12:34, that *out of the abundance of the heart the mouth speaketh*. We try to put words in the sinners mouth. I wonder how many people were forced into praying a prayer for salvation when they had no genuine faith. Our job is to present the Gospel. The Holy Spirit will convict, and draw those whom he sovereignly chooses. We can not do the job of the Holy Spirit.

We can do a great deal of damage, though. By exerting pressure, we can force someone into making an insincere decision. We then give them assurance verses, and convince them that they are enjoying a relationship with the Creator, when in fact nothing has been changed at all. I know it is very difficult not to push at this time. But we have to exercise restraint.

Remember the Jewish wife we mentioned earlier who was seeking marriage counseling? She insisted that we only use the Jewish Scriptures. I learned the most marvelous lesson, as the Lord was working in her heart. We showed her the Gospel in the Jewish Scriptures. After reading Genesis 15:6 together I really was not sure what to do next. I asked if we could look at the New Testament. I was quite surprised that because she had been so adamant about only using her Bible earlier, now she made no objection.

After looking through her Bible, the Jewish Scriptures began to convict her of sin, and she became more open. I turned to Romans 10:9-10. After reading the verse out loud, I was for a brief moment speechless, an unusual situation for me. I was thinking how I would phrase my challenge to her. I wanted to say something like where do you stand in relation to that verse, or what does that verse mean to you? While I was thinking about what to say, she interrupted my thoughts with, " I can do that; I can confess with my mouth that Jesus is Lord and I believe in my heart that God has raised Him from the dead."

I was shocked! Most of the Jewish people I had dealt with had great struggles with the Deity of Jesus, and we usually spoke nothing about the resurrection from the dead at all. Yet she read Romans, and said that she could do what it asked. It was obvious that the Spirit of God was working in her heart. We showed her the Scriptures, and He convinced her that the Scriptures were true. She chose to believe them in her heart, and made confession with her mouth. I was still thinking, however, that she had to pray to receive Christ! So I asked her if she would like to pray. She readily agreed and then instantly folded her hands and bowed her head. I was going to explain the ground rules. You know how it goes, "pray this little prayer after me." But with her head bowed and with her eyes closed, I felt sacrilegious saying anything.

I thought for a moment that if I began to pray, she would know to pray after me, if I used the proper inflection in my voice, and if I paused long enough. Or perhaps, I thought, I should pray, Father, I'm going to pray, and she is going to pray after me. While I was thinking about what I should do, she began to pray. She prayed the most theologically sound prayer that could have been rendered at the time. She confessed her sin, using the Biblical terminology she had just learned. She thanked the Lord for sending Jesus, and she acknowledged her need of Him for salvation. She expressed her faith in Jesus, and she thanked the Lord for allowing her to have the faith.

Since that night I have tried to learn to get out of the way of the Holy Spirit and allow Him to work. After showing people the Gospel I say little. I let them talk. They usually express reluctance to make any decisions or changes. I will rehearse for them what we have seen in the Scriptures, and I will encourage to act quickly. I will mention what is at stake, and how costly delay can be. However, I believe that we should not be looking for another notch on our Spiritual belts. I give them some breathing room. If the Spirit is working we will know. If they believe in their hearts, then out of the abundance of the heart the mouth will speak. We can encourage, we can add information, but we cannot push their decision.

I have had the blessing of being present at the birth of each of our four children. There was a moment at each birth where there was a tremendous urge to push, but at that moment my wife was instructed not to do so. I remember the apparent overwhelming urge, and the severe prohibition to abstain.

The urge to push a potential convert into making a decision can be extremely compelling. To do so can be destructive, and we must overcome the urge. Salesmen tell me that after the presentation of the product there is an awkward moment of silence. They say that the first one to break the silence loses. After presenting the Gospel there is also an awkward moment of silence. It is best to let the silence be broken by the unbeliever. If they are still searching they will tell you. If they are ready to make a decision they will not be able to hide it. If they are not ready to make a decision at this time, then they will share the reluctance. It is a delicate moment. We need to pray to be sensitive. I think we can try to discover what might be holding them back. We can try to remove obstacles with the truth, but we cannot force a decision.

A new missionary working at Temple university campus and I had a little disagreement about this issue. We showed a Jewish student the Gospel in the Old testament, and then I preceded to wait for a response. My new missionary companion could not contain himself. He aggressively jumped all over the guy. It soon became good missionary versus bad missionary. I admit that I might have made him look bad in front of an unbeliever, and that was a poor tactic. I could have been more thoughtful, but my missionary friend was incredibly thoughtless. He then accused me of not being evangelical enough. He thought that my reluctance to push was an evidence of a lack of commitment in my life. I tried to explain that if we push we lose. There is no benefit in coercion. If the person is ready to be saved no coercion on our part is needed. If he is not ready only two things can happen; we could force him into a superficial confession, and we all realize the terrible ramifications that could produce. Or he will refuse to be moved by our pressure. If that happens, inevitably we will reach an impasse, and all communication between us becomes futile. We will lose our friendship, and where we have worked so hard to break down barriers, we will have erected an insurmountable one. Where there was once a comradeship, there now is hostility.

It is usually eleven years between the time a Jewish person hears the Gospel and when he finally come to faith. The most important thing is to keep the friendship. My missionary friend and I were discussing this as we were walking up Broad street. Two students were approaching us, and as they came within eye contact they started to cross the street in the middle of the block. Broad street is a tough street to get across. Crossing in the middle of the block requires some athletic ability; you have to be quick and alert, but most of all, you have to be committed. As soon as they got half way across the street, my missionary friend recognized them. He said, "I was witnessing to those guys just the other day."

As we continued up the block two fellows who were across the street started to cross the street in the middle of the block. They trotted up to us and said "hey how you been?" I did not recognize them at first. But then I realized that they were two Jewish students that I had been witnessing to a year ago. I thought that it was a confirmation of what we had been discussing. Two people he had been witnessing to crossed the street to avoid him. Two students I witnessed to a year ago ran across the street to say hello. When you push, you become obnoxious and destroy the relationship, at best; at worst, you force someone into a false decision.

FIVE

Bible Prophecy

The Warning label

When I first came to Philadelphia I was invited to teach a Bible class that was run by a missionary from another ministry. He was called out of town on deputation, and since I was the new kid on the block they thought they would give me a call. The group I was addressing was about 20 in number. The twenty people were all professing Jewish believers. The group, although small in number, was a fairly good cross section of the Jewish community. Both men and women, old and young, former orthodox, conservative and reform were present that night.

Early in the presentation I started to get a lot of negative feedback. When you say something unpopular to a Jewish audience, you usually find out quickly. I said that we are all sinners. They didn't like that. I tried to clarify the statement by explaining how by nature we are sinners, even though we have been born again. The clearer I made myself, the more they disliked it. After a while I became aware that there wasn't another born-again person in the room. None of them knew about sin, none of them knew about depravity. All of them were, however, professing believers.

We later discovered what happened. The well-meaning missionary had used Messianic prophecy to convince these Jewish folks that Jesus was the Messiah. They knew nothing about sin and true salvation, but they were intellectually convinced as to the nature and character of Jesus the Messiah.

Most Jewish people need to make two distinct decisions in regards to Jesus. Most Jewish people are raised to think of Jesus in a negative way. They need to be brought to the place where the Gentiles start out. Gentiles begin with a positive attitude about Jesus. They are convinced that Jesus is legitimate, but that does not make them saved. If you were to go door to door to take a survey asking the average Gentile who he thought Jesus was, I am certain you would get some very sound Biblical answers. One would say he is the son of God, the second person of the Trinity, etc. If you were to ask those same people how to get to heaven, you would get some very Biblically incorrect answers. They will say you must do good works, ring bells, and if you are not good you will come back as a frog. Most Gentiles know who Jesus is, but they have no true idea as to the nature of man or the reality of the Gospel by faith. Most Jewish people have no understanding of Jesus. There are over three hundred prophecies predicting the Jewish Messiah. Through these prophecies our missionary friend brought this group of Jewish people to the place where most Gentiles are already.

These Jewish people had to make some tough decisions. If Jesus is the Messiah, then they needed to make the appropriate changes in their lives. What had happened was that Orthodox Jews were converted to become liberal Protestants. The subsequent changes in their religious lives was misread as evidence of salvation. The intellectual agreement about the Messiah was misunderstood as a confession of faith for salvation. They were convinced about Jesus and that was an important step in the right direction. But they were never taught that they were sinners or that the Messiah died for their sins. Messianic prophecy is a valuable tool to help a Jewish person make a big step in the right direction. Biblical prophecy can substantiate intellectually the validity of the Scriptures. The danger is, however, that we assume that the intellectual change is the only change that is needed. Many professing Jewish believers are professors only. They are convinced in their minds through prophecy, but they are not converted in their hearts through Biblical conviction. Salvation is by faith, faith that is an act of the will, an act of the will that comes when they are confronted with the bad news. Then they must reach out and personally trust in the good news for themselves.

Prophecy regarding the land

One would expect that the Jewish people would be excited about the prophetic Scriptures concerning the establishment of the State of Israel. Jewish people, however, are usually unknowledgeable about Bible prophecy. As we have already mentioned, there are over three hundred prophecies about Jesus in the Jewish Scriptures. If you are not going to believe in Jesus, you are not going to believe in Bible prophecy. The Jewish people would rather appeal to modern day politics and current history for the right to the their homeland before they would consider the Scriptures.

Showing the Jews the Biblical basis for the restoration of the land can accomplish at least three things. First, we can confirm the integrity of the Scriptures through prophecy and fulfillment. I was speaking with a Jewish believer about new age stuff. After showing him several prophetic texts, he replied, "Well that's not a big deal; after all, God is in control, so it isn't spectacular when He predicts the future." Unfortunately, this guy is only impressed when Edgar Casey gets close. The point is, God is in control, and He has revealed the future in the Scriptures.

Second, in addition to showing the character of the Scriptures, prophetic passages that deal with the land of Israel can initiate a conversation about the character of God. We can show how He has been faithful to his ancient people. Despite all the attempts to destroy the Jews, the Lord has preserved His own. The existence of the people of Israel is a testimony to God's care and faithfulness. We always delight in mentioning that if you want to see how the Babylonian lived, how the ancient Assyrian lived, how the Canaanite lived, you must go to a museum. If you want to see how the Jew lives go to Borough Park.

The third benefit from Bible prophecy is that it presents an opportunity to discuss eternity. After showing the prophetic Scriptures as they relate to Israel to your Jewish friend, it will be natural to begin discussing what the Bible has to say about the future. From a discussion of the future, it is easy to discuss what the Scriptures have to say about heaven and hell.

Jeremiah 30:3 *For, lo, the days come, saith the LORD, that I will bring again the captivity of my people Israel and Judah, saith the LORD: and I will cause them to return to the land that I gave to their fathers, and they shall possess it.*

Ezekiel 38:8 *After many days thou shalt be visited: in the latter years thou shalt come into the land that is brought back from the sword, and is gathered out of many people, against the mountains of Israel, which have been always waste: but it is brought forth out of the nations, and they shall dwell safely all of them.*

Amos 9:14 *And I will bring again the captivity of my people of Israel, and they shall build the waste cities, and inhabit them; and they shall plant vineyards, and drink the wine thereof; they shall also make gardens, and eat the fruit of them.*

Prophecy regarding the Messiah

Many Jewish people think of the concept of messiah in legendary terms. The Messiah is not thought of as a real person. Showing them the basis for the Messianic beliefs can serve a great purpose. We can begin to give them the Biblical picture of the Messiah, and slowly remove them away from the legendary perspective. Showing them the Scriptures begins to establish both the validity of the Scriptures, as well as establishing the historicity of the Messiah.

His Genealogy

From Abraham -Genesis 12:2
And I will make of thee a great nation, and I will bless thee, and make thy name great; and thou shalt be a blessing
From Isaac -Genesis 17:9

And God said unto Abraham, Thou shalt keep my covenant therefore, thou, and thy seed after thee in their generations.

From Jacob -Numbers 24:17

I shall see him, but not now: I shall behold him, but not nigh: there shall come a Star out of Jacob, and a Sceptre shall rise out of Israel, and shall smite the corners of Moab, and destroy all the children of Sheth.

From Judah -Genesis 49:10

The sceptre shall not depart from Judah, nor a lawgiver from between his feet, until Shiloh come; and unto him shall the gathering of the people be.

From Jesse -Isaiah 11:1

And there shall come forth a rod out of the stem of Jesse, and a Branch shall grow out of his roots

From David -2 Samuel 7:5

Go and tell my servant David,... 2 Samuel 7:16 *And thine house and thy kingdom shall be established for ever before thee: thy throne shall be established for ever. Psalm 132:11 The LORD hath sworn in truth unto David; he will not turn from it; Of the fruit of thy body will I set upon thy throne.*

The Virgin Birth: Isaiah 7:14

Therefore the Lord himself shall give you a sign; Behold, a virgin shall conceive, and bear a son, and shall call his name Immanuel.

The Place of Birth: Micah 5:2

But thou, Bethlehem Ephratah, though thou be little among the thousands of Judah, yet out of thee shall he come forth unto me that is to be ruler in Israel; whose goings forth have been from of old, from everlasting.

The Timing of the Messiah: Daniel 9:25

Know therefore and understand, that from the going forth of the commandment to restore and to build Jerusalem unto the Messiah the Prince shall be seven weeks, and threescore and two weeks: the street shall be built again, and the wall, even in troublous times.

His Nature

His nature would be eternal (Micah 5:2), and also divine (Isaiah 9:6). Most Jewish people do not think about the Messiah. During the years of diaspora, the belief was that the Messiah would lead them to the promised land. Now that the Jewish people have been returned to the land of Israel, there is little urgency in the coming of a Messiah. The Jewish belief, contrary to the Biblical picture, has historically been that the Messiah will be a man. *"As legend pictured him, the Messiah would be a human being of very special gifts: strong leadership, great wisdom and deep integrity. These he would use to stimulate a social revolution that would usher in an era of perfect peace. But there was never any suggestion of divine power brought to bear. The Messiah was envisioned as a great leader, a moulder(sic) of men and society, but for all that, a human being , not a God"*[17]

The above quote probably reflects the opinion of many of the Jewish people you will meet. Notice the use of the word "legend." When believers speak of Messiah, they speak of a person, a friend, a savior; never a legend. When they speak to the source of their beliefs, they quote Scriptures; they do not say, "according to the legend." Many Jewish people have a dim view of spiritual things. That is why we use Biblical prophecy to show them that the Scriptures are indeed miraculous. The average Jewish person is really very secular, and is often close to the so-called "New age" philosophy. *"Today, only the extreme orthodox still cling to the literal belief in the coming of a Messiah. In the modern city of Jerusalem, many such believers gather in their synagogues to pray for a redeemer to return to Zion. Most Jews, however, have reinterpreted the age -old belief in a Messiah, not as an individual Redeemer, but as mankind collectively, who by their own acts can usher in a Kingdom of Heaven. When humanity has reached a level of true enlightenment, kindliness and justice, that will be the day of the Messiah."*[18]

---

[17] *What is a Jew*, Rabbi Morris Kertzer, Macmillan Co. p. 38
[18] Ibid. p. 39

Notice the language that Rabbi Kertzer uses. When he refers to the orthodox community, he is compelled to call them extreme. The use of the word "extreme" reveals Rabbi Kertzer's philosophy. He is a secular humanist. Anybody who holds to religious convictions is considered an extremist. Rabbi Kertzer's views are similar to those of Jewish folks I know. His thinking is typical. If the Jewish people view the orthodox of their own community with that kind of disdain, we can begin to appreciate what they think of the fundamentalist Christian.

This mind set needs to be dealt with before Jews can be brought to the Lord. Our love and genuine concern for them will, with prayer, in time give us opportunities to show them the Scriptures. The prophetic texts can be used to establish the integrity of the Scriptures. The Scriptures can be used to show them the promises of the Messiah. They will learn that Jesus' credentials to be that Messiah are impeccable. The right line, the right place, the right time, and the right character will bring them to the place where they are no longer negative about the Lord. Then we simply show to them the Gospel in the Jewish Scriptures and wait for the positive response.

The Second Advent

Why isn't there peace on earth? Why are there wars? Why is there sickness, suffering and death? If the Messiah is Jesus, if the Messiah has already come, then why? I marvel that people who think of the Messiah in legendary terms can suddenly become so adroit when it comes to Messianic expectation. One Jewish friend once quipped that if Jesus is the Messiah, then he certainly didn't do a very good job. Another Jewish friend finds the condition of the world to be very depressing. He thought that it would be more hopeful to be waiting for a Messiah to come rather than to believe in one who has been here already.

The answer to these questions and complaints can be found in the second advent. The difficulty is that there is little mention of the second coming of the Messiah in the Jewish Scriptures. There are numerous prophecies that speak of the Messianic age. There are also messianic prophecies that deal with the first advent. These two messianic themes that are evident in the Scriptures have been interpreted by the Rabbis to be teaching that there is a second messiah; the first is the suffering messiah, whom they refer to as Messiah Ben Joseph.[19] There is little mention of the second messiah today, and few are familiar with the concept.

The dual aspect of messianic prophecy is evident from the Scriptures. That the Messiah will come twice is not referred to as frequently. However, it is clearly taught in the Scriptures. Hosea 3:4-5 *For the children of Israel shall abide many days without a king, and without a prince, and without a sacrifice, and without an image, and without an ephod, and without teraphim: 5 Afterward shall the children of Israel return, and seek the LORD their God, and David their king; and shall fear the LORD and his goodness in the latter days.* In Hosea chapter three we read how the Messianic rule of King David will come after a long period of time without a king in Israel. In Genesis 49:10 *The sceptre shall not depart from Judah, nor a lawgiver from between his feet, until Shiloh come; and unto him shall the gathering of the people be.* We see that a Judean king will be on the throne when the Messiah comes. The only way to reconcile these two verses is to admit two comings. The first coming occurred when the king was on the throne, then He was rejected; subsequently the Jews were dispersed. When the second coming occurs, the Kingdom will be restored.

This is precisely what we see being taught in Hosea 5:15-6:3 *I will go and return to my place, till they acknowledge their offence, and seek my face: in their affliction they will seek me early. 1 Come, and let us return unto the LORD: for he hath torn, and he will heal us; he hath smitten, and he will bind us up. 2 After two days will he revive us: in the third day he will raise us up, and we shall live in his sight. 3 Then shall we know, if we follow on to know the LORD: his going forth is prepared as the morning; and he shall come unto us as the rain, as the latter and former rain unto the earth.*

The Lord is speaking, and he says that he will return to His place. Where is the Lord's place? It is heaven. God says that He is

---

[19] Babylonian Talmud Sukkot 25:a

going to return to heaven. In order to return, he first has to leave. Hosea is teaching that the Lord is going to leave heaven and come to earth. He is then going to leave earth and return to heaven. He is going to stay in heaven until the Jewish people recognize their offense.

Notice the close of verse three. The coming of the Lord is likened to the rain in Israel. In Israel, there are two rainy seasons. The Messiah comes twice, once to fulfill the four Spring feasts of Leviticus 23:4-21, and a second time as the latter rains, after the long dry summer, to fulfill the three fall feasts of Leviticus 23:23-36. In verse 15 we read how in their affliction, they seek Him early. In the great tribulation the nation of Israel is brought to the place where they are made ready to receive the Messiah. This is what is being revealed in Zechariah 12:10, and what Jesus was referring to in Matthew 23:39, when He said, *Ye shall not see me henceforth, till ye shall say, Blessed is he that cometh in the name of the Lord*. The Scriptures do indeed teach that the Messiah is going to come to the earth twice. The prophesies that have not yet been fulfilled by the Lord Jesus await the second coming. The first time our Messiah came, He fulfilled the role of the suffering servant. He was rejected, and he died for our sins. The second time He will return to establish the long awaited Messianic kingdom. We will discuss these verses again in the Apologetics section.

SIX

Evangelistic Techniques

In the great commission, the imperative is to make disciples. The English translations render the passage as if the command was "to go." The word translated *go* is really a participle. However, the participle can in some instances have an imperative force. Many see the stress of the passage to be that of going. They emphasize missions, and special evangelical programs. Others see the word *go* as an adverbial participle. The command is "to make disciples." When do you make disciples? You make disciples while you are going. While you are going to school, while you are going to work, as you are going through life, you make disciples. How do you make disciples? You make disciples by teaching, and by baptizing.

The two different ways of understanding the text has produced two different approaches to evangelism. There is " witnessing as you go," and there is "going out to witness." Actually there is a third option, which is by far the most popular of all. This is to do neither, because most have opted for neither. By neither witnessing as we go, nor going out to witness, we have failed miserably. The Church has failed to make a significant impact into the Jewish community. For that reason we can no longer afford the luxury of an "either/or" mentality. We must adopt an aggressive policy of "both/and," both witnessing as we go, and going out to witness.

Witnessing As You Go

I recently heard a preacher ask the congregation about the chief end of man. We have all heard that the chief end of man is to glorify God. This preacher suggested that there will be greater glory to God once we are in glory. It will be easier to serve God in heaven because in heaven His will is always done. If we can serve the Lord and glorify Him better in heaven than on earth, why then are we left on earth? One preacher's suggestion was that we were left here for one simple reason. While we are here, we can reach the lost. We are the vessels through whom the Lord has chosen to work, to bring others to Himself. That makes the life-style evangelism of witnessing as you go both one of the most natural as well as one of the most supernatural things a believer can do.

Advantages

The advantages of witnessing as you go are obvious. There are no travel expenses and no ministry costs. The contacts come in normal situations, and are easy to make. Conversations develop spontaneously and without effort. I was sitting in Jiffy Lube this morning when I noticed a New York license plate on the car in the next bay. I turned to the lady in the waiting room, and asked if she was from New York. She said she lived up-state outside of Syracuse. She explained to me how she was visiting her mother. I spoke with her about her mom, and then casually asked her if she went to church in Syracuse? She said she didn't. I chided her mildly, in a joking way, and then preceded to tell her what Jesus had done for me. My car was finished, we exchanged pleasantries, and I was on my way knowing that I had left her, and those in the waiting room, with a small witness to think about.

Disadvantages

When you are called to make disciples, every person is a potential student. I know that I often take great liberties in class, however. As relaxed as I might appear in the classroom, I am very much aware that I am in front of those who are learning. That has to make a difference in what I say, and what I do.

The lost are learning about Jesus as they watch us. What we do speaks louder, and leaves a more lasting impression than what we say; our lives are examples for others. We are always on display, and we have no time off.

Most Christians are aware of these draw backs. They do not want to be inconvenienced. They do not want to have to live up to demanding standards. So they avoid speaking up for the Savior. When the door to witness opens up, they look the other way. In America we have been accustomed to our rights. Each is entitled to life, liberty, and the pursuit of happiness. That phrase has been translated to mean a less than 40 hour work week and two weeks paid annual vacation. When you witness as you go, you have **no** time off.

Another distinct disadvantage to witnessing as you go is the lack of accountability. When you go out to witness, you make plans to meet, you begin with prayer, and you are accountable. If you do not show, you have to explain yourself. Witnessing as you go allows for many "no shows." There is no one who will ask of your efforts, at least not in this life.

Procedure

Daily Prayer: Colossians 4:3

Begin each day by asking the Lord to open your eyes to the unsaved people you come in contact with. Then ask the Lord to open opportunities to communicate the Gospel with them. Ask God to burden your heart for them, that you might be able to recognize their need. Throughout the day evaluate the witness with the Lord. Ask if you have been missing opportunities, or if you might have been too anxious, or too reluctant. Scriptures say we have not because we ask not. Be certain that if you are not seeing souls come to Jesus it is not because you have neglected to pray about it.

Personableness

As we discussed earlier, it does not cost anything to be nice. It can pay off in grand dividends. Take an interest in others, ask questions, find out their interests, and look for needs that you can minister to.

Carry and lend literature

"Boy, Mitch you are really cheap; can't you afford to give out Gospel tracts?" Well I might be cheap, but frugality is not the reason why I do not give out literature. When we give literature away, it often gets tossed in the kitchen drawer with the used Mollie screws, and there it sits, picking up antique value as the years go by. When you lend literature, people will be more inclined to read it. They know that you are going to ask for it back, and you will probably ask them what they thought of the material, so they will have to read it. At least they will scan it. You will get more mileage out of your materials by lending them out. Sometimes you will even receive a piece of literature back, and give it to someone else.

Share your testimony

As we discussed earlier, share you testimony. Share it early and frequently. The personal testimony is like the jab in boxing. Develop a good one; it is an essential weapon. Develop and use it; it opens doors, and it makes things happen.

Volunteer for Everything

If they need help, you become the helper. If they need company, you agree to go with them. Visit the sick, the prisons, go to the children's games, and attend the recitals. At first they will think you are forward, and even a bit obnoxious. After a while, however, they will grow more comfortable with you, and it won't be long before they will be taking advantage of your willingness and kindness.

Going out to witness

Disadvantages

Outreach Programs are costly and time consuming. Most ministries involve volunteers, and that means training, and giving up control of aspects of the ministry. As well, programs are often non-productive. A good meeting involves much work. There is publicity, which can include the making of flyers and posters, mailing, handing out flyers, posting posters, and the making of radio or local television ads. There is the set-up of the location, which involves decorations, and if the program is in a church building, in Jewish ministries, setting up means taking down and camouflaging any and all potentially offensive objects. Finding a suitable location can involve meetings, calls, visits and mailings. Transportation, a children's program, nursery care, refreshments and, finally, the program must be planned. Music ministry, message, skits, and testimonies all take time and effort.

The total number of man hours invested in an outreach program can be staggering. The best meeting I can remember included about seventy new, unsaved, Russian-speaking Jewish people. Many meetings had none, and most had less then five. Can you imagine what kind of results the church would see if we would invest the same amount of time, prayer, care, and effort into witnessing to our neighbors? I think the results could be staggering.

Any kind of program is going to be less effective than witnessing as we go. Going door to door, or distributing tracts on the boardwalk or in the streets, can all be unnatural situations that can produce hostility and opposition. You cannot do evangelistic programs alone, so you have to work with others. Others have a tendency to be unreliable, unspiritual, and unprepared.

We were having a Hanukkah party in a church. We had about seventy people coming to the party, and that included about half a dozen unsaved Jewish folks. My pianist and song leader was a very talented young man. He sang and he played traditional Jewish songs in the most charming way. Every bobeh* that attended would just love him. The meeting was scheduled for Friday night. My charming musician called me Friday afternoon to tell me he had to work that night and couldn't make the meeting. He said that he could lose his job. We had cleared Friday night with his boss, and I was wondering what went wrong. What my friend didn't tell me, was that on Wednesday night, he had stayed up all night saving the princess in the Super Mario Bros. video game. He called in sick on Thursday, and then his boss had to rearrange the schedule so he was rescheduled for Friday night. He explained to me that I shouldn't be so upset. "God is in control, why can't I just trust the Lord?" Sure we can always sing acappella. But we also could have

---

* see glossary of terms

brought a delightful and charming music package to some lovely unsaved Jewish folks. I could have scheduled other music, but I was counting on him.

Advantages

One of the advantages of program evangelism is you get to work with others. Okay, so you noticed. Working with others is a disadvantage. It can also be a great advantage. It is an advantage to be a part of a team, to have comrades who share the pressure, to have others to divide the burdens. If you have a team, you will share with them the victory of a successful ministry.

After the meeting, campaign, or program is completed, you get to go home. When you are going out specifically to minister, there comes a time when the ministry is over. When the work is done, you can sit down, and have a word of prayer with your workers. You can evaluate the ministry, and then you can go home and kick your shoes off and relax.

There is also a greater potential. Now I know I said that programs are never as effective as witnessing as you go. That is always true. We can accomplish more if we invest the same amount of time and energy in our personal evangelism. However, since we often do not get involved in personal evangelism, programs do expand our outreach. One person can only do so much, but a team of people can do so much more.

Often when people see the difficulty of a program, they then learn to appreciate the opportunities that they have in their everyday life. Standing on a street corner for two hours handing out tracts can be very boring, and that experience can go a long way to making a person eager to see an open opportunity to share.

Aggressive programs attract attention. The publicity that is done for the meetings can be a witness in and of itself. The responses may not always be positive, but the notoriety can open up doors. People who have heard about us may be growing in curiosity, they may be open to hear what we are all about.

In the planning and the conducting of a program, you get to multiply yourself. The workers are learning how to run a program themselves. The workers and volunteers often become independent, continuing the programs and ministries on their own, and in many cases, have gone on into full time Jewish work.

Procedures

The STTJ Conference

The first thing we need to do in any location, is to train the believers to be more effective in Jewish evangelism. The " Speak Tenderly To Jerusalem " booklet is a great tool. It lends itself very nicely to seminars in local churches.

The first step in any program is prayer. Psalm 127:1 *Except the LORD build the house, they labour in vain that build it*. We need to pray about who attends. In some seminars we have had people with a bad spirit. Their negative attitude proved to be a discouragement throughout the meetings. We would hope that those who come, come because of a burden to reach the lost sheep of Israel.

Sometimes believers invite unsaved Jewish people to the STTJ conference. A seminar on how to reach the Jewish people can be offensive to an unsaved person. The STTJ is designed for believers, and is not designed for the unsaved. One Jewish woman entitled the seminar "the care, feeding, and mating habits of Jewish people." Yet when we bathe the program in prayer, marvelous things can happen. We have been blessed to see Jewish people come to the Lord as we were training Gentiles in Jewish evangelism.

In most cases we will be doing the training under the auspices of the local church. Their authority must be maintained. The ministry must belong to the church. We assist them, we are their servants, and their guests. We must guard against the tendency to take charge of the work. We have to move at their pace, and we cannot start ministries that they are not prepared to undertake.

The "STTJ" should not be done during a worship service. It is not a program for the entire church. We are hoping to train those who have a desire to reach the Jewish community. The seminar is suited for an elective Sunday school class. The material can be adequately covered in about six hours, with ample time for discussion and questions. It is also possible to present it as a Saturday workshop with special music and testimony. We have also met one night a week for a month, for a few hours each session.

Often there are people from other churches who want to learn how to reach their Jewish friends. We welcome multi-church participation, but we must insist on single church authority. One church is going to be responsible for the ministry, and we are going to make ourselves responsible to the leadership of that church. As well, everyone who attends should be there with the hearty approval of the leadership of their respective congregations. We will not be a party to anarchy.

There is plenty of Satanic attack on Jewish ministries. We therefore need all the protection we can get. That is why we bathe every ministry and every meeting with prayer. As well, it is the reason why we bring ourselves under the authority and within the gates of the local assembly. Matthew 16:18 18 *And I say also unto thee, That thou art Peter, and upon this rock I will build my church; and the gates of hell shall not prevail against it.* (KJV)

Literature Distribution

The best way to get out the most amount of information in the shortest period of time is to hand out tracts on a busy street corner. Before you select your corner, day, time, personnel, and the literature you want to distribute, pray. It is the only way to start every missionary endeavor.

• The Literature

Literature distribution can be thought of as the heavy artillery phase of the campaign. It is a terrific way to let the neighborhood know that we have arrived. We can announce programs, like English as a second language classes, or Hebrew tutoring. We can publicize the Purim party, or alert the community to some Messianic prophecies in the Jewish Scriptures.

After prayer, select the literature. When I know what we are using, I can better decide on who would be best suited to hand it out. There are a variety of literature types that you could distribute. The literature can include everything from meeting announcements, gospel presentations, or pre-evangelistic tools. The selection of the literature has to do with the purpose of the ministry, who you are trying to reach. The literature can be in Yiddish or

Russian, but if you choose literature in a foreign language, you have to find a location where that language is used predominately, and you have to be certain that your workers are familiar with the material.

Cost effectiveness is an ever present consideration. In the past it was in vogue to use mimeographed hand outs. The were reproduced cheaply, and they could be tailored to the ministry. Broadsides were most effective back in the sixties, however, when "the Hippies" roamed the earth. The long haired flower children liked the cheap, mimeo look, because it had an anti-establishment appearance. Today the same broadside looks unprofessional and are often unsuccessful. They communicate a totally different message. Today's "Yuppies" like things that are well done, expertly printed, and show some style. A professionally printed pamphlet is going to be more costly to hand out in quantity, but it will get a better reading on today's streets.

With the graphics of a PC and with a color printer, you can design a very attractive piece of literature that says exactly what you want to communicate. Be creative, but be careful; read and reread everything that is going to be handed out. Look for any possibly offensive language; if something can be misunderstood, it will be. If any thought can be taken the wrong way, that will be the way it is remembered.

Over the years we have made several embarrassing errors. Once we invited people to the high "hoy" day services. We left the "L" out of holy. We distributed literature in Wilmington, Delaware, inviting people to a meeting in Harrisburg, Pa. One year volunteers were late getting the art work on a flyer. I had to approve a flyer over the phone. In my mind, I pictured it printed on our stationary, with the letter head that said " proclaiming Israel's Messiah, sacrificed, risen, and returning." They described the text and the drawing and it all sounded fine, so in a rush I said, "Go ahead and print it." It went out on plain paper. There was not a single thing in the flyer to announce that we were believers. The tract showed a Jewish prophet and some scrolls, and invited folks out to a conference on prophecy from the Jewish Scriptures. Nowhere was there any mention of our beliefs, and no reference to salvation was made in the final copy of the pamphlet. An unsaved Jewish person could have come to the meeting and thought it was sponsored by the local synagogue.

The chief rabbi of the area was furious. He accused us of deliberate deception. The pastor of the sponsoring church agreed to accompany me as I went to the rabbi's study to apologize. The pastor showed up with his hat in his hand. He showed real class, since the mistake was totally mine. We explained to the rabbi how it was an oversight not to clearly identify ourselves and the true nature of our beliefs, and not a deliberate omission. I asked him if he knew of any other incident of this kind in our ministry in the past. The Rabbi had to admit that we had until then been fairly clear about who we were, and what we were doing. We told him that if he wanted, we would bring all further literature in for his approval first, before we distributed it. He almost agreed, then at the last minute declined. I was hoping he would do it. I could always use another editor to correct misstatements and typos. Besides, who would be better than a rabbi to spot any potentially offensive language. We could even add to the bottom of all our literature: "approved by the head of the board of Rabbi's."

Carefully read and edit every piece of literature that is to be handed out. Make sure it includes a local PO box that people can respond to. We recommend a post office box as opposed to a local address. The bomb threats are greatly diminished that way.

• Location

Choosing the right place to hand out tracts is really a science. We are not looking for just a busy corner; we are looking for the place where the most people that we want to reach are. If you want to reach the Jewish people, then discover their travel habits. Locate the public transportation vehicles that service the Jewish community. Find out where and when they arrive in the city, and then look for the best available legal place to access the most people you can.

The best opportunities are during the morning and evening rush hours, and during lunch time. At peak hours of traffic, you need to be careful to not block the flow of pedestrians. Some local ordinances may exist relating to handing out literature. You have a constitutional right to be on public streets, practicing your religion. Learn about the local ordinances, and abide by them; usually it only involves filling out forms, or buying a permit. Your attitude in sacrificing your rights, with a submissive spirit, speaks louder and longer than the literature you are dispensing.

• Personnel

There is an art to handing out literature on the street. On the same corner in the same time slot, one person can hand out over 700 pieces of literature, while another will only accomplish half that number. Some of that is personality, some of it is "know how." Those who are going on the street should be trained and adequately prepared. They have to make a good appearance. They should dress neatly and comfortably. Remember, on the street they are ambassadors. The appearance of the believers handing out the literature on the street is itself a testimony. They must be willing to follow instructions and display a submissive spirit. They must have a heart agreement in doctrine and policy with those who they work with.

• Procedures

Keep tracts in a shoulder bag. Place the tracts upright in the left hand, so that people can see them as they approach you. Take the tract off the top of the pile and hand it to the person directly into his hand. Never place a track into someone's bag or purse, unless we are asked to by that person because it is an invasion of privacy. If a person refuses a tract, we do not offer the same tract to the next person; simply place it on the bottom of the pile, and then offer the top tract. It is not much but each person is entitled to a fresh tract. Make eye contact with the people as they approach you. Be as friendly as possible. People tend to be followers, and crowds tend to move in waves. If the first person in the wave takes a piece of literature, then the rest of the people in that wave are more likely to do so. If the first person in the wave does not take the tract, then the rest of the people in that wave will be more reluctant.

As you see people approaching try to spot someone who is getting ready to take the literature. They'll start to shuffle their packages or will be looking at the tract. Pamphlet those that seem to want to take the material. If you get several refusals in a row, turn around and start working the other direction. As a rule though you should have one major direction, that you are focused on, those who are coming from the train or bus or whatever, and you concentrate on them

The track-handlers should be organized into groups of two. For every six people on the street, there should be one team leader. The person who is the worst at distributing the literature might be the best to serve as leader. Two workers should be positioned diagonally across from each other at an intersection. The leader will travel from one group of two to another. The leader is trouble shooting. It is the leader's job to remove as many distractions as possible, so the teams can continue to distribute the literature. The leader will keep an account of all the tracts distributed, and will compile any names that were collected on the street. It is the leader's job to make sure everyone is well supplied with literature. The leader also will spell the workers for bathroom and refreshment breaks.

The people should be trained to concentrate on distributing the literature. They have a job to do, and should stick to it. If someone asks questions, continue to hand out tracts. Explain that you cannot talk right now. Remember there is an address on the pamphlet where they can direct any questions they might have. Each person should carry a pad and pen. Try to get folks to leave their names and addresses, and then get back to them. One thing to guard against is a person on the street who expresses an interest in hearing the gospel. Everyone ceases to hand out pamphlets, and starts to engage the one person in conversation.

The biggest problem on the street is usually boredom. The second biggest nuisance is well-meaning believers who engage workers in conversations. On rare occasions there is hostility. Meet it with softness. Apologize for any and all offenses. Take a defensive posture, and if struck never strike back. Cry out for help, run for help, pray, witness, but never raise you hand offensively. We are representing Jesus, and if there ever was a time to turn the other cheek, this is the time. This is the time to be as wise as serpents, and as meek as doves. In all the occasions I've had on the streets, I have never been hit. I was punched at only once. Unfortunately the missionary who was standing next to me can't say that he had never been hit. I was involved in a heated discussion with a chassid. The missionary next to me was doing his job distributing literature. The chassid became enraged at me and swung out in fury. I ducked, and my co-worker got clipped in the ear.

Tracts produce little in the way of results. There are, however, some by-products to the ministry of tract distribution. The ministry tends to build comrades. Standing on the street corner can build faith, and confidence in your ability to serve, and as we mentioned before, once out on the street, people tend to be more aggressive in their personal evangelism.

Of course thousands of pieces of literature have been handed out, and the Lord can work through the printed word. Someone once called us from a tract that he found on the top of a trash bin in Atlantic city. The tract was handed out in Philadelphia, over five years earlier. How did a tract get to Atlantic city from Philadelphia, and where was it for five years? That tract might have some amazing stories to tell as it went from one to another on its five-year trek.

There will be some contacts made on the street, but for the most part we have little opportunity to follow up on the literature we hand out. We have found that the more exposure one has to the Gospel the greater the chance for a positive response. That being the case it is a shame we cannot find a way to contact the people we have given pamphlets to.

Mailings

The best way to distribute a large amount of literature and then follow up on those who receive the tracts is through mailings.

• Prayer

The first step in any and every ministry is prayer. We need to pray about the development of the mailing list, the selection of personnel, the materials to be sent out, and the raising of funds. Every aspect of a mail ministry needs to bathed in prayer.

• Mailing list

The first people to place on the mailing list are the most open contacts, the contacts that believers have made through everyday life. Our neighbors, friends, co-workers, family members, doctor, dentist, and lawyer are the first to be placed on the list. The next group to place on the list are the contacts made through evangelism; the folks we have met on the street, and those who have come out to programs and meetings. The bulk of the mailing list will be names from the phone book.

We have compiled a three page list of Jewish sounding last names. Everyone on the list has a Jewish sounding name, but everyone on the list isn't Jewish. We had Jacob Abrahamson on our list; he wasn't Jewish. Every Jewish person doesn't have a Jewish sounding name. I know a Simon Smith; he is Jewish. So everyone with a Jewish name isn't Jewish, and everyone Jewish doesn't have a corresponding name. That means any mailing will miss many, and include some outside the area of our focus. I will still place loads of literature in front of Jewish people, however. Some have compiled mailing lists from the newspaper. They use names from wedding announcements, Bar and Bat Mitzvah notices, and even the obituary columns. The advantage of using the newspaper is that the literature can be suited to a specific situation.

If possible, we mail everything out with a first class stamp, and as much as possible, we try to address every envelope in ink, and by hand, because a significant amount of mail is discarded immediately, or perused with a view to discarding, when it is sent bulk rate, and the address is computer generated.

• Personnel

The mailing ministry is a great place for the shy quiet type to serve. We need people to do clerical work. As well, we need people to do technical work. The mailing ministry could use an editor and chief, someone who can take charge of the ministry, and keep people on schedule. This person must insist on a standard of excellence in the material.

The technical responsibilities. The first and foremost task of the technicians is to produce the mailing. Each month we are going to send out a gospel presentation. The graphic artists need to design the flyer, and the theologians need to insure that the material is Biblically sound. The grammarians will be checking for linguistic clarity, and accuracy, while the evangelist will be developing material that is the most effective in communication.

This part of the work allows for creativity. Folks who find it difficult to speak out might really enjoy putting their message in print. We have seen some marvelous prose, poetry and art from some very gifted workers over the years. I also have seen some colossal blunders. I'm amazed at how good a poem can sound at 3 A.M., and how tragic it can read the next morning after a good night's sleep, unfortunately, after it was rushed to the mail box.

The clerical work. This work is less glamorous. It involves good eyes or a good magnifying glass. It requires patient and faithful laborers. The mailing list must be painstakingly compiled. The list must constantly be updated, with additions, subtractions, and corrections. The flyers must be folded, the envelopes addressed, stuffed, sealed, stamped and posted. We throw a letter sending party each month, and include a free lunch.

• Procedures

In addition to other ministries, we know that the word is going out through the mails. There will be folks who will ask to be removed from the mailing list. When that happens we always honor their request. We remove them from the mailing list, and place them on the visitation list. The next month we hand deliver the flyer to their door, and announce how we could not mail them this letter, so we had to bring it over personally. This part of the work can be very invigorating. However, if the staff has produced a fine piece of literature, it makes it easy to say I really wanted you to have this, and since I couldn't mail it, I'd thought I would just drop it off.

Phone Ministry

The most successful phone work we have seen was in Harrisburg, Pa. Folks had distributed a simple business card that read " Hear O Israel." Beneath the text was a phone number. Those who called heard a taped Bible message, followed by an invitation to leave a name and address for free literature. They were receiving hundreds of calls per week. People were listening to the message, and asking for the literature. The same ministry was attempted in Brooklyn, and it wasn't nearly as successful.

• Prayer

The first thing to do in a phone ministry is pray. We need to pray for the right kind of ministry, the right location, the messages on the machine, the tracts, the workers, and the follow-up. We need to pray for the right callers, and for the right attitude when we call. We need to pray that we won't get people at inopportune times. We need to pray that the callers will find folks to whom we can minister. Every aspect of the ministry needs to be bathed in prayer.

• Active Calling

Calling can be done by either individuals or by computer. The computer can contact more people in less time, but most people find the computer call to be obnoxious. But the right message, in the right location, might be a viable option. Many different companies have turned to phone solicitation. That means that more people are being pestered by phone calls. Cold calling can turn people off. However, companies do it because it produces results. We should have callers ministering in our outreach programs. The best use of the callers, however, is to remind folks of meetings. The night of the meeting they might need a ride or a baby sitter. We should also ask if someone else they know may be interested in being invited. It is always much easier to say that your friend asked if you could give him a buzz, rather than trying to call a stranger "cold turkey."

The callers should be friendly and cheerful. Some folks are great phone people. They love to talk on the telephone. They seem to be well received, and they get the job done. When we call we should always look for opportunities to minister. Ask if there is anything we might do to help. People may need a ride to go shopping, or to the doctors, or perhaps they need someone to help them around the house.

• Passive Phone Ministry.

The passive phone ministry is area sensitive. In some locations, it works, but not in others. In this work, the equipment does most of the labor. We humans have a subordinate role. Actually the machines let us get involved in two areas.

The Message. A short message is preferred to a longer one. It should raise interest and questions. We cannot expect to give answers at this level. Our hope is that we will create enough of an interest that they will request more information. The message should be changed frequently. Meeting announcements and season greetings are always appropriate. A brief two person dialogue, if well done, can be humorous and very effective.

The Material. You have to advertise the phone number. You can use a business card with the number on it. You should be up front about what you are doing. The card should identify the message in some way. Something like "Oops, did I forget to mention The Messiah has come; call 555-5555 and we'll tell you what we found." By identifying the topic, up front, you run the risk of turning some people off, some who might have been drawn into listening had they made the call. It is better to offend them early, rather than offend them later. Other ministries have used things like "Hear O Israel," as we mentioned earlier, with good results. There is a danger in not identifying yourselves. Don't make it easy for anyone to accuse you of being deceptive.

We are Jewish, and therefore have the right to use Jewish terminology. It is good for us to enjoy our culture. It is alright for us to use trappings from our culture in our advertising. However, we are first and foremost believers. As believers we have the responsibility of identifying ourselves. It is wrong for us not to declare who we are, and who we stand for. We must avoid having someone call thinking the message was sponsored by the local synagogue, and then becoming embarrassed or enraged. To advertise the phone ministry we can use flyers or posters. Posters can be hung, with permission, all over town. The flyers can be distributed in tract distribution, or through the mail ministry, or through visitation. Each ministry is interrelated.

Visitation

• Prayer

Matthew 9:38 *Pray ye therefore the Lord of the harvest, that he will send forth labourers into his harvest.* We need to pray for workers. We need to pray for contacts. We need to pray that they will find open doors and open hearts. We need to pray for protec-

125

tion, safety as they travel, and the actual visit. We need to bathe every aspect of the visitation ministry in prayer.

• Personnel

All of our visitation workers should have adequate training. They must be able to present the gospel from the Jewish Scriptures, and they all need to be competent in sharing their own personal testimony. Send workers out in teams of two. It is good to have a Jew and a Gentile on each team. Do not send a man and a woman out visiting together. Never send a man out to visit a woman. Never send a woman out to visit a man.

Ideally each team will meet on a different night of the week. If they have no one to visit that night, they get together for prayer and fellowship. Each night we have a team of men and a team of women ready to visit. A fully staffed visitation team should consist of twenty people: five Jewish men, five Gentile men, five Jewish women, and five Gentile women, teamed up two by two. They should be ready to visit on their respective week night, "prayed up," and armed with the gospel.

• Procedure

This ministry needs a company commander, a person who can recognize the gifts in people, and can team them up so that they are well suited to each other. The leader also needs to keep good records. You need to keep track of who needs a visit, who has been visited, by whom, when, what was said, and what literature was left.

The company commander should have a street map and keep a record of any tricky directions. Once, by the time I got to the unsaved persons house, I needed spiritual guidance more than they did, even though I had left in plenty of time armed with a map, directions, and an idea of where they lived. As it grew darker, I found it more difficult to read the street signs. I can't read and drive at the same time, so I kept having to pull over to read the map or the directions. Then I needed to get back into traffic, turn around, try to read the street sign, pull over, and check the map. I was getting dizzy and growing more frustrated and annoyed as the time grew later. Those bringing the good news should arrive more cheerfully.

Good record keeping is an essential. I know because I keep everything in my head. I'm constantly losing numbers, losing addresses, and driving my fellow workers crazy. Once when we were visiting one person, we had promised to come back to a house up the street. I'm always saying things like, "it's the second street, on the right, or was it the third? Well, I know it's the second house from the corner, or was it the third?"

We all need to be aware of the witnessing that the other is doing. It makes for a better prayer life when we can pray knowledgeably for each other. Sometimes we need to substitute for each other. We can't jump in very well if we aren't aware of what is going on in the witness. If a worker gets transferred out of town, the ministry should be able to continue. Therefore we need to keep everyone informed, and the best way to do that is through good record keeping. The ministry needs a data base of its very own, or at least a well organized shoe box filled with neatly written 3" by 5" cards.

Cold Turkey. "Cold Turkey" is walking up to a total stranger with the express purpose of proclaiming the gospel. I love it! Knees knocking, heart pounding, tongue stammering, stuttering, shaking, and quaking, Christ is preached. Those things are constant. The only things that change are where we do it and what materials we use. In any situation, at the mall or on the campus, we need first to get the person's permission to speak with him. When you go door to door the first thing you do, after prayer, is to knock on the door. If a person doesn't want to be disturbed he has the option of ignoring you, and not answering the door. We must give the same option to those at the mall or on campus. We have to be courteous and allow them to ignore us. The first step we take, after prayer, is to stand close enough to him for him to look up. If he makes an effort to look away, he does not want to be disturbed, if he looks up at you he will open the door. Once the door is open, then we need to ask for permission to come in. We introduce ourselves, explain who we are, and ask him if he has time to discuss the Scriptures. If he does not want to discuss the Scriptures, then we show him a gospel tract, and ask him if he would like to read it at his leisure. If he takes it at least he will have the chance to read how to be saved, and he can always contact us through the address on the tract.

Door to door. In the door to door ministry, record keeping is essential. You have to keep accurate track of which homes were contacted, who was spoken to, and what was said. When visiting in the home try to discover as much information as possible. Look for opportunities to minister. Be alert to needs in the homes that you could possibly help to meet.

Some people like to use tracts or surveys. If you are going to use a religious survey as a tool to share your faith, be certain that the survey is legitimate. If the survey is just a ploy, and the data is not being sincerely compiled, then you are guilty of deception. The end does not justify the means. The Lord will honor forthright methods.

Inviting people to a meeting personally is a great thing to do door to door. It gives you an opportunity to identify yourself, to share a few words, to leave a flyer, and then to return, say we missed you, or we hope you had a happy holiday. If an opening to present the gospel presents itself, then, grab it. Until then share your testimony, listen, love, and serve.

Going door to door is a bit unnatural. You can ease the pain by making it as natural as possible. Do not feel you need to obligate yourself to a gospel presentation at each location. The goal you should set is to establish a relationship with folks in your community that will allow you to return. If I'm going to make a hundred visits, I think it is more productive to visit twenty people five times than it is to visit a hundred different people, only once each.

A few years ago I was invited to a wedding. I wasn't surprised, as I had been to several family affairs over the years. At the reception, people began asking me how I was related to the newlyweds. I had become a close friend of the family; in fact many considered me to be a part of the family. I was there at funerals and unveilings. I sat Shiva* with them. I prayed with them, visited in the hospital with them, and counseled with them. Few of the relatives knew that my first encounter with the family was handing

---

* see glossary of terms

128

out literature door to door. I just got to know them. I had chances to befriend them, and I grew to be part of the family. I always tell people a missionary is like fungus; we grow on you.

Shop to Shop. As always a ministry should be the work of the Holy Spirit. Inevitably the plans of men are doomed to frustration. In our frustration we cry out to God looking for His direction. After floundering around in our own plans, we stumble into God's will. Then we experience great blessing, and start teaching others how they too might be blessed. There is no such thing as a foolproof program. What works in one location might not prove to be a good method in another. We need to be sensitive to God's leading, willing to serve, and flexible.

We were visiting door to door each week night in Northeast Philadelphia. We were frustrated that we could only get a few visits in during the evening hours. We wanted to make better use of our time, so we began visiting door to door during the day. We soon became frustrated by two factors. On the one hand we found large numbers of people who were not at home. The second problem was that when we did find someone at home, it was often a woman home alone, and that made for many uncomfortable situations.

In Northeast Philadelphia, there a row homes with stores beneath them. As we were visiting the homes, we began to stop in at the shops. This marvelous ministry of shop to shop evangelism developed. I've tried to duplicate this ministry in other locations and communities with little success.

This ministry strives on the main street of a small town. It especially flourishes when there is a nearby coffee shop, doughnut shop, or cafeteria where you can set up your office. The splendid thing about this ministry is, someone is always there. If you are visiting from 9-5 during the week, you'll never find a closed door. There is always someone to talk to. If you are in a Jewish neighborhood, the someone you are talking to is usually Jewish. Often it is the head of the house that your ministering to, and he is always suitably dressed, which is a great advantage over the door to door work.

129

You start cold turkey. You revisit, and you establish relationships. You need to begin to prioritize your visiting. If you are certain that everyone is hostile in one shop, then you should stop visiting there. After a while you become like a salesmen. You establish a route, and you make your scheduled stops in your territory. You deliver tracts and take prayer requests; you grow to be the chaplain of the street.

One of the great detriments to "shop to shop" evangelism is the rise of the shopping mall. The mall is replete with problems for the evangelist. The Jewish shop keeper who thrives on Main street is missing from the mall and its chain stores. The malls are all business. You can't close the store with a be back in ten minutes sign, and run down to the coffee shop.

The most productive visit is the revisit. For the most part cold turkey ministry is seed sowing. Revisiting involves watering and reaping. Compile the names of all those folks that have been brought under conviction, those who have spoken with other believers and who have been reached through other ministries. The folks who have heard the gospel and have seen the dynamics of the new life are on this list.

There is a great deal of excitement and some adventure in bringing the gospel to a person for the first time. We also realize that those who have heard the gospel have a chance to believe it later. There is not the same kind of urgency to return to someone who has already heard the word. Yet we are called to make disciples; making disciples requires revisiting. We affectionately call the would-be disciples "the hot list." You need to make new contacts all the time, breaking new ground, sewing seeds. But you must not overlook the importance of watering, nurturing, and weeding. You must commit yourselves to the tedious things that will eventually allow you the joy of reaping.

The Outreach Meeting

• Prayer

The first thing we do in a meeting ministry is pray. We need to pray for the date and place of the meeting. We need to pray about workers, publicity, and decorations. We need to pray about the program, and we need to pray about the follow up. We need to pray against demonic intervention because meetings seem to be where the attacks occur. Every aspect of an outreach meeting needs to be bathed in prayer.

• When

One of the most critical decisions to make is when to have a meeting. You certainly do not want to have a meeting in a room that seats 150 with six people in attendance. Be thankful for the six, but it sends out a message that you aren't very popular or successful. Do not have a meeting until the community is ready.

We never really know how many people are going to come out to a program. Therefore, it is a bit difficult to be certain about when we might be ready to have a meeting. However, the Lord usually lets us know when the time is right. The first Passover Seder we did in Hightstown was planned for the unsaved. Unsaved people began asking us what we were doing for Passover that year. We knew that we were going to have a good number in attendance before we even began to plan the meeting.

The next difficulty after deciding when you are ready to have a meeting is to decide on the occasion. The best programs for an outreach meeting are Hanukkah, Purim, Passover, and a " Thank God For Israel Day." Purim and Hanukkah are the easiest holidays to plan a date because neither is a very sacred holiday, and so you have some latitude in finding a night to celebrate. Hanukkah gives us eight days to choose from; that's the good news. The bad news is that all of those eight days occur in December. That means you have to contend with the Christmas hype, and in the Northern hemisphere the gorgeous weather conditions. Every Jewish meeting presents its own set of problems. Weekends are always the ideal time for a program. However, with a Jewish outreach, you have to be considerate of the Sabbath. Religious Jews cannot travel from sundown on Friday night until the first stars are visible after sundown on Saturday. It's true that there won't be many very religious Jewish people coming to our meetings, but if they are the people you are trying to minister to, then the meeting has to be held on a week night or Sunday.

If you are scheduling a Seder, there is a whole new set of things to consider. In Biblical times, there were two holidays established, Passover, and the Feast of Unleavened Bread. Today the two have grown together. What has remained is a tradition of celebrating on two nights, first Seder and second Seder. Often folks will celebrate first Seder at his mom's, and then do second Seder at her mom's house. If you opt to have your Seder on either first or second Seder, you will be competing with the family meetings. The only people who would be free to come would be those who do not have families. You want to reach out to them, but you do not want to exclude the others. If you choose another night, either just before Passover or during the week, people will think that you are so ignorant of Judaism, that you don't know when the holiday occurs. Our ministry can survive quite nicely no matter how little people think of our knowledge of Judaism. Our ministry can't survive without decent attendance. That means that in most cases you will be conducting Holiday meetings on "off" nights. Remember your purpose is to bring Jewish people under the influence of the gospel. You need to conduct your programs at their convenience.

• Where

After deciding on the night, you then need to consider where you are going to hold your meeting. The church often has excellent facilities. Using the church has the added bonus of the right price. The church building, however, may contain symbols or signs that could offend an unsaved Jewish person. In most cases you could simply remove, cover, or camouflage most of the offensive things, but that can raise another problem. In covering or removing sacred objects, you run the risk of offending your host. Some of the folks in the church could be upset if you remove the things that they hold dear. Remember, you are under their authority, and you are only a guest. If it looks like it might be a difficulty, then meet somewhere else.

Private homes may be large enough for some special meetings, but watch out for ample parking facilities and handicap accessibility. The home is normally the easiest to decorate, often provides the most comfortable atmosphere, and is usually ideally suited to the weekly Bible study.

Renting a hall is always an option. However, use it as a last resort. It is true that the rented hall will have ample parking, wheel chair accessibility, and won't have any religiously offensive objects. The rented hall, however, also has atmosphere that is extremely secular. There is usually drinking, loud music nearby, detracting from the atmosphere of worship. Before spending the money on a hall, research your community to discover what kind of free, or almost free, rooms there are. Often the library, a bank, or an apartment complex has a suitable community room available.

College Ministry

There are usually other organizations that focus on the college campus. If a Biblically sound ministry is already established on a campus, then it would be foolish to start a competing ministry. Often we can assist them, train them, or give them some expertise in reaching the Jewish students.

• Prayer

Prayer is an absolute essential in campus ministries. Back in the early seventies, we started a ministry at Temple University. We were shocked by the tremendous amount of evil that permeated the campus. There were two different organizations that catered to the homosexual. Besides them, there were " the students for chairman Mao," and "the students for democratic society," both of which were communistic and atheistic. Some of the other off-campus organizations included Islam, the standard cults, and witchcraft. We weren't prepared for that amount of Satanic activity. The only way to be able to deal with that volume of demonic action is dynamic prayer. We need to pray about the people that we work with; they must be spirit filled. We need to pray for protection for our workers and for their families. We need to pray for the college administrators, and the decisions they make. We need to pray for contacts, for meetings, and follow-up. Campus ministries need prayer.

• Permission

Most colleges have established policies about who can and who can't be on campus. The first step is to discover the rules and to comply with them. There will always be other organizations that take short cuts or worse. They may seemingly get away with that kind of activity, but we believe that if the Lord wants us there, He will open up the doors. Our scheming, plotting, and corner cutting are not the way ministry doors are opened.

In filling out applications it is an imperative that we declare our purpose. The school is looking for clubs that reflect the interests of the students and organizations that will meet student needs. Evangelical organizations that proselytize are usually viewed in a rather dim light. There is a strong tendency to misrepresent ourselves so that we meet their criteria.

There will probably be evangelical students on campus, and we will reflect their interests. We will be meeting many needs of students, through instruction, fellowship, and counseling. However, we cannot deny ourselves, and we can't deny our Lord. Proverbs 3:6 *In all thy ways acknowledge him, and he shall direct thy paths*. If the campus rules prohibit our activity, we can pray, we can appeal, we can reapply, but we must acknowledge Him. God will then open or close doors, and in so doing he will direct our paths.

• Consistency

One of the more popular campus ministries is the publicity table. Outside groups who have met with the campus rules are allowed to set up tables on campus at certain locations throughout the week. Our table had a sign announcing who we were and literature that would draw Jewish people to the reality of Jesus. Whether you use the publicity table or not, the important thing is to find a place on campus where you can be counted on to be. Any suitable nook can serve as an office. The student who is being drawn by the Spirit of God will seek you out. However, he needs to know where you are, and when you are going to be there.

Working the table can be a real adventure. As exciting as the table can be, though, it is a pretty easy ministry. It may involve hostility and argumentation, but the students for the most part will be approaching you. The more difficult ministry will be going out from the table and witnessing to strangers on campus.

• Workers

The Gideons sometimes come on campus to distribute Bibles. These men are all over fifty, and they wear ties and jackets. I thought that because of their age, and because of their dress, they

134

would never be able to reach the students. I may have been more wrong about some things in my life, but I don't remember when. They made a tremendous impact on campus. They were so popular that they had completely exhausted their supply of Bibles by noon. They had to scramble to resupply twice during the day.

Although anyone can minister on campus, college age youths will be the most effective. The workers need to be adequately trained and prepared for the work, but who they are isn't as important as who they know. Genuine concern and love for the lost is a must. Their prayer life and their integrity is everything. College students seem to be very leery of hypocrisy, and workers need to be the genuine article.

• Follow Up

A college ministry can produce a multitude of decisions. As much as possible these students should be funneled into the college and career group of the local church. New believers are going to be reluctant to speak with their parents about their faith. They are going to need encouragement to do the right thing. We have seen Jewish students who were threatened with losing their financial support. It is a tough choice for a young person to make, and many find it too difficult to do that which is right.

Many organizations have good follow up materials for new believers of the college age. The best possible follow-up program would be for the new believer to transfer to the Institute of Biblical Studies. Unfortunately everyone won't be able to attend, so for those can't come on campus we have the correspondence courses.

New believers will be hungry for the word of God. We should be certain that they are being fed. We should provide situations for them to serve. As soon as possible they should get involved in the work of the Lord.

Community Ministries

There are far too many different ways of ministering to the Jewish community to develop them all. A missionary can become a volunteer chaplain almost anywhere, such as hospitals, nursing homes, retirement communities, police departments, athletic leagues, youth ministries, and family counseling centers.

Like every other work, we get full permission to serve by being completely open in regards to our agenda. We offer advice, hope, counsel, encouragement, prayer, support, and understanding. But we also preach the gospel, and everyone needs to know that. If that prohibits us from serving, then we need to take our service somewhere else. We establish the gospel first and foremost; we never sneak it in later and hope to get away with it.

Whatever ministry location we are led toward, and whatever tools we are led to use, and no matter what the medium of communication is, prayer must start, permeate, surround and complete every work. Whether we are doing a puppet show in the nursing home, a magic show on campus, showing a movie at the community hall, or bringing a devotional to the little league, we need to be serious about the prayer time in preparation and in the performance of the program.

• The Weekly Bible Study

After the outreach meeting, phone ministry, visitation, and mailings, we invite those who have questions and those who have interest to a home Bible study. If we put a mailing out to 3500 people, we might see as many as 35 attend an outreach meeting. If we have 35 new folks out at a meeting, we might see three, four, or five attend the Bible study. That means we are reaching about one in a thousand. That is one in a thousand over a period of a couple of years, from the first mailing until the first Bible study. That doesn't sound very good. So let's hear some good news. Every Jewish person who has attended the Bible study for the ten weeks has come to know the Lord.

Prayer. We need to pray for those who attend, we need to pray about the location, we need to pray about the lesson, and we need to pray for protection against demons. We need to bring every aspect of the Bible study to the throne in prayer.

The Location. The best place for the weekly Bible study is a private home. The home needs to be adequate to accommodate comfortably all who will attend. The home needs to be accessible to the people who are going to attend. The hosts need to be committed to the ministry. Their doors have to be open, and their house has to be ready every week that we meet. Use great discernment in the selection of the ideal home. Often people will make a commitment to volunteer their house, but they can't keep that commitment. Both may have jobs, they might have children, and they might find the weekly meetings are becoming a real drag. We need to anticipate that before we select the right house.

Sometimes we meet in a modest home, and then someone will suggest that we move to their house, which is more luxurious. Select mature and sincere believers over flash. If the facilities are adequate, then modest is fine. But we can't have a host who wants to show off their house one week, then begrudges the people who use or perhaps abuse it the next.

Length of Meeting. There are two things to be considered here. First, how long does each meeting last, and second, how long will we continue to hold the Bible study. The meetings need to be over in two hours. That is more than enough time for prayer, fellowship, discussion, and instruction time. Everyone may seem to be enjoying themselves, but the next morning they may rue the night before. We have to discipline ourselves to end the meetings at the right time. It is far better to cut a meeting short so that everyone wishes we had spent more time together, then it is to run the meeting too long so that folks wish that they had stayed home.

The second thing to consider is the number of weeks to run the Bible study. We recommend a ten week course of study. We don't want to become a small church. If after ten weeks, there is an interest in continuing the fellowship, then perhaps the local church can take over the meetings. Unsaved people are afraid of making a life-long commitment. They won't come to a meeting that they think they will be trapped in for the rest of their lives. We need to set up the ground rules early. We are going to meet for ten weeks to discuss the Jewish Scriptures to find some answers to questions that many of us have been asking.

The Material. The course of study must be the Old Testament. We recommend the life of Abraham. It is a study from the Torah that includes messages on faith, commitment, tithing, worship, prayer, witnessing, separation, and family. In Abraham's life we see the doctrines of the Triunity of God, the promised messiah, the promise of a nation, and salvation by faith.

SEVEN

Messianic Congregations

This topic is a volatile one. It is unfortunate that we are so bitterly divided over this issue. One would hope that once we Jewish people have found faith in our messiah, that we would rejoice together. Unfortunately almost every Jewish believer I know has taken a position on one side or the other, and everyone seems to be rather passionate about the position they have taken. There seems to be little ground for agreement. Emotions run high, and accusations rule over reason. Those in traditional evangelical churches are accused of being anti-Semitic, and those who go to messianic congregations are called Judaizers. The subject needs to be addressed, since Jewish people will have to worship somewhere when they come to faith. We will attempt to approach the issue as objectively as possible.

First we need to define what a messianic congregation is. In many communities groups of Jewish believers have left the local church and have started to worship in a Jewish setting. Many of these Jewish churches have abandoned the use of Christian terminology, and have substituted Jewish equivalents. Instead of a church, it is a congregation, instead of Christian, it is Messianic; hence the Christian church is now called a messianic congregation.

There are three organizations of messianic congregations in the United States. The first is the Messianic Jewish Alliance or

M.J.A. The second is the Union of Messianic Congregations, or U.M.J.C. Both of these see themselves as a fourth branch of Judaism, and both allow for charismatic congregations to join in the organization. These two groups probably account for over 80% of the congregations in the United States. The third group is called the Federation of Messianic Congregations, or F.M.C. This group is lesser know, and is considerably smaller than the other two. The F.M.C. is non-charismatic, and doesn't see itself as a movement within Judaism.

For definition purposes we will say that a messianic congregation is any affiliate member of one of the existing messianic organizations. I know of some fellowships that are sensitive to Judaica in their practice, but are independent and Baptistic. We will consider them to be Baptist churches with funny names.

Strengths

Comfortable

I know that "comfortable" does not sound very important, but it is. It is important because messianic congregations are not just comfortable, they are very comfortable. To a Jewish person a church service can be oppressive. Most messianic congregations are like a good friend's living room. You never seem to notice how fast the time goes by. Unsaved people feel welcome, and believers feel relaxed.

Unity

Here is where most messianic congregations are terribly misunderstood. They are always criticized for dividing the body of Christ. This criticism most likely comes from those who have never been to a messianic congregation. If an evangelical church has a hundred people in attendance, the likelihood is that the congregation will include less than five Jewish people. If a messianic congregation has a hundred people in attendance, the congregation will probably be around fifty/fifty; half of the folks will be Jewish, and half will be Gentiles. Now that's unity. Messianic congregations are not dividing the body of Christ; they are uniting Jews and Gentiles together in worship.

Worship

Messianic congregations are a great place to worship the Lord. There is usually some Hebrew liturgy, and plenty of up-beat choruses, Scripture set to music, as well as traditional hymns. There is always sincerity and joy. The service usually has plenty of great music and will often include Davidic dancing.

The Scriptures encourage us to be lifting up holy hands. 1 Timothy 2:8 *I will therefore that men pray every where, lifting up holy hands, without wrath and doubting*. Evangelical churches are usually afraid of being labeled charismatic. Their worship is generally more reserved, and even restrictive. The messianic congregation worships with more abandon.

Judaica

Some would consider Judaica as a negative. Every evangelical church I know celebrates Easter. Every evangelical pastor I know knows the origin of the pagan holiday. We all know that the celebration of the resurrection of the Lord was separated from its original date, so that the Catholic church could keep a distance from the Jewish rituals. The resurrection historically occurred during the week of unleavened bread, not the first Sunday after the first full moon after the spring equinox. However, Easter isn't the only pagan ritual in the church. We have Halloween parties, Christmas trees, Sunday Sabbaths, and St. Valentines day. These extra Biblical traditions are shunned in the messianic congregations. Their liturgical year is found in Leviticus 23. Their Sabbath is on Saturday.

Weaknesses

Destroys City-wide Outreach

The first thing we do when we come into a city is train a church in Jewish evangelism. Once one church is trained, we then train another. After several churches are equipped to share the gospel with the Jewish people, we then begin meetings. Each of the churches will move at its own pace, and in its own direction. Some may do Passover Seders, others "Thank God for Israel" banquets. Some will have monthly meetings, others yearly, or even less often. These churches, through their programs and through their witness, begin to see results. Jewish people start hearing and start believing the gospel.

The numbers are small at first, but they begin to grow, and they grow geometrically. The more churches involved, the more points of witness exist in the city. The more Jewish people who get saved, the greater the testimony to the Jewish community. The first year there might be only one decision, the next year three, then eleven, the following year twenty seven. There may be over forty Jewish people worshipping in eight different churches.

Then the messianic congregation is planted. The forty Jewish believers leave the eight churches and they all attend the messianic congregation. All the gentile believers who are excited about Jewish evangelism leave their respective churches for the congregation as well. Now instead of having eight points of witness to the Jewish people, we have only one. The following year there are seven Jewish people who find the Messiah at the congregation. Admittedly that is a great number. No one church ever saw seven Jewish decisions in one year before this. However, that number represents all the decisions in the city. Had the eight churches kept up their outreach programs the number could potentially have been five times larger.

The evangelistic results of the messianic congregation levels off at about three or four a year. That's still pretty good, but it unfortunately is all there is. The city-wide witness was growing geometrically, and now it has ceased to grow. All of the witness to the Jewish community has been centralized into one congregation; the rest of the churches in the city have ceased to be effective in Jewish evangelism. Not only have the churches ceased to be effective in Jewish evangelism, but they may continue to be ineffective for years to come. It is like a volcanic eruption; it takes years for the soil to be able to bear fruit again after it has been contaminated by the lava.

The pastor and leaders of the respective churches have all been hurt. They have expressed love and service to many Jewish believers, and in return the Jewish people have stormed off and left the church. Not only have they left, but they have taken some dynamic young families with them. That church is reluctant, to say the least, to start any Jewish outreach programs.

Doomed to Grow More Jewish

I know that I said Judaica is good. However, the messianic congregations are doomed to acquire too much of a good thing. I say doomed because it can't be helped. You can write to prevent it in the constitution, try to protect against it in the by-laws, warn about it in the purpose statement, and watch out for it in practice, and at best you can stem the tide a bit.

When a Jewish person embraces Jesus Christ, that person can't help but feel some guilt. In the early 70's I was present at what was called in those days the F.C.T.J. conference (the fundamentalist Christian testimony to the Jews). I had a new believer with me that year who was preparing to enter into Jewish work. Many Jewish believers were present. My new friend was struggling with his identity as a believer. As we were walking, we passed two Jewish ministers that I knew. One was dressed like a chassid, complete with tallit, beard, and kippah. The other fellow was wearing a leisure suit. I told my friend that one of the two men had been raised in an orthodox Jewish home, the other was raised Episcopalian, and didn't discover his Jewish roots until after he became a believer. At the time he immediately assumed that the one dressed in the traditional garb of the ultra orthodox was the one who was raised in the orthodox home. In reality, it was reversed. The reason is natural. The one was secure in his Jewish culture. He knew he was a good Jew, and he also knew that the bondage to the Jewish traditions didn't draw him any closer to the God of Abraham. He was delighted to be free, and he readily embraced his brothers and sisters in the church. The other man felt that his faith in Jesus showed that he really wasn't a good Jew. He felt that he had to prove his Jewishness. So he shrinks away from all that is not Jewish and embraces the Jewish garb and traditions. I know the guilt feelings and the desire to prove how truly Jewish you are. It stems from pride, and it is propelled by guilt. Here are two different individuals, one of whom was fairly comfortable with his identity as a Jewish believer in Jesus. Why can't a Messianic congregation be populated with folks like him? The answer is that he was coming from practicing Orthodox Judaism. Over 90% of the Jewish people are not practicing Orthodox. That means most Jewish believers are going to be experiencing guilty feelings about their new found faith.

Beyond the natural tendency to usurp the first birth over the second, there exists now a theological teaching within some of the congregations. Some are teaching that Jewish people, within the body, are to maintain their Jewish distinctive. Gentiles need not keep kosher or wear the traditional Jewish garb, but Jewish believers should. They say that being Jewish is not just a privilege but a responsibility.

Fill a room up with guilt ridden new believers. Remove the influence of Gentile leadership. Stir in a little pride in Judaica, add in a pinch of bad theology, and let simmer for several months, and then you will have ultra Jewish tendencies brewing.

Don't Prioritize Christian Edification

Years ago we ran a children's and teen camp each summer. We had a fellowship of Jewish believers, but our youth were all affiliated with local churches. The rest of the kids in the camp all came from messianic congregations. The young people and the teens from the local churches were lacking some skills and some training that the other kids obviously had. The kids from local churches did not know any of the messianic dances, they were a little weak on their Hebrew, and weren't as familiar with the Sabbath prayers and liturgy. However, in Bible knowledge, the local church kids swept every category. The most helpful youths, the most spiritual, and the most prayerful were the kids who came from the local churches. That only makes sense. You only have them for a few hours a week. If you are going to spend your time practicing Judaism, you can't be studying the New Testament. I know of one messianic Rabbi who literally lost his congregation because of this problem. Each week he taught the importance of Judaica. He stressed the rules of Kasherute. He never spoke about prayer, family, or marriage, and eventually he starved the flock.

Ephesians 4:11&12 *And he gave some, apostles; and some, prophets; and some, evangelists; and some, pastors and teachers; For the perfecting of the saints, for the work of the ministry, for the edifying of the body of Christ.* The purpose of the local church is to edify the saints to the work of the ministry. The purpose of a messianic congregation is to worship the messiah, in a Jewish context, to provide an atmosphere within which Judaica can be maintained by those who know the Lord.

Conclusion

We never discussed the weaknesses of the evangelical church. Some of those weaknesses contribute to the messianic movement. We need to look at the strengths of the messianic congregation, and to learn from them. They do many things well. Evangelical churches are, as a rule, rather intolerant. They need to be that way. They want to protect against doctrinal heresy from creeping into the church, so they view all change suspiciously. However they need to recognize between doctrinal changes and cultural changes. They need to distinguish between beliefs, which can't change, and practice.

Couldn't they have Friday night meetings in the church for those who are interested? Couldn't they celebrate Passover Seders? Couldn't they incorporate some Jewish-style music into the worship service? Could they pray for the peace of Jerusalem? How about a small-group fellowship that emphasizes Jewish outreach programs, or maybe a Jewish-interest Sunday school class?

Jewish believers will bring changes to the church. The pastor who wants to feed his flock will encourage those changes. Jewish believers, however, need to recognize the priorities. Messianic congregations are great fun, but the submission to the authority of the local congregation comes first.

The theological position of the messianic movement states that Jesus gave to Peter the authority to continue the oral tradition, that the authoritative tradition still comes down to us. If that is true then the tradition comes down to Peter, to the Roman Catholic church, through the Catholic church, to the reformers, from the reformers to the evangelical church that brought us to faith in Jesus. Hebrews 13:7 *Remember them which have the rule over you, who have spoken unto you the word of God: whose faith follow, considering the end of their conversation.*

Now we know how to "mish," we know why we do it, what to say, and where it can be done. The only thing left to do is do it. Go get em, be prayerful, and be in love when you go.

SECTION TWO
JEWISH APOLOGETICS

INTRODUCTION

I have been ministering to Jewish people since 1972. In that time span I have heard numerous objections to the gospel. Most of them, however would not come under the category of an attack on Christianity. Phrases like "I was born a Jew, and I'll die a Jew," or as Aryeh Kaplan writes, "Conversion to another faith is an action of religious treason," and "A Jew must give his life rather than embrace Christianity."[20] These statements may show reasons why Jewish people would be reluctant to explore the truth of our faith, but they do not constitute an attack on our faith.

The attacks on our faith leveled by Jewish people fall into two major categories: (1) general attacks, and (2) specific Jewish attacks. Many Jewish people are atheistic and humanistic. The attacks they bring against Christianity are those that could come from any none religious person. Questions regarding evolution or the issue of suffering in God's creation are not handled here. Instead, we are addressing the specific Jewish attacks from those who profess to believe the Jewish Scriptures, the miracles, and the God of Abraham. Attacks of this nature hit the very core of our faith. These attacks object to the Christian book, the Christian beliefs, and the Christian behavior.

There are several books that are currently in print that endeavor to destroy the basis of the Christian faith, from the Jewish perspective. Our ministry listed every objection raised, categorized them, and attempted, by the grace of God, *to give an answer to every man* (1 Peter 3:15)

I am perpetually misplacing keys, wallet, eye glasses, and Bible. Therefore I'm frequently involved in a frantic process of searching the house, car, and premises for any and all of the aforementioned items. Before beginning a search, I already know that I'm eventually going to find what I'm looking for. Any feigned panic is usually designed to elicit as much sympathy and help as possible from the family. The missing item has to be hiding somewhere. With some strategy planning and several

---

[20]*The Real Messiah*, Aryeh Kaplan , NCSY New York, NY 1976 p24

possible solutions in mind, I begin my search until someone else in the family has finally discovered the item I was looking for. Although I know that the item will be found, and that there are several possible solutions, I still don't feel really good. I do not feel right until I have what I'm looking for in my chubby little fist.

Answering objections to the Gospel can be like that. We know there is an answer; we have several possible solutions. However, we don't feel really good until we know the answer. Sometimes we can't be sure as to which is the correct answer, so we don't feel right about it. Assemble enough of these questions together, and the results can be doubts in the *faith which was once delivered unto the saints* (Jude 3). To prevent that from occurring, we need to remember the overwhelming case for Christianity. Our faith is what provides a solution to the problem of man's depravity. (Jeremiah 17:9) Our faith is consistent with and is based upon the prophetic Scriptures.

Our Messiah was born of a virgin (Isaiah 7:14) as predicted, was cut off at the time predicted (Daniel 9:26), for the reasons predicted (Isaiah 53:8), and in the way predicted (Psalm 22). Our Messiah exhibited the character that the Scriptures predicted, and is of the nature that the Scriptures predicted. Our Messiah *died for our sins according to the scriptures; he was buried, and... he rose again the third day according to the scriptures* (1 Corinthians 15:3-4).

One can level attacks at the Christian faith. But there is nothing else to offer. There are no other faiths and no other religious systems that can offer the hope. The Temple of Judaism lies in ruins. The tomb is empty. The testimony of the millions of changed lives, changed societies, changed calendars, and changed countries lends weight to the words of Peter when he says in John 6:68 *Lord, to whom shall we go? thou hast the words of eternal life.*

EIGHT

Attacks On The Christian Book

Inconsistencies with the Old Testament

The virgin birth

In Matthew 1:18-23 we read: *Now the birth of Jesus Christ was on this wise: When as his mother Mary was espoused to Joseph, before they came together, she was found with child of the Holy Ghost. Then Joseph her husband, being a just man, and not willing to make her a publick example, was minded to put her away privily. But while he thought on these things, behold, the angel of the Lord appeared unto him in a dream, saying, Joseph, thou son of David, fear not to take unto thee Mary thy wife: for that which is conceived in her is of the Holy Ghost. And she shall bring forth a son, and thou shalt call his name JESUS: for he shall save his people from their sins. Now all this was done, that it might be fulfilled which was spoken of the Lord by the prophet, saying, Behold, a virgin shall be with child, and shall bring forth a son, and they shall call his name Emmanuel, which being interpreted is, God with us.*

Many Jewish people believe the source of the virgin-birth concept is seated in pre-Christian mythology. As Pinchas Stolper writes "Nowhere does the Bible predict that the Messiah will be born of a virgin. In fact virgins never give birth anywhere in the Bible. This idea is to be found only in pagan mythology."[21] Rosenberg, in his book, The Christian Problem, goes on to suggest that the mythology is that of Mithraism.[22]

First of all, let us clearly establish our position. Christianity does not begin with the book of Matthew. Biblical Christianity begins with the book of Genesis. The so called pre-Christian cults and myths that our faith is supposed to be based upon are not pre-Christian at all. The truth of the virgin birth is taught in the Scriptures. Look as far back as Genesis 3:15 *And I will put enmity between thee and the woman, and between thy seed and her seed; it shall bruise thy head, and thou shalt bruise his heel.* Where else do you see the seed of a woman referred to in Scripture?

The concept of the seed of a woman is only spoken of here in the Jewish Scriptures. It is an unusual expression and could be a reference to the virgin birth. Also, in Isaiah 53:2 *For he shall grow up before him as a tender plant, and as a root out of a dry ground.* The mention of a root out of dry ground could also be referring to the virgin birth. Instead of looking into pagan sources, we look to the Scriptures. If Christianity were truly dependent upon pagan beliefs, then why would Matthew quote the book of Isaiah?

The vocabulary is also seen as an inconsistency. The Jewish position is to take a rather dim view of Matthew's interpretation the prophet Isaiah. In Stuart Rosenberg's book, "The Christian Problem," he writes, "The remarkable Christian dogma of the 'Virgin Birth,' is based four-square on a faulty translation of a Hebrew word. *Almah,* 'meaning young woman,' is incorrectly rendered in the Greek Bible version by the word parthenos - (παρθενος) a virgin."[23] Notice that Rosenberg offers no proof for his statement. He simply waves his magic pen to dismiss the seventy

---

[21] Ibid p45

[22] The Christian Problem (A Jewish View) Hippocrene Books New York, NY. 1986

[23] Ibid.p68

Jewish Rabbis who translated the Hebrew Scriptures into the Greek language. They are simply wrong because he says so. He then quotes a few modern-day liberal Christians to support his view.

Rosenberg, and the liberals he quotes, are removed from the source by over twenty five hundred years. Those seventy men whose translation he ignores were over two thousand years closer to the scene then he is. How is it that he and the liberals can be so certain this far removed from the scene? If they were looking for the truth they would have to at least consider the virgin meaning.

None of the Jewish apologetic books even investigate the Hebrew word עלמה. They only assume that the Christian interpretation is incorrect and their assumption is enough. Let's take a look at the Scriptures, and see what we can learn when we study the word of Matthew when it refers to Isaiah 7:14; this is clearest passage for the virgin birth in the Scriptures. *Therefore the Lord himself shall give you a sign; Behold, a virgin shall conceive, and bear a son, and shall call his name Immanuel.*

There are several words used for a woman in the Hebrew Scriptures. The most common of these is the Hebrew word *ishah* אִשָׁה. *Ishah* is used 686 times in the Tenach. The next most frequently used word for a woman in the Scriptures is *naahrah* נַעֲרָה. The word *naahrah* occurs 57 times, and is usually translated as young girl, or perhaps a servant girl, and as a young woman only in Ruth 4:12. In the Hebrew Bible the word that is used to denote a woman whose chief characteristic is chastity is *bithulah* בְּחוּלָה. The word *bithulah* appears 50 times in the Tenach. The word that is translated "virgin" in Isaiah 7:14 is the Hebrew word *almah* עַלְמָה. Noticed *almah* is used only seven times in the scriptures.

Apparently *almah* is an exclusive word. As we look at the various words for a woman in the Hebrew Scriptures we see how they become more specific as they are used less frequently. *Ishah* is a woman in general. *Ishah* can refer to a woman who is either young or old. *Naahrah* is a special kind of *ishah*. She is a young girl, a young woman who could also be a virgin. Her chief characteristic is her youth. The word *bithulah* is a special kind of young woman. She is a young woman whose chief characteristic is her chastity. The word *almah* refers to a specific kind of *bithulah*. *Almah* refers to a young woman who is a virgin, who is also in the state of betrothal.

The first place where the word *almah* occurs in the Scriptures is in Genesis 24:43. ***Behold, I stand by the well of water; and it shall come to pass, that when the virgin cometh forth to draw water, and I say to her, Give me, I pray thee, a little water of thy pitcher to drink.*** There is a principle in Scriptural interpretation called the law of first usage. It is a rule that is more important in a word that is used infrequently like *almah*. *Almah* is obviously an exclusive word. The law states that the way a word is used the first time it appears in the Scriptures sets the standard for its usage throughout the rest of the Bible. In the Genesis passage the word *almah* refers to Rebekah. It is interesting to note that in this passage Rebekah is referred to by all three of the more specific terms for a woman. In Genesis 24:16 ***And the damsel was very fair to look upon, a virgin, neither had any man known her: and she went down to the well, and filled her pitcher, and came up.*** She is called a *naahrah*, here translated damsel, and she is called a *bithulah*, translated a virgin.

As Eliezer, Abraham's servant, retells the story in verse 43 ***Behold I stand by the well of water; and it shall come to pass, that when the virgin cometh forth to draw [water], and I say to her, Give me, I pray thee, a little water of thy pitcher to drink,*** he changes the word that he formally used to describe the virgin Rebekah. Now instead of calling her a *bithulah*, the more general term for virgin, he chooses the word *almah*, a more specific kind of virgin. What has transpired between verse 16 and ver 43? In what way has Rebekah changed? Two significant things have happened that contribute to the change in Rebekah's status. The first is in verse 22. ***And it came to pass , as the camels had done drinking , that the man took a golden earring of half a shekel weight, and two bracelets for her hands of ten [shekels] weight of gold.*** Rebekah accepted the Jewelry from Eliezer, Abraham's commissioned servant, who was sent to find a bride for Isaac. The second thing is that her brother and her legal guardian Laban approved of the jewelry and apparently the contract was sealed.

Genesis 24:30 *And it came to pass, when he saw the earring and bracelets upon his sister's hands, and when he heard the words of Rebekah his sister, saying, Thus spake the man unto me; that he came unto the man; and, behold, he stood by the camels at the well.* Rebekah is called a (*bithulah*) virgin until she accepts the jewelry. When her guardian approves of the jewelry her status changes. From then on the *bithulah* has become the *almah*. She is still a virgin, but now she is a specific kind of a virgin; she is now a virgin who is in the state of betrothal. The first time the word *almah* is used in Scriptures it refers to a virgin who is betrothed; this sets the standard for the usage of the word *almah* throughout the rest of the Scriptures.

The next time the word *almah* is used is in Exodus 2:8. *And Pharaoh's daughter said to her, Go And the maid went in and called the child's mother.* The word *almah* is here translated "maid." It is referring to Miriam, the sister of Moses. There doesn't seem to be any significant details in regards to the marital status of Miriam in the text. However, there is a Midrash[*] on the passage that could help with additional historical information. According to the Rabbis, Miriam was betrothed to be married, and her father didn't want her to go through with the marriage because he didn't desire to see more Jewish children born into captivity.[24] Now we can't be certain as to the historical accuracy of the Midrashic literature. However, we can be fairly certain that the insight we get from them on word usage is accurate.

Even if the Rabbis are inventing companion stories to the Scriptural accounts, they certainly wouldn't devise tales that are inconsistent with the Biblical language. If the word *almah* couldn't mean a virgin betrothed to be married, then they would never have contrived a story where Miriam is a betrothed virgin. So according to the Rabbis the word *almah* means a virgin betrothed. If the incident that the Midrash records is historical then the Scriptures

---

[*] see glossary of terms
[24] Midrash Rambam

use the word *almah* to refer to Miriam, who is a virgin in the state of betrothal. So the Rabbis teach that the word *almah* means a virgin in the state of betrothal. If the Midrashic literature is historically accurate, then the Scriptures use the word *almah* in both the first and the second usage, to refer to a virgin who is betrothed.

The third time the word *almah* appears in the Scriptures is in Psalm 68:25 ***The singers went before, the players on instruments followed after; among them were the damsels playing with timbrels.***

We began the mailing ministry in Bucks County, PA in the late 1970's. Almost every month a letter went out to Jewish homes or at least to the homes of people with the last names that often belonged to those of Jewish descent. After being on the mailing list for over a dozen years, Richard finally decided to call us. Richard, who went by his Hebrew name of Rachmiel, was a practicing Chassid.* We developed the most unusual friendship. We would talk about everything, and we would talk for what seemed to be forever.

When Richard decided it was time to seek a wife, he went to a Yenteh* , a woman who arranges marriages professionally. She sought out a good Chassidic family and according to ancient tradition, a marriage was arranged. I had the privilege of being the best man at the wedding. Unfortunately some of the Rabbis present recognized me. The ultra-orthodox community put a great deal of pressure on my friend, and we were forced to sever our relationship. But the wedding, ah what a wedding it was. I suppose that there is nothing in Psalm 68 to indicate exactly what is being referred to. But if you had seen Richard's wedding, you would have thought of the procession of girls who accompanied the bride. The wedding included singers, musicians that preceded the girls as they made their entrance into the hall, followed by the damsels playing on the timbrels.

There is a glimpse of a royal wedding in the Scriptures in Psalm 45:13-15. ***The king's daughter is all glorious within: her clothing is of wrought gold. She shall be brought unto the king***

---

* see glossary of terms

in raiment of needlework: the virgins her companions that follow her shall be brought unto thee. With gladness and rejoicing shall they be brought: they shall enter into the king's palace. The virgins in the procession in Psalm 45 are referred to by the Hebrew word *bithulah.*

Psalm 68 might also be a picture of the wedding procession. Each of the damsels in this procession are called *almah.* They are virgins, as those in the procession of Psalm 45 were, only here the fact of their betrothal status is also pointed out, probably so we can appreciate their joy more completely.

The next time we see the word *almah* is in Proverbs 30:19 *The way of an eagle in the air; the way of a serpent upon a rock; the way of a ship in the midst of the sea; and the way of a man with a maid."* The Rabbis insist that in this passage the word *almah* cannot mean virgin. There are four things being compared, and according to the Rabbis, what they each have in common is that they leave no trace. Their argument is that the way of a man with a virgin would leave a trace and that almah here can't refer to a virgin. The Rabbinical position assumes sexual intercourse has transpired. If there was no sexual intercourse, then there would be no trace. However, the leaving of no trace is not the central thought that connects these four ideas. In Proverbs 30:20, *Such is the way of an adulterous woman; she eateth, and wipeth her mouth, and saith, I have done no wickedness*, we read how the four different situations of verse 19 are compared to the way of an adulterous woman. The adulterous woman tries to remove all traces of her behavior, but the Scriptures teach that there will always be evidence that remains. Your sin will find you out (Numbers 32:23). Even in Proverbs we see how the activity of the Harlot takes its toll on her. She losses her femininity and develops masculine traits. She becomes loud and stubborn in Proverbs 7:10, and even in this passage we can see that she eats like a man.

It doesn't seem that the thread that connects all the incidents together in Proverbs 30:19-20 is that of "being without a trace." There is something marvelous about each. The way of an eagle in the air is indeed a marvel to behold. The way of a serpent on a rock, the way it moves is marvelous. The ship in the midst of the seas, what powers it? In each of these there is a hidden force, an unseen power at work, something marvelous. Although it is a bit different even in the adulterous woman there is an unseen force at work, a hidden power that is being wielded, and it too, is a marvel to behold. If that is the context of Proverbs 30:19, then the very specific meaning of *almah* that we have already seen in the Scriptures adds to the text. It is marvelous to see the way of a man with his bride to be. The unseen forces at work, the hidden power that compels him, is a marvel to behold.

The next two times we see the word *almah* is in Song of Solomon 1:3 and 6:8 *Because of the savour of thy good ointments thy name is as ointment poured forth, therefore do the virgins love thee.* There is little in this passage that reveals information about the character of the virgins that are mentioned. However, there is something of note in the 6:8 passage. *There are threescore queens, and fourscore concubines, and virgins without number.* Each of the kinds of women mentioned have a relationship with the king. The queens are his wives, the concubines are his possessions. To be consistent, the *almah*s should also have some relationship to him as well. It seems that the only relationship left would be that of betrothal. Once again we see that the best understanding of the word *almah* is that it refers to virgins who are betrothed to be married.

The context of Isaiah 7:14 is also seen as a problem. In all other usage in the Scriptures the word *almah* has meant a virgin in the state of betrothal. We can only assume that the usage here in Isaiah is the same. The question is, who is the betrothed virgin who is being addressed? Isaiah is instructed to meet Ahaz in verse three. He is instructed to take with him his son She-ar-jash-ub. She-ar-jash-ub could be a disciple of Isaiah, called a son, or he could be a son by a former wife, but in all likelihood he is the son of Isaiah and the wife in the context. If that is the case, then she couldn't be the virgin in question. In chapter 8:18 Isaiah writes that he and his children are for signs. There are two children mentioned, and each of them is a sign. The first was She-ar-jash-ub. He was a sign to Ahaz in regards to the Syrian empire and their conspiracy with the Northern kingdom, Israel against Judah. Before he is old enough to know right from wrong, both the lands were to be forsaken by both their kings. The second sign was Ma'her-shal, al-hash-baz. Before he is old enough to speak, both lands will be ransacked of their spoils by Assyria.

There is in the context a third sign, the sign of the virgin birth. In verse eleven the Lord asks Ahaz to ask for a sign. The verse reads *ask thee a sign*. The word translated thee is a second person singular pronoun. In verse fourteen the Lord is no longer speaking; Isaiah is speaking. He records that the Lord will give a sign. The verse reads *the Lord himself shall give you a sign*. The word translated you is plural, not singular. The sign of the virgin is not the same sign that was spoken of in verse eleven. The sign of verse fourteen is sent out to the plural house of David, and not to the individual king Ahaz. In verse sixteen Isaiah writes about She-ar-jas-ub. The sign there is again promised to a singular person. This is the continuation of the sign to Ahaz. None of the Jewish commentaries mention the change of number from the singular second person pronoun in verse eleven to the plural in verse fourteen.

In Isaiah 7:15-16, we read, *Butter and honey shall he eat, that he may know to refuse the evil, and choose the good. For before the child shall know to refuse the evil, and choose the good, the land that thou abhorrest shall be forsaken of both her kings*. Gerald Sigal asks " When did Jesus eat curds and honey,... could Jesus as a sinless god-man choose the evil."[25]The answer is that the sign spoken of in verses 15 and 16 have nothing to do with Jesus. These verses are speaking of the sign to the individual Ahaz, and not to the plural house of David. Conversely the sign of the virgin birth in verse 14 is not to the singular Ahaz, but rather to the plural house of David. It is not to be fulfilled within the life time of Ahaz, but will wait for the fullness of time.

Jewish people also have theological reasons to doubt the virgin birth as well. Most Jewish people think of the virgin birth as a Catholic fairy tale. They tie the concept in with the perpetual

---

[25]*The Jew and the Christian Missionary: A Jewish Response To Missionary Christianity* By Gerald Sigel pg 27

virginity of Mary and see the entire doctrine as puritanical. To them it is preposterous. You'll hear them quip, "everyone knows that it takes two to tango." They will marvel at how we can believe what is, in their opinion, so much nonsense. In The Real Messiah, Pinchas Stolper writes "Nowhere does the Bible predict that the Messiah will be born to a virgin. In fact, virgins never give birth anywhere in the Bible. This idea is to be found only in pagan mythology. To the Jewish mind, the very idea that G-d would plant a seed in a woman is unnecessary and unnatural. After all, what is accomplished by this claim? What positive purpose does it serve?"[26] That is precisely the right question to ask. Of course a virgin birth goes a long way towards authenticating the Messiah. His parents, their friends, and the immediate family will certainly know for sure that he is the promised one of God. We believe, however, there are at least two significant reasons beyond that of clear identification.

One reason is the royal line. The Rabbis will readily agree with us that the Creator could certainly accomplish a virgin birth. God can do anything. The question is, why would He want to? As we have already seen, the Messiah is to come from the tribe of Judah, and from the root of Jesse, and from the house of David. This is what the Scriptures teach, and the Rabbis agree.[27] Jeremiah 22:24-30 *As I live, saith the LORD, though Coniah the son of Jehoiakim king of Judah were the signet upon my right hand, yet would I pluck thee thence; 25 And I will give thee into the hand of them that seek thy life, and into the hand of them whose face thou fearest, even into the hand of Nebuchadrezzar king of Babylon, and into the hand of the Chaldeans. 26 And I will cast thee out, and thy mother that bare thee, into another country, where ye were not born; and there shall ye die. 27 But to the land whereunto they desire to return, thither shall they not return. 28 Is this man Coniah a despised broken idol? is he a vessel wherein is no pleasure? wherefore are they cast out, he and his seed, and*

---

[26]*The Real Messiah* NCYC p45

[27]Babylonian Talmud Berekoth 99, Sanhedrin 93b Sukkoth 52a Baba Bathra 75 b

are cast into a land which they know not? 29 O earth, earth, earth, hear the word of the LORD. 30 Thus saith the LORD, Write ye this man childless, a man that shall not prosper in his days: for no man of his seed shall prosper, sitting upon the throne of David, and ruling any more in Judah. We can see how the last king of Judah, who was a direct descendent of David, is decreed never to have a physical descendent of his own to sit on David's throne.

The Scriptures declare that the Messiah will be from the royal line of David, and the Scriptures also declare that the last king in that royal line will never produce seed that will reign. That is a bit of a problem, but not one beyond the power of the Creator. The Messiah could be a descendent of David through another line, escaping the curse on Jeconiah, but then he wouldn't be in the royal lineage. The Messiah could be an adoptive son, and that way he wouldn't be included in Jeconiah's curse. But he'd still, even though adopted, have some parentage, and that genuine physical parentage would disqualify him from being the Messiah, from both Biblical and rabbinical standards. [19]

There might be other solutions, but the one that the Creator ordained was to have an adopted son who had no physical father. His mother would be from David's house, his adopting father would be from the royal line, and there would be no physical father to tie him to Jeconiah, or any one for that matter except for the Creator Himself. That's one theological reason why there might be a virgin birth. It eliminates any would-be pretenders to the office of Messiah, and goes a long way toward establishing who the genuine promised anointed one of God really is.

The other theological reason is the natural line. It necessitates a physical death. The curse on Jeconiah is not the only curse that has to be circumvented in the lineage of the Messiah. There is an existing curse on all mankind. In Genesis 2:17 we read *But of the tree of the knowledge of good and evil, thou shalt not eat of it: for in the day that thou eatest thereof thou shalt surely die.* If Adam were to disobey the Creator then he would die. In Genesis 3:22, *And the LORD God said, Behold, the man is become as one of us, to know good and evil: and now, lest he put forth his hand, and take also of the tree of life, and eat, and live for ever.* We see that the Creator has separated man from access to the tree of life so that man would no longer live forever. Something happened to man in the third chapter of Genesis. He became a dying sinner, and he reproduced after his own kind. The difficulty is that the Scriptures teach that the Messiah is to be everlasting.

Micah 5:2 *But thou, Bethlehem Ephratah, though thou be little among the thousands of Judah, yet out of thee shall he come forth unto me that is to be ruler in Israel; whose goings forth have been from of old, from everlasting.*

Isaiah 9:6 *For unto us a child is born, unto us a son is given: and the government shall be upon his shoulder: and his name shall be called Wonderful, Counsellor, The mighty God, The everlasting Father, The Prince of Peace.*

In addition we read in Ezekiel 18:4 that *the soul that sinneth it shall die.* As we learned earlier, man has inherited a sin nature from Adam so that all men sin, and therefore all men die. Yet the Messiah is called *everlasting father,* and the *one whose goings forth [have been] from old, from everlasting.* The Messiah is an eternal being. Yet all the descendants of Adam are temporal beings. The virgin birth allows the Messiah to be a man, who is free from Adam's curse and Adam's condition.

The natural line also necessitates a spiritual death. As we have already discussed, the Scriptures teach that the nature of man is wicked. Jeremiah 17:9, *The heart is deceitful above all things, and desperately wicked: who can know it?* Yet when we consider the prophecies regarding the Messiah, he appears to be quite different.

Isaiah 11:3-5 *3 And shall make him of quick understanding in the fear of the LORD: and he shall not judge after the sight of his eyes, neither reprove after the hearing of his ears: 4 But with righteousness shall he judge the poor, and reprove with equity for the meek of the earth: and he shall smite the earth with the rod of his mouth, and with the breath of his lips shall he slay the wicked. 5 And righteousness shall be the girdle of his loins, and faithfulness the girdle of his reins.*

How do we reconcile what Isaiah 11 says about the Messiah with what Isaiah 64:6 says about the righteousness of man? Again the virgin birth solves the problem.

In Romans 5:12 *Wherefore, as by one man sin entered into the world, and death by sin; and so death passed upon all men, for that all have sinned.* We read about the imputation of the sin nature. If my wife's interpretation is correct, the children get their nature from the father. Without a human father there would be no inherited old sin nature. The virgin birth would allow the Messiah to fulfill the prophetic picture.

So what must be our conclusion on the virgin birth? We believe in the virgin birth on the basis of the Scriptures. I realize that the Septuagint is inconsistent, and therefore unreliable. But we can't assume that it is always wrong. For us to declare that the Septuagint is incorrect we must do a word study. The word study we have done shows that the Septuagint is indeed correct in Isaiah 7:14.

The theological discussion shows that there is indeed a reason, a purpose for the miraculous teaching. The context of Isaiah 7 with the change of address from the singular king, to the plural house of David allows for the prophecy to be fulfilled beyond the time of Isaiah. This is not designed to be proof. It is simply an attempt to show just cause for our convictions. Our Jewish friends obviously have come to a different conclusion than we have. Some have declared that our beliefs are based on pagan teachings. We wanted to show that our conclusions are consistent with the teachings of Scripture, and there is no inconsistency between the teaching of Matthew in the New Testament, and the teaching of Isaiah.

Matthew's two donkeys

I was sitting on the cement staircase leading down to the basement of the students activity center at Temple University. I don't know why I was sitting. My recollection of those days was that I was always on the run. I would be carrying books back and forth from Mitten hall to the SAC building, or manning one of the publicity tables, or talking to a student, or training a worker. Rarely would I be able to just sit down. It's possible that I was sitting down to talk with Michael, but as it seems to me, Michael discovered me sitting there and sidled up and sat down beside me. Michael was a professional anti-missionary. He was very good at what he did. Michael sat down beside me and showed me Matthew 21:1-5 *And when they drew nigh unto Jerusalem, and were come to Bethphage, unto the mount of Olives, then sent Jesus two disciples, Saying unto them, Go into the village over against you, and straightway ye shall find an ass tied, and a colt with her: loose them, and bring them unto me. And if any man say ought unto you, ye shall say, The Lord hath need of them; and straightway he will send them. All this was done, that it might be fulfilled which was spoken by the prophet, saying, Tell ye the daughter of Sion, Behold, thy King cometh unto thee, meek, and sitting upon an ass, and a colt the foal of an ass.*

The verse Matthew quotes is Zechariah 9:9, *O daughter of Jerusalem: behold, thy King cometh unto thee: he is just, and having salvation; lowly, and riding upon an ass, and upon colt the foal of an ass.* My friend Michael pointed out to me that the Hebrew Scriptures in Zechariah 9:9 indicate one animal. The Septuagint translation mistranslates two animals in the verse. Matthew, who quotes from the Septuagint translation, tries to make the story sound Biblical so he invents two animals in his fulfillment story.

As I thought through Michael's explanation, it sounded so plausible. Then I thought through the ramifications of the view. If Matthew is unreliable, then the New Testament is unreliable, and with it the whole of the Christian faith is totally undermined. Before I could think of a response, Michael patted me on the shoulder, and he walked into the student activities center. I was left sitting on the steps. My head was down, and I was feeling embarrassed. I was ashamed because I had been caught off guard; I wasn't familiar with this objection, and I didn't have an answer prepared.

The mention of the second animal by the Septuagint could reflect a misunderstanding of the Hebrew. The mention of a second animal by Matthew, however, doesn't necessarily imply misunderstanding, nor does it need to include any error. Sigal says that "Matthew in his eagerness to use Zechariah 9:9 as an example of how Jesus fulfilled prophecy, misses the point that Biblical poetry makes frequent use of synonymous parallelism."[28] In actuality Sigal in his eagerness to discredit Matthew misses the point. The point is that the Messiah enters the city in meekness. Most of the rabbinical scenarios have the Messiah entering Jerusalem as a king and a conqueror.

Obviously Jesus is only riding one animal. He certainly isn't pictured by Matthew as entering Jerusalem as some kind of circus acrobat deftly astride two donkeys at the same time. There were, however, two animals involved. As we read in Zechariah "the ו is epexegetical (1 Samuel xvii 40), describing the ass as a young animal, not yet ridden, but still running behind the she-asses. The youthfulness of the animal is brought out still more strongly by the expression added to עַיִר, viz. בֶּן־אֲתֹנוֹת i.e., a foal, such as asses are accustomed to bear."[29] The foal mentioned both in Zechariah and in Matthew would have still been of nursing age. An animal of that age would never be separated from its mother. The mention of the foal demands the presence of the mother, and Matthew mentions the presence of both animals.

The picture is one of tremendous humility: the Messiah, entering the city riding side saddle on a nursing baby donkey. This is not the rabbinical picture, but that is the Messiah the Scriptures predicted. The scene is similar to what we read in 1 Kings 1:33, 38-40 *The king also said unto them, Take with you the servants of your lord, and cause Solomon my son to ride upon mine own mule, and bring him down to Gihon: So Zadok the priest, and Nathan the prophet, and Benaiah the son of Jehoiada, and the Cherethites, and the Pelethites, went down, and caused Solomon to ride upon king David's mule, and brought him to Gihon. And Zadok the priest took an horn of oil out of the tabernacle, and anointed Solomon. And they blew the trumpet; and all the people said, God save king Solomon. And all the people came up after*

---

[28] The Jew and the Christian missionary, Sigal page 79
[29] Keil-Delitzsch Commentary on the Old Testament, Eerdmans volume 10 p 334

him, and the people piped with pipes, and rejoiced with great joy, so that the earth rent with the sound of them.

Matthew's account is not an attempt to reconcile a mistranslation, but is indeed consistent with what would have had to have occurred historically, given what we know about the life cycle of the donkey. If Matthew had only mentioned the one animal, an anti-missionary of Michael's stature would have probably published a book, trying to discredit the New Testament on being historically inaccurate. They would be clamoring for an explanation for the missing donkey.

The Elijah Problem

The difficulty according to Sigal is "Jesus considered Malachi's prophecies concerning Elijah, the harbinger of the Messiah, as completely fulfilled in John. For Jesus, Elijah had come in the person of John."[30] Matthew 17:12 *But I say unto you, That Elias is come already, and they knew him not, but have done unto him whatsoever they listed. Likewise shall also the Son of man suffer of them.* Sigal needs a little help here. Why can't we agree that John was Elijah, that he was reincarnated? That would be consistent with the Chassidic teaching of "Gilgal" , so what would be the problem? The problem is, if Elijah was John, then the New Testament is in error in John 1:21 *And they asked him, What then? Art thou Elias? And he saith, I am not. Art thou that prophet? And he answered, No.* If Elijah wasn't John, then Jesus is mistaken. Matthew 11:13 &14 *For all the prophets and the law prophesied until John. And if ye will receive it, this is Elias, which was for to come.*

Jesus refers to the Scriptural teaching of Elijah in two different ways. In Matthew 17:10 & 11, we read *And his disciples asked him, saying, Why then say the scribes that Elias must first come? And Jesus answered and said unto them, Elias truly shall first come, and restore all things.* The Greek verb ερχεται translated "shall come" is really in the present tense, but the verb for "will

---

[30]*The Jew and The Christian Missionary* P 83

restore," αποκαταστησει is in the future tense. That clearly places the fulfillment of this phrase in the future.

The Rabbis get annoyed every time we refer to the second coming. However, it is not our fault that the prophets predict two distinct advents of the Messiah. We will discuss the second advent as a separate topic. But Jesus clearly is teaching here that Elijah will come before the second advent.

It is interesting to note that in Matthew 17 verse 11, Jesus taught that Elijah is to come, present tense, and to do things in the future, but in verse 12 Jesus taught *that Elias is come already*, and employs the second aorist, a past tense verb. The answer is both. In some way, the role of Elijah has already been accomplished, and Elijah will of certainty have a role in the future.

We have resolved one aspect of the problem, in regards to the future. The other aspect, regarding the nature and character of Elijah, as it relates to John at the time of Jesus, is resolved in Luke 1 :17. Here we read what the angel has to say about the nature and character of John *And he shall go before him in the spirit and power of Elias.* John clearly was not Elijah, but was to come in the spirit and power of Elijah.

All four Gospels equate the ministry of John to Isaiah chapter 40 *The voice of him that crieth in the wilderness, Prepare ye the way of the LORD, make straight in the desert a highway for our God.* The Isaiah passage makes reference to both the first and second advents of the Messiah. Notice "the voice" here is not named. It could be Elijah as the Rabbis thought, or it could be someone else, in the spirit and power of Elijah. In Matthew 11:14, Jesus said *And if ye will receive it, this is Elias, which was for to come.* He was clearly speaking of John, but he clarifies his statement by saying *if you receive it.* Receive what? Earlier we see the things that the kingdom of God must suffer for man's sake. Perhaps Jesus is saying that if you receive the kingdom, then the ministry of John would count as the forerunner for the Messiah.

In Malachi the prophet Elijah is clearly named. Malachi 4:5-6 *Behold, I will send you Elijah the prophet before the coming of the great and dreadful day of the LORD: And he shall turn the heart of the fathers to the children, and the heart of the children to their fathers, lest I come and smite the earth with a curse.* This passage is a clear reference to the second coming and can only refer to the end times.

John is the forerunner of the Messiah at his first coming. Elijah is promised to have that role at the second coming. If any would be searching for Elijah and messiah at the time of Jesus, the ministry of John in the spirit and power of Elijah would direct the searcher to find the true Messiah Jesus.

Rachel weeping for her children

In Matthew 2:14-19 we read the account of the events that took place following the birth of Jesus. *When he arose, he took the young child and his mother by night, and departed into Egypt: And was there until the death of Herod: that it might be fulfilled which was spoken of the Lord by the prophet, saying, Out of Egypt have I called my son. Then Herod, when he saw that he was mocked of the wise men, was exceeding wroth, and sent forth, and slew all the children that were in Bethlehem, and in all the coasts thereof, from two years old and under, according to the time which he had diligently enquired of the wise men. Then was fulfilled that which was spoken by Jeremy the prophet, saying, In Rama was there a voice heard, lamentation, and weeping, and great mourning, Rachel weeping for her children, and would not be comforted, because they are not.*

Matthew concludes by saying that these events were a fulfillment of what was mentioned by the Prophet Jeremiah in chapter 31:15-19 *Thus saith the LORD; A voice was heard in Ramah, lamentation, and bitter weeping; Rachel weeping for her children refused to be comforted for her children, because they were not. Thus saith the LORD; Refrain thy voice from weeping, and thine eyes from tears: for thy work shall be rewarded, saith the LORD; and they shall come again from the land of the enemy. And there is hope in thine end, saith the LORD, that thy children shall come again to their own border. I have surely heard Ephraim bemoaning himself thus; Thou hast chastised me, and I was chastised, as a bullock unaccustomed to the yoke: turn thou me, and I shall be turned; for thou art the LORD my*

God. Surely after that I was turned, I repented; and after that I was instructed, I smote upon my thigh: I was ashamed, yea, even confounded, because I did bear the reproach of my youth.

The attack asserts that the New Testament is invalid because the reference in Jeremiah seems distinct from the incident of Matthew chapter 2.[31] Matthew's use of the Old Testament seems a bit forced and unusual. However, his liberty with the Scripture is completely consistent with Jewish Rabbinical commentary. What is unusual is that a Jewish scholar would make mention of it. The Midrashic literature, the Targums, the Mishnah, and the Rabbinical commentaries are replete with interpretations that can border on the fantastic. In the light of the traditional Jewish writings it is ludicrous to bring accusation against Matthew.

In his commentary on Matthew 2:18-20 John Broadus writes "He and his Jewish readers had the general conviction that everything in the history of the nation of Israel was sacred and significant, and wherever Matthew saw a resemblance between an event in the history of Israel and an event in the life of Messiah, he might consider that this resemblance was divinely designed and wish his readers to take the same view."[32]

In Jeremiah chapter 31 we are being shown how the ten tribes of the northern kingdom are going to be restored in the Messianic age. Both Judah and Israel are going to go through much suffering due to their sin, but ultimate deliverance is assured. Rachel is the mother of the ten northern tribes. Her weeping in Ramah is significant. Ramah is where those of Judah who were to be carried away captive were gathered. However, Rachel is not weeping for those of Judah, but rather for her children of the northern ten tribes. Ramah is a lofty border city where the cries of Rachel for Israel's sins could be heard throughout the land of Judah. Israel's rejection of the reign of Judah's king made possible the ultimate exile of both Israel and Judah. Therefore the wail and agony of Rachel could not be comforted. Rachel, the mother of both Benjamin and Joseph, is pictured as matriarch of both Judah and

---

[31] Ibid page 189

[32] *Matthew*, John Broadus, Judson Press. Valley Forge Pa . pg 25

Israel. In Jeremiah, however, her agony will end in the times of the Messiah when both nations will be delivered, restored and united.

In Matthew the situation repeats itself. Herod, an Idumite, is rejecting the true king of Judah. Because of this the children of the southern kingdom suffer. Again the sins of the northern kingdom bring a great burden to the southern kingdom, and to the matriarch of both. Again their cry is heard throughout the land of Judah. Out of the depths of the despair, however, there is the Messianic hope of restoration. In Matthew the long awaited Messiah appears.

Which Zachariah

In Matthew 23:35 Jesus makes a reference to the death of a man named Zechariah. Matthew 23:35 *That upon you may come all the righteous blood shed upon the earth, from the blood of righteous Abel unto the blood of Zacharias son of Barachias, whom ye slew between the temple and the altar.* The way the Old Testament books were ordered at the time of Jesus is a little different than they are today. At that time the last book in the Jewish Scriptures was Second Chronicles. The two deaths that Jesus refers to occur in the first and the last books of the Jewish Scriptures.

Genesis 4:8 *And Cain talked with Abel his brother: and it came to pass, when they were in the field, that Cain rose up against Abel his brother, and slew him.*

2 Chronicles 24:20-21 *And the Spirit of God came upon Zechariah the son of Jehoiada the priest, which stood above the people, and said unto them, Thus saith God, Why transgress ye the commandments of the LORD, that ye cannot prosper? because ye have forsaken the LORD, he hath also forsaken you. And they conspired against him, and stoned him with stones at the commandment of the king in the court of the house of the LORD.*

The difficulty is that the man who was slain in Second Chronicles is the son of the Priest Jehoida but Jesus refers to Zechariah the son of Berechiah. The prophet Zechariah is the son of Berechiah. We don't know how he died. He could have also been slain between the altar and the temple. Zechariah the son of

Jehoida was slain because of unpopular spirit-filled preaching. Zechariah the prophet could have been slain also because of unpopular spirit-filled preaching. He lived and died in the same time frame, and is mentioned twice in the book of Second Chronicles, 26:5 and 29:1. If this were a possible solution to the problem, it would allow for the Genesis to Second Chronicles continuum, but it is unlikely. However, the Old Testament is replete with name problems. In fact the Prophet Zechariah is stated to be the son of Berechiah in Zechariah 1:1 *In the eighth month, in the second year of Darius, came the word of the LORD unto Zechariah, the son of Berechiah, the son of Iddo the prophet, saying,* and then in Ezra 6:14 he is referred to as the son of Iddo. *And the elders of the Jews builded, and they prospered through the prophesying of Haggai the prophet and Zechariah the son of Iddo.*

We can see from Zechariah 1:1 that in reality Berechiah is the son of Iddo, and Zechariah is the grandson. Perhaps Zechariah the son of Jehoida is also the grandson of a man named Berechiah. We don't know; it might be a case of a scribal error in the New Testament text, but there is no evidence of that.

We don't have a single certain answer. But we also don't have a reason to discard the New testament. In 1 Samuel 17 we read the of the incident when David slew the Philistine Goliath. However, in Second Samuel 21:19 we read: *And there was again a battle in Gob with the Philistines, where Elhanan the son of Jaareoregim, a Bethlehemite, slew Goliath the Gittite, the staff of whose spear was like a weaver's beam.* Who slew Goliath? Was it King David or this other guy? In First Chronicles 20:5 we get a partial answer. 1 Chronicles 20:5 *And there was war again with the Philistines; and Elhanan the son of Jair slew Lahmi the brother of Goliath the Gittite, whose spear staff was like a weaver's beam.* Here we see that Elhanan actually slew the brother of Goliath. But we still don't know why the Scriptures read incorrectly in Second Samuel. We can assume a scribal error, but there are no texts to my knowledge that render an alternate reading.

Two wrongs don't make a right. We can find some problems and confusion in both Testaments but that does not answer any questions or solve any difficulties. However, if a practicing Jewish person is going to assign authenticity to the Jewish Scriptures in spite of some minor difficulties, he cannot honestly discredit the New Testament on the basis of the same kind of minor difficulty.

Which High Priest

In Mark 2:25-26 Jesus refers to an incident in the life of King David. *And he said unto them, Have yea never read what David did, when he had need, and was an hungered, he, and they that were with him? How he went into the house of God in the days of Abiathar the high priest, and did eat the shewbread, which is not lawful to eat but for the priests, and gave also to them which were with him?*

The difficulty is that as far we know the incident took place while Abimeleck was high priest. Meanwhile Jesus says that the high priest was Abiathar. It is not unusual to refer to the High Priest Abiathar in relationship to David. Those days could easily be called the days of Abiathar. Abiathar is better known than his father and is often thought of in relation to King David. Again we don't have all the information. There are many kinds of dual regency of the high priest, and often a high priest would have to be temporarily side-lined due to defilement. The Midrashic literature speaks of a time when Aaron became unclean, and Eliezer had to minister in his stead. However, Eliezer then became unclean, and Ithamin had to minister in his place.[33] Who then would be called the High Priest, Aaron, Eliezer, or Ithamin? We don't know if that was the situation at the time of Abiathar or not. We are too far removed from the incident. However, the Gospel of Mark is a great deal closer to the event than we are. Why should we assume an error when we are lacking full information? We don't attack the Old Testament on every point of disagreement between Kings and Chronicles. We assume that there must be some means of reconciliation, howbeit unknown to us. Why can't we make the same assumption for the Gospels?

---

[33] Midrash Rabbah Numbers 11:26 Pg. 63

Hate your enemies

In Matthew 5:43 *Ye have heard that it hath been said, Thou shalt love thy neighbour, and hate thine enemy.* According to one Jewish apologetic "There is not a word anywhere in the vast literature of Judaism which indicates this."[34] Without even looking through the Talmud or the Midrash or any of the Targums we can find indications in the Scriptures themselves.

Psalm 97:10 *Ye that love the LORD, hate evil: he preserveth the souls of his saints; he delivereth them out of the hand of the wicked.*

Psalm 101:3 *I will set no wicked thing before mine eyes: I hate the work of them that turn aside; it shall not cleave to me.*

Psalm 119:104 *Through thy precepts I get understanding: therefore I hate every false way.*

Psalm 119:163 *I hate and abhor lying: but thy law do I love.*

Psalm 139:21 *Do not I hate them, O LORD, that hate thee? and am not I grieved with those that rise up against thee?*

In Psalm 97:10 those that love the Lord are instructed to hate evil. The question is, what is evil? Things are not evil of themselves. People can be evil, and we are instructed to hate evil. We must hate the work of wicked men, every false way, and lying. David, in psalm 139:21, declares that he hates those that hate the Lord.

The psalms quoted above qualify as being somewhere within the vast literature of Judaism. The Torah itself admonishes us to love our neighbors. Because the neighbor is singled out for love, probably the enemy is not entitled to the same kind of treatment.

Beyond that even if these verses didn't qualify, we would still have to assume that perhaps those at the time of Matthew were aware of literature within Judaism that we aren't aware of. It is rather unlikely that Jesus would publicly declare that there was a teaching of that sort when there was no such known teaching within Judaism.

---

[34] *A Jew Examines Christianity*, by Rachel Zurer, Jinnac Press NY. 1985 pg. 84

Paul's ignorance of Hebrew (seed)

In Galatians 3:16 Paul wrote *Now to Abraham and his seed were the promises made. He saith not, And to seeds, as of many; but as of one, And to thy seed, which Christ.* [35] *because nowhere in the Hebrew Bible is the word seed used in reference to human descendants. To that objection we need only to look at Genesis 4:25 And Adam knew his wife again; and she bare a son, and called his name Seth: For God, said she, hath appointed me another seed instead of Abel, whom Cain slew.* Here we see a clear usage of the Hebrew word seed where a single individual is meant.

The objection continues to insinuate that Paul was ignorant of the Hebrew language. Sigal declares that Paul did not understand the collective force of the Hebrew word זֶרַע which is translated seed. It is unlikely that Paul would be unfamiliar with the collective sense of the Hebrew word, since the Greek word σπερματα has the same force.

The Hebrew word for seed always appears in the singular; however, the word seed can have both a singular usage as in Genesis 3:15. *And I will put enmity between thee and the woman, and between thy seed and her seed; it shall bruise thy head, and thou shalt bruise his heel,* or it can have a plural usage as in Genesis 17:8. *And I will give unto thee, and to thy seed after thee, the land wherein thou art a stranger, all the land of Canaan, for an everlasting possession; and I will be their God.* Whether the word is to be understood as singular or plural is a matter of interpretation. Paul asserts that his understanding of the Scriptures is not a personnel point of view. In Galatians 1:12 we read, *For I neither received it of man, neither was I taught it, but by the revelation of Jesus Christ.* In fact Paul begins the book of Galatians by asserting his divine appointment. Galatians 1:1 *Paul, an apostle, (not of men, neither by man, but by Jesus Christ, and God the Father, who raised him from the dead;)*

---

[35] *The Jew and the Christian Missionary* Pg. 8

Later in Galatians 2:2 Paul speaks of receiving revelation *And I went up by revelation, and communicated unto them that gospel which I preach among the Gentile."* Sigal says that Paul's usage of the Hebrew is fallacious. We see that Paul's usage of the Hebew is consistent with the Hebrew Bible. The difficulty isn't in translation but in interpretation. Paul claims to have authority to interpret the Scriptures.

Rather than attack Paul's knowledge of Hebrew the objection should come against Paul's assumed authority. Paul is stating that because the promise culminates in a singular Messiah, a singular word is used. He is referring to typology, which is prevalent in Rabbinical thinking. Paul was making a theological and grammatical interpretation. When you realize the amazing liberties the Rabbis take with the understanding of a text in the field of Gemmatria, an objection of this sort becomes comical.

No Nazarene

In Matthew 2:23 we read, And he came and dwelt in a city called Nazareth: that it might be fulfilled which was spoken by the prophets, He shall be called a Nazarene. Sigal states that at no point in the Old Testament is Messiah referred to as a Nazarene,[36] as Matthew 2:23 says. Sigal then mentions one of the possible solutions. Sigal says it has been speculated that Matthew is referring to Netzer,[37] a branch or shoot, as mentioned in Isaiah 11, and implied in Zechariah 3:8 (Isaiah 11:1) *And there shall come forth a rod out of the stem of Jesse, and a Branch shall grow out of his roots:* Zechariah 3:8 *Hear now, O Joshua the high priest, thou, and thy fellows that sit before thee: for they are men wondered at: for, behold, I will bring forth my servant the BRANCH.*

Sigal mentions a second explanation. He linguistically shows how the second alternative is impossible. However, Sigal nowhere refutes the first suggestion that Matthew is equating the region with the Hebrew word for branch, a term which clearly refers to

---

[36] Ibid. Pg 191
[37] Ibid.

175

the Messiah in the Scriptures. As well the Nazarenes were apparently people from a region that was despised. Nazareth was a place of contempt. As we see in John 1:46 *And Nathanael said unto him, Can there any good thing come out of Nazareth?* The Messiah is depicted as the rejected one in Isaiah 53. So there could be a possible reference to the rejected one from the rejected region.

We certainly don't have all the information. Matthew was trying to show the authenticity of Jesus by relating him to the Jewish Scriptures. If the Messiah was never referred to as a Nazarene, what possible advantage could Matthew gain for his cause by saying so? We might not at this distance be able to ascertain exactly what Matthew was referring to, but we can be sure that his readers had some frame of reference.

Inconsistencies within the New Testament
Acts 15 & Matthew 5

The difficulty is that Jesus never advocated disobedience of the Torah law. As we can see in Matthew 5:17 *Think not that I am come to destroy the law, or the prophets: I am not come to destroy, but to fulfil.* Yet in Acts 15 the council of elders introduces some dramatic changes, and the Gentiles are not required to obey the Torah law from that time forward.[38] Acts 15:28-30 *For it seemed good to the Holy Ghost, and to us, to lay upon you no greater burden than these necessary things; That ye abstain from meats offered to idols, and from blood, and from things strangled, and from fornication: from which if ye keep yourselves, ye shall do well. Fare ye well. So when they were dismissed, they came to Antioch: and when they had gathered the multitude together, they delivered the epistle.*

When Jesus refers to the law, he is not speaking exclusively of the law of Moses. It is more likely Jesus is testifying to the continued acceptance and authenticity of the Hebrew Bible. We can see that usage of the terms elsewhere in Matthew's Gospel. In Matthew 11:13 *For all the prophets and the law prophesied until John,* and again in Matthew 7:12 *Therefore all things whatsoever*

---

[38]*You take Jesus , I'll Take God,* Samuel Levine Hammorah Press LA, CA. 1980 pgs .79-80

ye would that men should do to you, do ye even so to them: for this is the law and the prophets.

It seems rather natural that when Jesus says that he came to fulfill the law, he simply meant that **all** that the Scriptures say about the Messiah will be fulfilled in his life and ministry. As we see in John 1:45, he is the one of whom the law and the prophets did write. *Philip findeth Nathanael, and saith unto him, We have found him, of whom Moses in the law, and the prophets, did write, Jesus of Nazareth, the son of Joseph.*

There is no contradiction between the Gospel of Matthew and the book of Acts because Matthew is referring to the entire Jewish canon, which Jesus fulfills by his life, ministry, and atoning work. The council that was convened in Acts 15 and the relationship between Christians and the Torah will be discussed under the topic "objections to Christian behavior."

The return of Jesus

The difficulty here, according to Aryeh Kaplan, is that the New Testament itself claims that the prophecies concerning the Messianic reign of Jesus [39] In three locations in the New Testament Jesus says *That generation shall not pass until all things are fulfilled.* In Matthew 24:34 *Verily I say unto you, This generation shall not pass, till all these things be fulfilled.* In Mark 13:30 *Verily I say unto you, that this generation shall not pass, till all these things be done,* and in Luke 21:32 *Verily I say unto you, This generation shall not pass away, till all be fulfilled.*

The references of Jesus to "that shall not pass away" are references to the people who are alive at the end time. As we can see clearly in Luke, we are being shown a prophetic look at the last days. Luke 21:20-25 *And when ye shall see Jerusalem compassed with armies, then know that the desolation thereof is nigh. Then let them which are in Judaea flee to the mountains; and let them which are in the midst of it depart out; and let not them that are in the countries enter thereinto. For these be the days of vengeance, that all things which are written may be fulfilled. But*

---

[39] *The Real Messiah*, Arayeh Kaplan ,NCSY, New York, NY. 1976, P46

woe unto them that are with child, and to them that give suck, in those days! for there shall be great distress in the land, and wrath upon this people. And they shall fall by the edge of the sword, and shall be led away captive into all nations: and Jerusalem shall be trodden down of the Gentiles, until the times of the Gentiles be fulfilled. And there shall be signs in the sun, and in the moon, and in the stars; and upon the earth distress of nations, with perplexity; the sea and the waves roaring. He then refers to Matthew 16:28 as proof of his point. *Verily I say unto you, There be some standing here, which shall not taste of death, till they see the Son of man coming in his kingdom.*

The generation spoken of in Luke 21:32 is clearly an end time generation. Jesus is not speaking about the people of his day. However, we do see language that does refer to the people who were alive and standing there at the time of Jesus. Jesus said that some of the people standing there would not taste of death until they saw him coming in his kingdom. Yet, it has been almost 2,000 years, and Jesus has not yet set up his kingdom. Was Jesus wrong?[40] This passage is a bit difficult. It's not a problem as far as faith is concerned, nor is it a discrepancy in the New Testament. The problem is in the difficulty of being certain as to exactly what Jesus meant. Some have suggested that he was referring to the Mount of Transfiguration, which Matthew describes in the very next verse. Others think that Jesus is referring to the destruction of Jerusalem in 70 CE. A third possibility is that Jesus is predicting the events that occurred when the Holy Spirit descended at Pentecost. The post resurrection appearances of Jesus to the disciples might also be a possible explanation.

John certainly saw the Lord coming in his glory in his vision at the aisle of Patmos. Perhaps Peter was given a similar vision, enabling him to write the prophetic material of his epistles. The New Testament teaches an imminent return of the Lord. He could come at any time. New Testament believers expected his return. We might not be certain as to what Jesus meant in Matthew 16, but we have more than enough possibilities. In Peter's second Epistle

---

[40]The Jew and the Christian Missionary, PG. 209

he speaks of those who would scoff at the second coming of Jesus. II Peter 3:3-4 *Knowing this first, that there shall come in the last days scoffers, walking after their own lusts, And saying, Where is the promise of his coming? for since the fathers fell asleep, all things continue as they were from the beginning of the creation.*

It is interesting to note that the New Testament, which is being attacked on the issue of the return of the Lord, accurately predicts the conditions we now find, and the attitude of the last day scoffers. It is difficult to disregard the New Testament, especially when it actually foretold the attack that was going to come.

Teachings on divorce

In Matthew Jesus declares there is one legitimate reason for divorce, and that is adultery.[41] In Matthew 5:32, we read *But I say unto you, That whosoever shall put away his wife, saving for the cause of fornication, causeth her to commit adultery: and whosoever shall marry her that is divorced committeth adultery*, and again in Matthew 19:9, *And I say unto you, Whosoever shall put away his wife, except it be for fornication, and shall marry another, committeth adultery: and whoso marrieth her which is put away doth commit adultery.*

Yet in Mark 10:9 and in Luke 16:18 there are no grounds for divorce.[42] Paul, according to Sigal, supports the more rigid, legalistic declaration, as found in Mark and Luke.[43] Although the words for adultery and fornication are frequently interchangeable, when they are used together whatever distinction there is between them would at that time be emphasized. In both Matthew 5 and in Matthew 19 both terms are used together. The term translated fornication is *porneia*. *Porneia* is a general word used for any kind of illicit or unlawful sexual intercourse. The word for adultery is μοιχεια Moichia. This word is more specific. It refers to sexual immorality that violates a marriage contract. Mr. Sigal has

---

[41]Ibid pages 190-195

[42] Ibid Page 200

[43] Ibid

misquoted Jesus when he mentions adultery as the only grounds for divorce. Jesus gave fornication as the only grounds.

In Biblical Judaism the state of betrothal was binding. There existed no grounds for divorcing the espoused wife. If on the night of the wedding, it was discovered that she had prior sexual relations, then the husband could, at that time, divorce her. However, her crime would technically be a premarital act. Once married, Jesus instructs them to remain so.

Those who were punished were forced into a life of adultery. They were left to harlotry, and they were looked upon always as the wife who was "put away." A woman, realizing the implications of indiscretion, would keep herself pure, and if the women maintain their purity, then the men would be pure as well. That would make for a distinct nation, a peculiar people.

Therefore there are no grounds for divorce after the wedding night. The only grounds for divorce that Jesus allowed for were for premarital unfaithfulness. Paul does not hold to the hard line of Mark and Luke, but actually adds new grounds. With the establishment of the church, there is a new scenario. People are getting saved and are joining the fold. Some are married to unbelievers, and others were already divorced. Paul's needed instruction in First Corinthians chapter 7 deals with these circumstances. We notice that Paul, when repeating previous teaching, says that the command comes from Jesus. *"And unto the married I command, yet not I, but the Lord, Let not the wife depart from her husband."* When Paul is giving the needed new information he sates that what he is now teaching is new, and was not previously taught by Jesus. *But to the rest speak I, not the Lord: If any brother hath a wife that believeth not, and she be pleased to dwell with him, let him not put her away.*

There are many differences among believers in regards to the divorce issue, but these differences do not stem from New Testament contradictions. The charges laid by Sigal are based largely on a misquote and on misunderstanding.

The anointing of Jesus

During the week before the cross, Jesus was invited to a dinner. On that occasion, he was anointed with expensive oil. The incident is recorded by all four Gospels. According to Mr. Sigal the discrepancies between the records cannot be reconciled. "Luke's version of the same event differs in quite a number of details. There is no doubt that Luke, though he changes the time and location of the event, is depicting the same occurrence. Luke is the only one who says the woman was a sinner. The synoptic gospels say she anointed Jesus with perfume, while John says it was spikenard ointment. Matthew and Mark say the woman anointed Jesus' head and Luke and John say that she anointed Jesus' feet. There is a decided lack of agreement between the four evangelists."[44]

Luke 7 36-48   *And one of the Pharisees desired him that he would eat with him. And he went into the Pharisee's house, and sat down to meat. And, behold, a woman in the city, which was a sinner, when she knew that Jesus sat at meat in the Pharisee's house, brought an alabaster box of ointment, And stood at his feet behind him weeping, and began to wash his feet with tears, and did wipe them with the hairs of her head, and kissed his feet, and anointed them with the ointment. Now when the Pharisee which had bidden him saw it, he spake within himself, saying, This man, if he were a prophet, would have known who and what manner of woman this is that toucheth him: for she is a sinner. And Jesus answering said unto him, Simon, I have somewhat to say unto thee. And he saith, Master, say on. There was a certain creditor which had two debtors: the one owed five hundred pence, and the other fifty. And when they had nothing to pay, he frankly forgave them both. Tell me therefore, which of them will love him most? Simon answered and said, I suppose that he, to whom he forgave most. And he said unto him, Thou hast rightly judged. And he turned to the woman, and said unto Simon, Seest thou this woman? I entered*

---

[44]Ibid pg 222

into thine house, thou gavest me no water for my feet: but she hath washed my feet with tears, and wiped them with the hairs of her head. Thou gavest me no kiss: but this woman since the time I came in hath not ceased to kiss my feet. My head with oil thou didst not anoint: but this woman hath anointed my feet with ointment. Wherefore I say unto thee, Her sins, which are many, are forgiven; for she loved much: but to whom little is forgiven, the same loveth little. And he said unto her, Thy sins are forgiven.

Sigal equates omission with contradiction. Luke's Gospel says nothing in regards to when this incident occurs. Luke, who is often a very detailed historian, remains silent here as to time. It is true that the other gospel writers clearly place the incident during the passion week. Luke records the incident in a context of events that occurred much earlier in the life of Christ. However, he does not indicate that he is recording things in an historical sequence. There is no language like, "on the next day," etc. The absence of such language by a usually careful historian implies that Luke is including the incident at this place because the lesson taught completes his lesson. The absence of those details do not constitute a contradiction. Luke simply states that a Pharisee invited Jesus for dinner. Mark names the host as Simon the leper. Luke later records Jesus addressing his host as Simon so there is no contradiction. There exists no contradiction as far as time, and there is no contradiction in regards to place.

As far as the events that occurred, Mary is called a sinner by Luke and isn't named while she is clearly identified in John's gospel. She is called a sinner in only one Gospel, and named in only one gospel; this is an example of an omission in the other gospels, and not a contradiction.

Now as to the details, Matthew and Mark record the anointing of Jesus' feet while Luke and John say that she anointed Jesus' head. Wow if it wasn't pathetic it would be funny. What if she anointed both Jesus' head and feet? Remember, omission is not contradiction.

What about the difference between spikenard ointment and perfume? All four gospels record that she used ointment. Mark and

John specify exactly what kind of ointment was used. The ointment was spikenard, a costly fragrant oil from the Orient. The only mention of perfume is in Sigal's book, not in the gospels. There are no contradictions as to the time, place, or details.

The potter's field

The incident is recorded for us in both Matthew 27:7-10, and in Acts 1:18-19. Matthew 7-10 *And they took counsel, and bought with them the potter's field, to bury strangers in. Wherefore that field was called, The field of blood, unto this day. Then was fulfilled that which was spoken by Jeremy the prophet, saying, And they took the thirty pieces of silver, the price of him that was valued, whom they of the children of Israel did value; And gave them for the potter's field, as the Lord appointed me.* Acts 1:18-19 *Now this man purchased a field with the reward of iniquity; and falling headlong, he burst asunder in the midst, and all his bowels gushed out. And it was known unto all the dwellers at Jerusalem; insomuch as that field is called in their proper tongue, Aceldama, that is to say, The field of blood.* Before we discuss the apparent difficulties between Matthew and Acts, we are presented with another problem. Matthew quotes from the prophet Zechariah, but attributes the quote to the prophet Jeremiah. There are several possibilities to explain this difficulty. The first is to simply assume a scribal error. There is no evidence of such an error, but it is easier to assume that an earlier copyist erred than to assume that the evangelist did.

Some suggest that Zechariah is in reality reproducing Jeremiah 18:2 and 19:1-2 and Matthew intentionally refers to the original source. If this is indeed the case, it would not be unusual for Matthew to give credit to the better known prophet. Jeremiah 18:2 *Arise, and go down to the potter's house, and there I will cause thee to hear my words.* Jeremiah 19:1-2 *Thus saith the LORD, Go and get a potter's earthen bottle, and take of the ancients of the people, and of the ancients of the priests; And go forth unto the valley of the son of Hinnom, which is by the entry of the east gate, and proclaim there the words that I shall tell thee.*

In his commentary on Matthew, John Broadus cites a suggestion from Lightfoot. *"Lightfoot quotes the Talmud as saying that, in the ancient order of prophetic books, Jeremiah stood first. So he thinks Matthew has quoted from the general prophetic collection as the book of Jeremiah; comp. Psalms of David, the Proverbs of Solomon. This is very ingenious. But no similar quotation is found in New Test. Hengstenberg and Cook ("Bib. Comm.") notice the fact that only Jeremiah, Isaiah, and Daniel are quoted by name in the Gospels, Zech. being several times quoted or referred to in the Gospels, and many times in the New Test., but never named"*[45]

In the Gospel of Matthew and the Book of Acts, the field that was purchased was called "a field of blood" for two different reasons. According to Matthew it was because it was the price of blood in the betrayal of a man, while Acts suggests it was so named because Judas met his bloody death there.[46] Actually, there are three distinctions between the account in Matthew and the record in Acts. Matthew says the chief priest purchased the field, while Acts says Judas did. However, all Judas got was a field. Matthew says he hanged himself, while Acts indicates a fall. It is not very difficult to imagine a possible solution. A man has to hang himself on something. Whatever he hung himself from could have broken. So if he hung himself from a branch, and the branch broke, then he would have suffered from a fall. So Matthew records a hanging and Acts describes a fall. It is possible that there were two reasons why the field was called by two different names. Matthew mentions one reason and Acts records the second.

The resurrection accounts

The resurrection sometimes provokes belligerent and absurd allegations. Sigal says, "The Evangelists could not have seen the resurrection event from different perspectives, since they did not personally witness the resurrection... no one saw Jesus rise from

---

[45]*Matthew*, John A. Broadus The Judson Press Valley Forge Pg 559
[46]"The Jew and The Christian Missionary Pg. 236

the dead... the empty tomb explains nothing."[47] Sigal does nothing to explain the empty tomb. Sigal does nothing to explain the testimony of the gospel writers. Sigal simply emphatically states that it never happened and his opinion is apparently all the evidence he needs.

Sigal insists that the New testament was written so long after the events that it is impossible to get a straight story. He insists that the resurrection is pure fabrication. But the opposite is true. If it was truly prefabricated, we would expect to find great sameness in the resurrection accounts, but instead we find different perspectives.

Sigal insists that these distinctions cannot be resolved. However, with surprising simplicity they are worked out rather nicely. Any good synoptic tool can do the reconciling.[48] The only problem is to sort out the proper order of events. The appearances of Jesus after the resurrection are as follows:

To Mary Magdalene when she returned to the tomb [John 20:11-15, Mark 16:9-11]

To the other women returning to the tomb a second time [Matthew 28:9-10]

To Peter in the afternoon [Luke 24:34, I Corinthians 15:5]

To the disciples on the road to Emmaus [Mark 16:12-13, Luke 24:13-15]

To the ten disciples [Mark 16:14, Luke 24:36-43, John 20:19-23]

To the eleven disciples one week after Thomas was present [John 20: 26-29]

To the seven disciples by the Sea of Galilee [John 21:1-23]

To 500 people as reported by Paul [I Corinthians 15:6]

To James the Lord's brother [I Corinthians 15:7]

To the eleven disciples on a mountain in Galilee [Matthew 28:16-20, Mark 16:15-18]

---

[47] Ibid Pg. 238-239

[48] *Life of Christ in Stereo*, Johnston Cheney, Western Cons. Bapt. Sem. 1969 Portland, Or. sec 161-167

At the ascension from the Mount of Olives [Luke 24: 44-53, Acts 1:3-9]

To Stephen (perhaps in a vision) [Acts 7:55-56]

To Paul on the road to Damascus [Acts 9:3-6, 22:6-11,26:13-18]

To Paul in Arabia [Galatians 1:12,17]

To Paul in the Temple [Acts 22:17-21]

To Paul in prison in Caeseria [Acts 23:11]

To John at the Aisle of Patmos [Revelation 1 :12-20]

Passover night

The trial and crucifixion take place in John on the day before Passover, but in the other three gospels these events occur on the first day of Passover.[49] John 13:1 *Now before the feast of the Passover, when Jesus knew that his hour was come that he should depart out of this world unto the Father, having loved his own which were in the world, he loved them unto the end.* John 18:28 *Then led they Jesus from Caiaphas unto the hall of judgment: and it was early; and they themselves went not into the judgment hall, lest they should be defiled; but that they might eat the Passover.*

Harold Hoehner suggests that the Sadducees kept a different calendar from that of the Pharisees. We know this is true for the calculation of the feast of Pentecost. According to Hoehner, the Pharisees, the Galileans, and the disciples of Jesus began their day at sunrise, but the Sadducees and the Judeans began their day at sunset.[50]

The 14th of Nissan began at sunrise for the Gallileans. That afternoon they could begin the slaughtering of the animals. Later that night they would begin the Passover meal. At sundown, while the Galileans were eating the Passover, the 14th of Nissan would begin according to the Judean calendar.

At Sunrise on the 15th of Nissan on the Galilean calendar, it would still be the 14th on the Judean calendar. That afternoon the

---

[49] *The Real Messiah* pg. 23-24

[50] *Chronological aspects of the Life of Christ.* Zondervan Publishing House.1977. Harold W. Hoehner Pg.88-89

Judaens and the Sadducees would sacrifice the animals. They would celebrate the feast that night on the 15th of Nissan.

This view allows for the disciples of Jesus to be celebrating the Passover the night before the Sadducees. Marvelously, in this scenario, Jesus not only ate the Passover with his disciples but was also slain at the precise time that the Passover lamb was sacrificed.

John is recording the events according to the Sadducees calendar, while the Synoptic Gospels are recording the events according to the calendar of the Galileans and the Pharisees. Thus two days are provided for the slaughter of animals. That resolves a tremendous logistical difficulty. It is difficult to image how such a large number of lambs could possibly be slain in one afternoon. This proposed interpretation "does justice to the data of the Synoptics, the Gospel of John, and the Mishnah."[51]

Inconsistencies in logic

Written too late

This objection assumes that because the gospels were written so long after the death of Jesus, they could no longer be counted on as reliable documents. That being the case there is no history, or at least no reliable history, of the life and times of Jesus. Scholars are frustrated that not a single word attributed to him can ever be verified. Nor has a single word by him or about him during his lifetime ever been found. "Scholars believe that there must have been an oral tradition on which Mark, the first gospelist, based his writing. The others copied some of Mark while John wrote a different kind of gospel altogether. The evangelists writing from forty to a hundred years after Jesus' death probably used some oral tradition, altered and edited to agree with what they thought he might have said or what they wished he had said, because the gospels were missionary documents, with each

---

[51] Ibid pg 88

evangelist presenting his own viewpoint and bias. In this respect Biblical scholars are generally in agreement."[52]

Notice how Rachel Zurer says that most Biblical scholars agree with her position. She has obviously been studying liberal theologians. I would love to ask her how she explains the phenomenal growth of the Christian faith. I would also like to have her explain exactly what motivated the gospel writers to invent these stories, and to perpetrate this hoax on mankind.

My apologies, we are not on the offense. Our assignment is not to cross-examine the witnesses. We are simply asked to give an answer for the reason of the hope that is within us. This objection is based purely on bias. If we were to apply the same principle to the Torah, Judaism would topple. Not a single word attributed to Moses can be verified.

Moses wrote the book of Genesis thousands of years after the creation. In the opinion of many it would be millions of years after creation. The gospels were written only a few decades after the resurrection of Jesus. Yet we do not discard the Torah because it was written late. As well, Moses was writing from a distinctly monotheistic point of view. He clearly had a religious bias. We don't assume that a religious bias on the part of Moses makes the Torah historically inaccurate.

If we are to allow the Torah to stand, we must allow the gospels the same amount of initial respect. We cannot dismiss them because they were written by Christians. We cannot assume that they are unreliable historically because they weren't written down instantly. The gospel writers were expecting the imminent return of the Lord. They didn't immediately realize the need for a preserved record of the world-changing events that they had witnessed.

John's uncertainty

In Matthew 3 13-17 we read how John the Baptist was present when the Father identified clearly who Jesus truly was. *Then cometh Jesus from Galilee to Jordan unto John, to be baptized of*

---

[52] *A Jew Examines Christianity* Jenna Press 1985 Rachel Zurer Pg. 12

him. But John forbad him, saying, I have need to be baptized of thee, and comest thou to me? And Jesus answering said unto him, Suffer it to be so now: for thus it becometh us to fulfil all righteousness. Then he suffered him. And Jesus, when he was baptized, went up straightway out of the water: and, lo, the heavens were opened unto him, and he saw the Spirit of God descending like a dove, and lighting upon him: And lo a voice from heaven, saying, This is my beloved Son, in whom I am well pleased.

Later in Luke's gospel we read about John's doubts about the true nature and character of Jesus. Luke 7:18-20 *And the disciples of John shewed him of all these things. And John calling unto him two of his disciples sent them to Jesus, saying, Art thou he that should come? or look we for another? When the men were come unto him, they said, John Baptist hath sent us unto thee, saying, Art thou he that should come? or look we for another?*

According to Sigal it is illogical that John would baptize Jesus, introduce Jesus, and later be uncertain as to who Jesus really was.[53] Sigal dismissed the validity of the New Testament on the basis of this inconstancy. If the New Testament were a trumped up document, it would not include this type of historicity. The very fact that it includes a record of doubters, including a doubt from a once avid supporter, is a credit to the document. It shows that it has not been tampered with to eliminate a potentially embarrassing record.

It is not particularly unusual to find John having second thoughts. He was a devoted follower of the Lord, and now he was in prison, and he was about to be beheaded for his efforts. John, like most of his day, was probably expecting a different kind of Messianic presentation. He probably expected David's son to establish David's throne through a military victory. It is not illogical that John had doubts about who Jesus really was, even though he baptized and introduced Him. It is simply human nature. The Jewish Scriptures could be criticized in a similar way.

---

[53]The Jew and the Christian Missionary pg. 92-93

The Jewish people were eye witnesses to many marvelous miracles. They were given more than enough evidence for them to be certain about the power of God. Their deliverance from Egyptian bondage proved to them that God loved them. Yet when they were challenged to conquer the promised land, they wanted to return to Egypt. As we can see in Numbers 14:3-4 *And wherefore hath the LORD brought us unto this land, to fall by the sword, that our wives and our children should be a prey? were it not better for us to return into Egypt? And they said one to another, Let us make a captain, and let us return into Egypt.*

Sigal certainly would not discard the Torah on the basis of this illogical situation. Yet he finds a reason to discard the New Testament on the same grounds, i.e., believers with doubts. This is simply human nature. It is accurately recorded, exactly as we would expect it to occur.

The temptation

In Matthew chapter 4 we read of the temptation of Jesus. According to Sigal, it is illogical for God to be tempted.[54] It is interesting that a man who does not recognize Jesus as Lord does not allow Jesus to be a man either. Jesus is also man, a man who was born in Bethlehem. That man had to be shown to be above temptation. Jesus is the same yesterday, today and forever, and He is incapable of sin. For the Christian faith to be sure, Jesus has to be above reproach, both now and forever. The temptation of Jesus proves that he cannot fail. Satan gave it his best shot, but Jesus shows himself to be Lord, above temptation.

Some might find it preposterous that Satan would attempt to test the Lord. However in the Jewish Scriptures we read of the rebellion of Satan against God's authority. Satan attempted to overthrow the dominion of God. If the record of Satan's rebellion isn't a reason for rejecting the Jewish Scriptures, then the record of Satan's temptation of Jesus also cannot be used as a reason to reject the New Testament.

---

[54]Ibid pg195

Don't judge

Jesus could not be the Judge of Israel referred to in Micah 5:1 *Now gather thyself in troops, O daughter of troops: he hath laid siege against us: they shall smite the judge of Israel with a rod upon the cheek,* because Jesus instructs us not to judge in Matthew 7:1[55] *Judge not, that ye be not judged.* Jesus' instruction for us to not judge others in no way disqualifies him from being the judge himself. According to the Scriptures, he is qualified to be judge by divine enabling. As we see in Isaiah 11:3-4 *And shall make him of quick understanding in the fear of the LORD: and he shall not judge after the sight of his eyes, neither reprove after the hearing of his ears: But with righteousness shall he judge the poor, and reprove with equity for the meek of the earth: and he shall smite the earth with the rod of his mouth, and with the breath of his lips shall he slay the wicked.*

We who are not so enabled ought not to be involved in executing judgment. The judge has a dual assignment. The first is to determine guilt, and the second is to assign a penalty. We believers must be involved in the recognition of evil; we need to discern right from wrong, and in that capacity every believer must exercise judgment. However, we are not to assign a penalty for crimes, real or imagined. It is not unusual to find the judge giving such advise. In the Scriptures Moses instructs not to commit murder, yet Moses took the life of an Egyptian. The same kind of thinking that would disqualify Jesus from being judge would certainly disqualify Moses from being the law giver.

Jesus died too soon

"The first question that probably has already crossed your mind is that the time is off. Jesus died around 32 AD and the Temple was destroyed in 70 AD. If Jesus died in order to offer us a chance to atone for ourselves because we need blood, then why did he die during the time when the Temple was still standing?

---

[55]*You Take Jesus, I'll take God* Hammorah Press, P.O. Box 48862, Los Angeles, Ca. 90048 1980 Samuel Levine pg. 35

Man did not need Jesus yet, so why did he die then? Did he die in advance? Thus this theory is incorrect historically."[56]

I would love to cross examine this witness. Why was the Temple destroyed? Doesn't the Talmud speak about the changes that occurred within the Temple, and within the sacrifice system at the time of Jesus? However, we are not attacking the Jewish faith, we are only on the witness stand, giving answers for the hope that is within us. The fact that the Temple was still standing does not negate the sacrifice of Jesus.

The Temple sacrifice was a temporary solution. There were no seats in the Tabernacle, there was no place for the priest to sit down. When our high priest offered himself, he sat down on the right hand of the Majesty on high. The sacrifice was finished.

The Temple remained standing after the sacrifice of Jesus. However, there were some significant changes, such as the veil was rent from top to bottom. The rent veil was left as a testimony to the sacrifice that had been completed and the way to God had been opened for all. The approximate forty years of time between the sacrifice and the destruction the Temple corresponds with the time in the wilderness. It is a time for the nation to repent and receive the Messiah that had been rejected.

The king of the Jews

"Why did the Romans put the words, 'King of the Jews' on the head of Jesus when he was crucified? That is what it says in Matthew 27:37, and it implies that the Romans killed Jesus for political crimes, and not religious crimes. Furthermore, if the New Testament is correct in its story that the Jews turned Jesus in to the Romans, then it becomes very difficult to understand. If the Jews turned him in, then they obviously did not like Jesus, so why would the Romans call him the King of the Jews right after the Jews turned Jesus in to the Romans? Something is obviously mixed up -the story was written by a poor reporter, or else by a fabricator who did not like the Jews."[57]

---

[56] Ibid pg.43

[57] Ibid pg 72

Levine is right; something is obviously mixed up. Unfortunately it is the assumption that Mr. Levine draws. The statement "the King of the Jews" does not imply that Jesus was crucified for political reasons. The fact that he was crowned with thorns shows that the Romans were mocking him; the title they gave him was one of sarcasm and derision. We may not be able to be certain as to exactly why the Romans placed the superscription on the cross. However, we cannot on the basis of the superscription assume that the author was a poor historian or a liar. We have to recognize that the author of the New Testament must have been closer to the event than Mr. Levine.

Conclusion

There are some general rules that we can apply to many of the objections raised in this section:

Is there a textual problem? They are infrequent, but they do occur.

In comparing Scripture to Scripture, are both texts properly translated?

In comparing Scripture to Scripture, are both texts properly interpreted?

In comparing Scripture to Scripture, is there an omission in one account? Omissions aren't contradictions.

If an attack in the area of logic is raised against the New Testament, could that same attack be used against the Old Testament?

NINE

Attacks on Christian Beliefs

Regarding the Messiah

His nature

The first complaint would be about his divinity. The complaint is that "no where does the Jewish Bible say that the Messiah will be divine."[58] This objection has to question the sincerity of the writer. Any Jewish scholar should be familiar with Isaiah 9:6. As well, a scholar should be aware of the traditional messianic view of the verse. Since Isaiah 9:6 is speaking about the divine character of a child who is to be born, and since the Rabbis teach that the child is indeed the Messiah, then the conclusion is that the Jewish Scriptures do indeed teach that the Messiah is to be divine.

If Mr. Kaplan were to say that he disagrees with the standard interpretation of Isaiah 9:6, that would be acceptable. If he were to admit that the passage is predicting a divine Messiah, but that Jesus is not the one spoken of, then I could understand his

---

[58] The Real Messiah Pg 45

position. However, Mr. Kaplan does not take either of these views. His position is to act as if that the verse is not in the Bible at all.

Isaiah 9:6. *For unto us a child is born, unto us a son is given: and the government shall be upon his shoulder: and his name shall be called Wonderful, Counsellor, The mighty God, The everlasting Father, The Prince of Peace.* Traditional Jewish literature assigns this verse to the Messiah. Targum Jonathan reads "For to us a SON is born, to us a Son is given: and He shall receive the Law upon HIM to keep: and HIS name is called of Old, Wonderful, Counselor, ELOHA, THE MIGHTY, Abiding to Eternity, THE MESSIAH, because peace shall be multiplied upon us in HIS days." There is no doubt that the Targum is teaching that the verse is a messianic prophecy. The use of the capital letters in the nouns and pronouns that refer to the Messiah show the respect that is reserved for God. Unfortunately, in the English translation of the Massoretic text, the Bibles presented to all Jewish 13-year-olds, a portion of this verse is transliterated rather than translated. What we read is "his name shall be called peleh joez el gibhor-abi-ad-sar-shalom."

There is no other passage in the Jewish Scriptures where a phrase is left untranslated. The more recent Jewish translations render the passage "the wonderful counselor of the Mighty God, of the Everlasting Father, Prince of Peace. The earlier lack of translation shows a deliberate effort to leave the passage in obscurity. The more recent translations are forced and prove that there is a definite agenda on the part of the translator. In the Jewish Scriptures, there is a tiny dash that is occasionally used to connect words. In the Hebrew Bible the word father appears before the word eternal. After the word father, and before the word eternal is that tiny dash. There is another dash after the word prince and before the word peace. Literally the phrase would read " wonderful counselor, mighty God, father eternity, prince peace." That is a bit rough in English, but with the dashes it is smoothed out. With the dash we read, " father (of) eternity, prince (of) peace. The Jewish translation renders "wonderful counselor of the mighty God of the everlasting father." That translation detracts from the deity of the child that is to be born. That translation totally ignores the dash. The dash doesn't appear between counselor and God, and it doesn't reappear between God and the word father. That translation is done with the same agenda that earlier left the phrase untranslated. Now it is translated but in an obscure manner.

The normal reading of the passage is not complicated at all. Each of the following English translations agree. The NIV reads *For to us a child is born, to us a son is given, and the government will be on his shoulders. And he will be called Wonderful Counselor, Mighty God, Everlasting Father, Prince of Peace.* (NIV)

The New King James reads, *for unto us a Child is born, Unto us a Son is given; And the government will be upon His shoulder. And His name will be called Wonderful, Counselor, Mighty God, Everlasting Father, Prince of Peace.* (NKJV)

The New Revised Standard Version *For a child has been born for us, a son given to us; authority rests upon his shoulders; and he is named Wonderful Counselor, Mighty God, Everlasting Father, Prince of Peace.* (NRSV)

And finally the American Standard version *For unto us a child is born, unto us a son is given; and the government shall be upon his shoulder: and his name shall be called Wonderful, Counsellor, Mighty God, Everlasting Father, Prince of Peace. (ASV)*

All of the English translations agree. They all testify that the passage is speaking about the deity of the child. The Traditional Jewish position is that the passage also speaks about the Messiah. The conclusion is that the Jewish Scriptures do indeed teach the deity of the Messiah.

Jews also question the tri-unity. In his book *You Take Jesus, I'll Take God,* Samuel Levine writes "It makes no sense whatsoever to say that the Father is equal to the son and the Holy Ghost, and yet call them different names."[59] Later he entitles an entire section "How can three equal one?."[60] There are two different objections to the tri-unity of God. The first is that it is

---

[59] You take Jesus , I'll take God pg 58

[60] Ibid pg 77

illogical. The Scriptures teach us that there are going to be things that are beyond our abilities. Isaiah writes *For my thoughts are not your thoughts, neither are your ways my ways, saith the LORD. For as the heavens are higher than the earth, so are my ways higher than your ways, and my thoughts than your thoughts.* From this passage you would expect some things of faith to be beyond the things of intellect. Apparently everything won't fit into a neat logical box. The Tri-unity defies reason. Although there are some analogies to it, there is no real explanation. God's ways are beyond ours.

The second objection to the Tri-unity is that it is unbiblical. This position is based on the teaching of Deuteronomy 6:4. This particular verse is chanted frequently in Hebrew at services and has become known as the undying watchword of the Jewish faith. It is called simply the Shema. The name is taken from the very first word of the passage, the word "to hear." Deuteronomy 6:4 *Hear, O Israel: The LORD our God is one LORD.*

The word translated one is the Hebrew word אֶחָד (echad). This word can have the idea of a collective one. For instance it is the word that appears in Genesis 2:24 *Therefore shall a man leave his father and his mother, and shall cleave unto his wife: and they shall be one flesh.* The word here is referring to a unity, a unity where two are combined, or included together as one. *"Echad"* could have the same meaning in Deuteronomy 6 as it does in Genesis 2. If it does, then the *shema* would read Hear O Israel, the Lord, Our God, the Lord is a unity. That means that the very verse that is being used to show the absolute oneness of God is actually teaching the plurality of God. The Tri-unity is being taught in the undying watchword of the Jewish faith.

Throughout the Scriptures we see other references to the plurality of God. In fact the very word for God *Elohim* is itself a plural word. Because of this we see that often a plural pronoun is assigned to it, as in Genesis 1:26 *God said, Let us make man in our image, after our likeness,* or as in Genesis 3:22 *And the LORD God said, Behold, the man is become as one of us, to know good and evil: and now, lest he put forth his hand, and take also of the tree of life, and eat, and live for ever,* or as we read in Isaiah 6:8 *Also I heard the voice of the Lord, saying, Whom shall I send, and who will go for us?*

In Genesis eighteen we read that the Lord appeared unto Abraham. It is interesting to note that what Abraham saw was three men. Genesis 18:1-2 *And the LORD appeared unto him in the plains of Mamre: and he sat in the tent door in the heat of the day; And he lift up his eyes and looked, and, lo, three men stood by him: and when he saw them, he ran to meet them from the tent door, and bowed himself toward the ground.*

In the book of Isaiah we see this idea of three, in connection to the character of God, in several different locations. In Isaiah 6:3 when Isaiah saw the Lord, the angels cried out *And one cried unto another, and said, Holy, holy, holy, is the LORD of hosts: the whole earth is full of his glory.* The whole earth is filled with his (singular) glory, yet He is three times Holy.

In Isaiah 11, the Spirit of the Lord is described in a threefold way. The spirit of wisdom and understanding, the spirit of council and might, and the spirit of knowledge and the fear of the Lord. (KJV) *And the spirit of the LORD shall rest upon him, the spirit of wisdom and understanding, the spirit of counsel and might, the spirit of knowledge and of the fear of the LORD.*

In Isaiah 48:16 we see a reference to the Lord, to God and to the Spirit. *Come ye near unto me, hear ye this; I have not spoken in secret from the beginning; from the time that it was, there am I: and 48:17 Thus saith the LORD, thy Redeemer, the Holy One of Israel; I am the LORD thy God which teacheth thee to profit, which leadeth thee by the way that thou shouldest go.* This verse is as clear a statement as one could ask. The Lord of Israel declares himself to be the Lord, the Redeemer, and the Holy One of Israel.

There is some significant Old Testament evidence regarding the Trinity. These several verses can not be ignored. The Jewish people must have recognized this truth of the plurality of God. When the New Testament teaches about the Tri-unity of God, it does not present the doctrine as a new truth. It simply continues to reference it as a matter of fact.

The Trinity might be beyond human understanding. The fact that it exists argues for the conclusion, that the doctrine could not be of human invention. The Trinitarian doctrine does not have its source in man-made religion. It is based on revelation. It is not a belief in three God's, but rather the faith in One God who exists as three persons. Or, as the Scriptures say, Hear O Israel, The Lord, our God, the Lord, is a unity.

The "super human" nature of the Messiah is a problem for some. We believe in a supernatural Messiah. Jesus is an anointed one who is more than prophet, or priest or king. According to some Jewish thinking, this idea of a supernatural messiah was never the traditional Jewish view. A supernatural messiah is a product of much later thinking.[61]

Stuart Rosenburg is not alone in his thinking. A large portion of the Jewish community does not believe in anything supernatural. They are scientists who think that Christian thought is filled with ancient naive superstitions. Christianity is regarded as a religion for the unsophisticated.[62]

Rabbinical Judaism, especially Hassidic Judaism, would fall quickly under the same criticism. The tales of Rabbi Israel Ben Eliezer, the Bal Shem Tov, are filled with miracles as recently as the 16th century. If the Christian believes the Bible is unsophisticated, then the Hassidim must be unsophisticated as well. Rosenburg is free to believe that fundamentalism is unsophisticated. However, when he states that supernatural beliefs are a late invention then we need to respond. There are numerous rabbinical sources we could refer to that show an early belief in a supernatural Messiah. We should only use the rabbinical material when absolutely needed.

The Talmud, the Midrash, and the Kabbalah are considered sacred by some Jews. When Christians cite from these texts it can be offensive and hurtful to those who hold these works in a high regard. Sometimes we need to refer to them to show that our interpretation is not foreign to Jewish thought. These tools are helpful, and we certainly can benefit from having a working

---

[61] *The Christian Problem* Stuart E. Rosenberg Deneau publishers Canada, 1986 Pg 34

[62] *You Take Jesus* I'll Take God, pg. 78

knowledge of them, but we must be respectful, and exercise great care, so that we do not cause anyone to feel insulted.

The Scriptures themselves have plenty to say about the supernatural messiah. The prophets show us that David's son is going to change the world drastically. His supernatural appearance at the mount of Olives changes the structure of the land surrounding the great city, as recorded in Zechariah 14:4. *And his feet shall stand in that day upon the mount of Olives, which is before Jerusalem on the east, and the mount of Olives shall cleave in the midst thereof toward the east and toward the west, and there shall be a very great valley; and half of the mountain shall remove toward the north, and half of it toward the south.*

In Isaiah we see that the Messiah will judge and rule, not by human, but by supernatural standards. *And there shall come forth a rod out of the stem of Jesse, and a Branch shall grow out of his roots: and the spirit of the LORD shall rest upon him, the spirit of wisdom and understanding, the spirit of counsel and might, the spirit of knowledge and of the fear of the LORD; And shall make him of quick understanding in the fear of the LORD: and he shall not judge after the sight of his eyes, neither reprove after the hearing of his ears: But with righteousness shall he judge the poor, and reprove with equity for the meek of the earth: and he shall smite the earth with the rod of his mouth, and with the breath of his lips shall he slay the wicked.*

The same passage continues to show us the new world that the Messiah will rule over. We can see a world of total peace. Perhaps Rosenburg believes that we can achieve peace amongst mankind through totally natural means. However, any naturalist would believe that leopards are designed to eat meat, and so there will always be violence in the animal world. Yet when the messiah comes there is predicted peace in the animal kingdom as well. *The wolf also shall dwell with the lamb, and the leopard shall lie down with the kid; and the calf and the young lion and the fatling together; and a little child shall lead them. And the cow and the bear shall feed; their young ones shall lie down together: and the lion shall eat straw like the ox. And the sucking child shall play on the hole of the asp, and the weaned child shall put his hand on the cockatrice' den. ⁹ They shall not hurt nor destroy in all my holy mountain: for the earth shall be full of the knowledge of the LORD, as the waters cover the sea.*

His ancestry

Since it is natural for animals to behave violently towards each other, then peace in the animal kingdom is supernatural. Since that peace is accomplished through the Messiah's reign, then that reign and that Messiah are predicted to be supernatural. These prophecies are made 700 years before Jesus. These prophecies are rather early, and show that a belief in a supernatural Messiah is far from a late Christian invention.

The first credential a Jewish person would doubt is his ancestry. This argument simply stated is this, if the father of Jesus is God, then Jesus can't be the true Messiah, because he wouldn't be a descendent of David.[63] Initially this argument sounds absurd. If God is indeed the father of Jesus, then Jesus is certainly the Messiah. However, the Jewish person who raises this objection doesn't believe that Jesus is the son of God; this person is attempting to show a problem with logic in the Christian faith.

Rabbinically, a person is established to be Jewish on the basis of the mother. If you are the son or daughter of a Jewish mother, then you are Jewish. However, the tribe to which a person belongs is established on the basis of the father. Therefore according to the traditional view, in order for Jesus to be a descendant of David, his father would have to be a descendant of David.

Of course this view assumes that there is an earthly father. With the unique circumstances regarding the virgin birth, there is no earthly father. Jesus only has a physical line from his mother's side. Many believe that the Gospel of Luke is recording the lineage of Mary. If that is the case then Jesus would be a descendant of David from the only earthly parent that he has. As well there is no reason why Joseph couldn't adopt Jesus, and in so doing make him a legal heir to David's throne.

Jesus would have no earthly father to disqualify him from being a true descendent of David. His only parentage comes through his adopting father and from his natural mother. Both of

---

[63] *You Take Jesus, I'll Take God* pg 78

these lines present him with the credentials needed to be the true Messiah of Israel. In addition, there is a curse that is placed upon the last reigning king of Judah. As we read in Jeremiah 22:30 *Thus saith the LORD, Write ye this man childless, a man that shall not prosper in his days: for no man of his seed shall prosper, sitting upon the throne of David, and ruling any more in Judah.*

It is interesting to note that the curse states specifically, "no man of his seed." Jesus is the seed of a woman. No one else could possibly present the proper credentials. Only the virgin born descendent of David and son of God, only Jesus is qualified to be the heir to David's throne.

His works

An objection about Jesus' works is drawn from Deuteronomy 13:1-9. *If there arise among you a prophet, or a dreamer of dreams, and giveth thee a sign or a wonder, And the sign or the wonder come to pass, whereof he spake unto thee, saying, Let us go after other gods, which thou hast not known, and let us serve them; Thou shalt not hearken unto the words of that prophet, or that dreamer of dreams: for the LORD your God proveth you, to know whether ye love the LORD your God with all your heart and with all your soul. Ye shall walk after the LORD your God, and fear him, and keep his commandments, and obey his voice, and ye shall serve him, and cleave unto him. And that prophet, or that dreamer of dreams, shall be put to death; because he hath spoken to turn you away from the LORD your God, which brought you out of the land of Egypt, and redeemed you out of the house of bondage, to thrust thee out of the way which the LORD thy God commanded thee to walk in. So shalt thou put the evil away from the midst of thee. If thy brother, the son of thy mother, or thy son, or thy daughter, or the wife of thy bosom, or thy friend, which is as thine own soul, entice thee secretly, saying, Let us go and serve other gods, which thou hast not known, thou, nor thy fathers; Namely, of the gods of the people which are round about you, nigh unto thee, or far off from thee, from the one end of the earth even unto the other end of the earth; Thou shalt not consent unto him, nor hearken unto him; neither shall thine eye pity him, neither shalt thou spare, neither shalt thou conceal him: But thou shalt surely kill him; thine hand shall be first upon him to put him to death, and afterwards the hand of all the people.*

Moses is warning the Jewish people not to believe a false prophet. In that warning he states that they should disregard his miraculous works. Jesus said in John 14:11 *Believe me that I am in the Father, and the Father in me*: or else believe me for the basis of the works he performs, and Jesus appeals to His works and asks to be believed on that basis.

Perhaps this doesn't seem like a very difficult challenge to some. However, I recall how much grief this passage caused me. It was during the time that we were ministering on the campus of Temple University. My friend Michael, the anti-missionary who was assigned to the campus, was conducting a seminar on combating evangelists. As an evangelist I thought it would be advantageous to be present.

Michael read Deuteronomy chapter 13 to the class. Then he asked me the following question. "If God wanted to warn the Jewish people not to believe in Jesus, what would he say differently?" How do you answer a question like that? It is a little bit like the old question, "when did you stop beating your wife?" If you never beat your wife, then you didn't stop. If you answer that you didn't stop, some would assume that you still are beating her.

The problem in Deuteronomy 13 is the worship of other gods. God is instructing us to disregard any work, sign, or miracle that is performed if the worker is directing us away from the God of our fathers. Jesus never taught us to worship other gods. Jesus directs us to worship the Lord God of Israel. In the temptation in the wilderness, Jesus quotes and affirms the Scriptures when he says in Matthew 4:10, *Then saith Jesus unto him, Get thee hence, Satan: for it is written, Thou shalt worship the Lord thy God, and him only shalt thou serve.*

In John when Jesus asks to be believed on the basis of His works, he is telling people to focus on the Father. Remember he started the statement by saying " believe me. I am in the father and the father is in me." Jesus began his life and ministry by pursuing the will of the father. He has always been about the father's business. Jesus has always promoted worship of the father, and at no time did he ever encourage worship of any other gods.

Some Jewish people believe that all Christians are guilty of idolatry. Since we believe that Jesus is God, and since they do not, then Jesus is to the Jewish person another god. If we believe in another god, then we Christians are guilty of idolatry. If Deuteronomy 13 were speaking to a false messiah who was claiming to be a god, then the passage would read quite differently. The passage would warn us not to follow after a false god who makes claims and boasts about himself.

However Deuteronomy 13 speaks about a false prophet who directs others to worship another. Even John the Baptist wouldn't fit the scenario, since he never performed miracles while directing people to Jesus. So even from the Jewish perspective, Deuteronomy 13 doesn't seem to be referring to Jesus, or any of the events that occurred at the time of Jesus.

His ministry

The Jewish people for the most part believe in a messianic age, not in a personal messiah.[64] Since Jewish people don't believe in a personal messiah, they can't believe in Jesus. This argument doesn't even begin to deal with the truth. It is based totally in the area of belief. It is a conclusion drawn from improper reasoning.

There is a basketball-size hole in one of my storm windows. I asked everyone in the house if they knew how the window was broken? Not a single person in the house knew anything about the window. Since no one knew anything about the window, no one in the house broke the window. The window could only have been broken by someone in the house. Since the window could only be broken by someone in the house, and since no one in the house broke the window, then the window was not broken. Therefore the basketball-size hole in the storm window does not really exist. Yet I can see the hole; I can feel the draft. The conclusion drawn that there can be no hole is based on false information. Just because no one would admit to breaking the window, someone had to break it,

---

[64] *The Christian Problem* Pg 93

because the window was indeed broken. Modern Jewish thought might exclude the belief in a personal Messiah; however, that in no way changes the truth of Scripture. The Bible predicts a personal Messiah and Jesus is that Messiah.

In Jeremiah chapter 31 we read about the new covenant. The Christian faith is based on the concept of a new contract. Jeremiah 31:31-34 *Behold, the days come, saith the LORD, that I will make a new covenant with the house of Israel, and with the house of Judah: Not according to the covenant that I made with their fathers in the day that I took them by the hand to bring them out of the land of Egypt; which my covenant they brake, although I was an husband unto them, saith the LORD: But this shall be the covenant that I will make with the house of Israel; After those days, saith the LORD, I will put my law in their inward parts, and write it in their hearts; and will be their God, and they shall be my people. And they shall teach no more every man his neighbour, and every man his brother, saying, Know the LORD: for they shall all know me, from the least of them unto the greatest of them, saith the LORD: for I will forgive their iniquity, and I will remember their sin no more.*

The objection is raised that if the birth of the Christian religion introduces the new covenant, then there should no longer be any need of anyone to teach the word of God, because the new covenant of Jeremiah declares that they shall no longer teach every man his neighbor.[65] The Lord declares that this covenant will be different from the one that He made with them at Mount Sinai, which the nation of Israel had already broken by the time Jeremiah was written. Because the covenant with God was already broken, the nation of Israel has no existing contractual relationship with the Lord. If this is true, Jews should be more concerned with the condition of the nation of Israel then with finding fault with the Christian faith.

The new covenant of Jeremiah 31 is made specifically with Israel, and must await that nation's future restoration. There are

---

[65] *You Take Jesus, I'll Take God.* Pg 14-15

many Christian positions that would insist that Jeremiah 31 is speaking to the church age. There is no need to defend these views. This attack is against faulty thinking. There are aspects of the new covenant that are evident in this age. That is a bonus.

The very mention of a new contract points to the ruined Temple, and that has to be explained by Judaism. All of Jeremiah 31 has yet to be fulfilled; but this is no embarrassment to Christianity. A new contract exists and many of the aspects of this contract have already begun. The forgiveness of sin is part of the contract and that is only made possible through the finished work of the Messiah. That points us to the empty tomb that proves the truth of our faith. Jeremiah 31 raises more questions for the Jewish position than it does for the Christian.

The objection is made that since Jesus at no time preached to the heathen, he could not be the king that is spoken of by the prophet Zechariah.[66] In Zechariah 9:9 we read of the lowly king Messiah riding into Jerusalem. In verse ten we see how that same king had a ministry to the heathen. We believe that the triumphal entry of Jesus into Jerusalem on Palm Sunday is the fulfillment of Zechariah 9:9. Zechariah 9:9-10, *Rejoice greatly, O daughter of Zion; shout, O daughter of Jerusalem: behold, thy King cometh unto thee: he is just, and having salvation; lowly, and riding upon an ass, and upon a colt the foal of an ass. And I will cut off the chariot from Ephraim, and the horse from Jerusalem, and the battle bow shall be cut off: and he shall speak peace unto the heathen: and his dominion shall be from sea even to sea, and from the river even to the ends of the earth.*

It is true that Jesus insisted that his disciples preach only to the lost sheep of the house of Israel, but that was only at the outset of his ministry. At the "great commission" Jesus sends his disciples into all the world, to teach and to make disciples in all nations. Judaism had failed to reach the world with the message of the one true God. Christianity has succeeded where Judaism has failed.

---

[66] Ibid. Pg. 20,23

The total dominion spoken of by the prophet Zechariah must await the second coming of the Lord. However the reaching out to the heathen has already occurred. The evangelization process has taken the gospel to every continent. The gospel missions are unlocking the language and cultural barriers so that the message can be proclaimed to every hidden group of people, to all people throughout the world.

The world-wide spread of the Christian faith does not disprove Christianity. The fact that the Gospel is preached throughout the world is a testimony to the universal appeal of the truth. That universal appeal was designed by the Creator to meet the human need.

An argument is raised from the lack of peace in the world. Few of the earlier objections are those that are raised by the average Jewish person. Most Jewish people are not very aware of the kind of things that are expected of the long awaited Messiah. However, most know about the prospect of world peace. One friend of mine in a public discussion with me once made a brilliant statement. He said that he would rather wait for a messiah who would bring world peace than believe in one who has failed.

The same Scripture which predicts the birth of Jesus in Bethlehem also shows him to be the man of peace. Micah 5:5 ***And this man shall be the peace, when the Assyrian shall come into our land: and when he shall tread in our palaces, then shall we raise against him seven shepherds, and eight principal men.***

Since Jesus did not bring that peace, then he could not be the one who was promised to be born in Bethlehem; he could not be the promised messiah.[67] Jesus himself addresses this issue. He tells us that we are not to expect Him to fulfill the prophecies regarding peace at his first coming. In Matthew 10:34 we read ***Think not that I am come to send peace on earth: I came not to send peace, but a sword.***

The advent of Jesus has brought division in nations and in homes, both within the Jewish faith and among the Gentiles. As with many of the promises about the messianic reign, this promise

---

[67] Ibid Pg. 35

must also wait for the return of Jesus for fulfillment. However, there are some significant areas where peace has been established with the first coming of Jesus. In Romans 5:1 we read about the new position that we have with God. *Therefore being justified by faith, we have peace with God through our Lord Jesus Christ.* Along with this peace which is not observable there is the peace from God in Philippians 4:7. *And the peace of God, which passeth all understanding, shall keep your hearts and minds through Christ Jesus.* This peace should be observable. The peace of mind that a believer can enjoy through exercising Biblical principles and producing fruit of the Spirit should be able to be seen by others. Certainly the lack of any such peace is known to others. Most people are filled with unrest. Worry, anxiety and stress permeate their day and fill their lives.

Believers can rest in the sovereign God. They are at peace with God, and they can be certain of his love for them. God has demonstrated his love towards us. Romans 5:8 *But God commendeth his love toward us, in that, while we were yet sinners, Christ died for us.* God assures us to continue to bless us on the basis of that love. Romans 8:32 *He that spared not his own Son, but delivered him up for us all, how shall he not with him also freely give us all things?* Being assured of these truths ought to make an observable difference in the way a person approaches life.

When the Messiah returns, he will set up a kingdom that will bring universal peace and even include peace in the animal kingdom. However, until that time the believer can enjoy an inner peace which is living proof that Jesus is indeed the promised prince of peace.

An argument is raised from the standpoint of exclusive revlation. This argument could possibly belong under the heading of logic. It seems that it is illogical that the Lord would not have revealed himself in a more general way. The question that is raised is this: If Jesus really did return from the dead, and if he really came in the name of grace and kindness, then why didn't he reveal himself to everyone?[68]

This argument stems from two different errors in thinking. The first has to do with the nature of God. Some believe that a loving God, a gracious and kind God, would establish some system of universal redemption. Apparently it is inconsistent in some people's thinking for God to allow any to be condemned.

The second mistake in thinking has to do with the nature of man. Some think that the only thing a man needs is information. If God were to make himself known, man would indeed make the proper response. The problem isn't with depravity, the problem is a lack of education. If God would only be a little clearer, man would behave a lot better.

The fact that there is a place of condemnation is very scary. The fact that God condemns is an awesome truth. However, that truth is taught in the Jewish Scriptures. It is indeed the word of God that reveals these facts to us. These same Scriptures show us our true nature. Increased information seems to make us more responsible, but not more likely to respond positively. We have inherited a nature that is opposed to the things of God; more information will not change our predisposition.

Look at the children of Israel in the wilderness, the miracles they were privilege to see, and the plagues that they escaped. Yet a whole generation died in the wilderness, and it wasn't for a want of revelation. They perished because of a lack of faith. Jesus' decision not to reveal himself universally does not disprove the resurrection. This same kind of question could be leveled against the Torah as well. If God is truly the Creator of all men, then why was the Torah given only to Israel? Why are the heathen allowed to continue in unbelief? The answer is we don't know. We don't know why some are seemingly given more advantages, and more opportunities than others. We believe that God is, and we can only expect that the Judge of the earth will do right. Because many remain in unbelief is not evidence against the existence of God. The fact that there is limited revelation does not speak against

---

[68] Ibid. Pg.70

God, nor does it speak against the truth of His son in the New Testament.

Another argument comes from the prophecies of the Messianic reign that remain unfulfilled. There are numerous predictions of the messianic kingdom that were not fulfilled when Jesus came. We recognize that these prophecies await the second coming of Jesus. The Jewish position is that there is no teaching in the Jewish Scriptures of any second coming.

Recently the Jewish position on Isaiah 53 has been that the passage is referring to the nation of Israel. Isaiah refers to the servant of the Lord 17 times. It is evident, however, that there are two different servants being referred to. The one servant is that of the nation of Israel. This servant is clearly identified in Isaiah 41:8 *But thou, Israel, art my servant, Jacob whom I have chosen, the seed of Abraham my friend.* There is a different servant in the book of Isaiah, however, and this servant is not identified as Israel. This servant is introduced in 49:6, and we can see immediately that this servant cannot be Israel because the servant restores Israel. Isaiah 49:6 *And he said, It is a light thing that thou shouldest be my servant to raise up the tribes of Jacob, and to restore the preserved of Israel: I will also give thee for a light to the Gentiles, that thou mayest be my salvation unto the end of the earth.*

This is the servant of Isaiah 53, the suffering servant who is cut off out of the land of the living for the transgression of the people of Israel. In a recent public discussion an anti-missionary stated that Isaiah 53 was speaking of Israel. Each time the prophet was referring to Israel as the servant, the prophet clearly identified Israel as the servant. Because the nation of Israel is not here identified could possibly mean that a second, and different servant was being spoken of.

At the end of the discussion, after most people had left, the Rabbi admitted that Isaiah 53 was speaking about a second servant, a suffering servant who was the messiah the son of Joseph. The Rabbi then explained the traditional Jewish position that there are two different messiahs. One is the son of David, who will reign and rule in Jerusalem, and a second messiah who was to suffer and die. He then went on to elaborate how Jesus could never be the suffering servant. It is true that what the Rabbis predict concerning the suffering servant has little to do with Jesus. Jesus is the fulfillment of the Scriptures, and has no relationship to the mistaken traditions of the rabbis.

The tradition of the rabbis, however, have recognized some truths. They have recognized a dual theme in messianic prophecy. To satisfy these themes they have invented a second messiah. Instead there is only one Messiah, but that Messiah comes to the earth on two occasions.

As we mentioned earlier, the Scriptures do teach about the second coming of the messiah. In Genesis 49:10 we read a cryptic verse, *The sceptre shall not depart from Judah, nor a lawgiver from between his feet, until Shiloh come; and unto him shall the gathering of the people be.* This verse is usually interpreted to mean that there will be a recognized Judean king reigning right up until the time of the messiah. This was true at the coming of Jesus as Herod was an independent Judean king. In Hosea 3:4-5 we read *For the children of Israel shall abide many days without a king, and without a prince, and without a sacrifice, and without an image, and without an ephod, and without teraphim: Afterward shall the children of king; and shall fear the LORD and his goodness in the latter days.* This passage teaches that there will be no king in Israel for many years before the messiah comes.

These two passages seem to contradict each other. One says that there will be a king up until the time of Messiah. The other passage says that there will be no king for a long time and then the Messiah will come. Jewish traditions do not explain the two passages. The Rabbis do not answer the question. The Christian position, however, handles the two passages quite nicely. Jesus the Messiah comes once while there is a king, but is rejected by his people. Because of the rejection, the people go into Diaspora, and live many years without a king, and after many years, Jesus the Messiah returns. This is what Hoses 3 was talking about.

As well we could look to another passage that deals with the issue. Hosea 5:15-6:4 *I will go and return to my place, till they acknowledge their offence, and seek my face: in their affliction they will seek me early. Come, and let us return unto the LORD: for he hath torn, and he will heal us; he hath smitten, and he will bind us up. After two days will he revive us: in the third day he will raise us up, and we shall live in his sight. Then shall we know, if we follow on to know the LORD: his going forth is prepared as the morning; and he shall come unto us as the rain, as the latter and former rain unto the earth. O Ephraim, what shall I do unto thee? O Judah, what shall I do unto thee? for your goodness is as a morning cloud, and as the early dew it goeth away.*

God is speaking in these verses, and He says that He will return to his place. God's place is heaven, and God says in Hosea that He is going to return to heaven. The only way He can return to this place is if He had previously left. This passage is clearly teaching that at some time after the writing of Hosea, God is going to leave heaven, then He is going to return to heaven.

However, God will not return to heaven for eternity. He will stay in heaven until the Jews acknowledge their offense. The people who are being addressed here are the people of Israel and Judah. The Christian interpretation would be that the offense spoken of is the rejection of the Messiah. This is what Jesus was speaking of in Matthew 23:39. *For I say unto you, Ye shall not see me henceforth, till ye shall say, Blessed is he that cometh in the name of the Lord.*

Both the first and second coming of the Messiah are mentioned in Hosea 5:15. The return to His place shows the first coming, and the word "until" shows the second coming. I was once discussing this verse with a Rabbi. The Rabbi said that he had to look it up. I asked what is there to look up? We were reading the passage in his Hebrew Bible. I asked him to simply explain what he thought the passage was saying. I never found out what the rabbinical response to Hosea 5:15 is. Rather than explain the passage to me, the Rabbi grew enraged and asked me to leave his study. Often people ask me what the Rabbis say about Hosea 5:15. The answer is simple. The rabbis say, "Get Out!"

In chapter 6 of Hosea, verse 3 we read how the Messiah will come as the rains come upon the land of Israel. The rain comes upon the land twice, the latter and former rain. The Messiah, according to Hosea, is God and will come twice as the rain comes twice. Our eschatology fits rather nicely with what is taught in the book of Hosea. We see the first and second advent, the Jewish rejection, the Church age, and the great tribulation. All are mentioned, and can easily be explained. The Jewish response is "Get Out!"

Some Jews believe that the Jewish Scriptures teach that Israel will be redeemed at the coming of the messiah.[69] When Jesus came the exact opposite happened. Israel was condemned when the Jews rejected Jesus. The messiah was expected to return the Jewish people to the land, and when Jesus was born the Jewish people were already living in the land. These two objections show us the philosophy that we must overcome. Some Jewish scholars equate rabbinical teaching with Scripture. What the Rabbis teach is the same as the Word of God. When Kaplan refers to the Scriptures he doesn't give the reference. We don't know what text of the Bible he is speaking about. That makes it a bit difficult to respond.

Jewish tradition has taught many messianic concepts. These concepts are in some cases built solidly on revelation. In some cases they are man-made. However, for Jewish tradition it doesn't matter. The man-made ideas are regarded with the same esteem as the Scriptural concepts. Jesus did not fulfill the Jewish expectations of the messiah.

A false messiah would have made certain that the traditional expectations were satisfied. If the New Testament was really a phony record, then wouldn't the authors have presented a Jesus that measured up to the Jewish anticipation? Jesus' failure to measure up to the tradition is evidence against any hoax.

The Scriptures weren't completely understood. They predict a Messiah that was significantly distinct from the man-made one. The Scriptural Messiah will come twice. Jesus fulfills the scriptural predictions. The things that have been left unfulfilled await his return.

---

[69] *The Real Messiah*, 45

Teaching on Sin

In a discussion a Rabbi once told a story about a burning house. He said that when a fire was discovered in the basement, the inhabitants fled to the first floor for safety. As the fire began to engulf the first floor, they hid on the second. They finally were destroyed hiding from the fire in the attack. The Rabbi then likened the folly of those in the household to the behavior of the early Christians. If there were a fire in the basement, the early Christians never would have moved upstairs.

His point was that since the early Christians built themselves upon the foundation of Judaism, they must have believed the foundation to have been sound. Since they thought that the foundation was sound then any difference between Christianity and the Jewish foundation must be an error in Christianity. With that kind of logic, we could never win any discussion because the very fact of difference declares us wrong. Many Jewish objections of the Christian faith are based in this kind of thinking. The mention of the difference is enough to show that the Christians are wrong. This kind of thinking seems to be prevalent in the subject of man's nature. The very fact that a difference can be shown between the Christian belief and the traditional Jewish position seems to be enough to prove to the Jew that the Christian is incorrect in his thinking.

The Christian faith indeed has roots in Judaism. This is a better analogy because the roots lie in darkness. The plant blooms in the light. As far as the house is concerned it has but one foundation. Our house is built on the rock. Ephesians 2:20 *And are built upon the foundation of the apostles and prophets, Jesus Christ himself being the chief corner stone.*

There is disagreement with the apparent moral pessimism. In the book, *The Christian Problem*, we read "The insistence that man is a sinner...seems to Jews to be a moral pessimism which is not in consonance with their way of thinking."[70] The fact that

---

[70] *The Christian Problem* Pg. 93

traditional Jewish thinking is in opposition to the teaching of Christianity isn't a problem for Christianity. The issue is not how uncomfortable the teaching on depravity may make a Jewish person feel. The issue is, what do the Jewish Scriptures teach about the nature of man?

We had mentioned these verses in section one, as we discussed the Gospel in the Old Testament. We use these verses frequently because we realize that the traditional Jewish thinking contradicts what is taught in the Word. Psalm 51:3 *For I acknowledge my transgressions: and my sin is ever before me.* Psalm 51:5 *Behold, I was shapen in iniquity; and in sin did my mother conceive me.* Psalm 51:10 *Create in me a clean heart, O God; and renew a right spirit within me.*

If one isn't going to believe in the sinful nature of man, I have no idea how he would interpret these verses. They clearly express that man is born into sin, and therefore his sin is before him. In Jeremiah 17:9 we read *The heart is deceitful above all things, and desperately wicked: who can know it?* The Hebrew word for heart is Leb. The Strong concordance shows the following ways that the word is translated in the King James Bible, and lists some of the possible meanings for the word leb {labe}: heart 508, mind 12, midst 11, understanding 10, hearted 7, wisdom 6, comfortably 4, well 4, considered 2, friendly 2, kindly 2, stouthearted

1) inner man, mind, will, heart, understanding
  1a) inner part, midst
    1a1) midst (of things)
    1a2) heart (of man)
    1a3) soul, heart (of man)
    1a4) mind, knowledge, thinking, reflection, memory
    1a5) inclination, resolution, determination (of will)
    1a6) conscience
    1a7) heart (of moral character)
    1a8) as seat of appetites
    1a9) as seat of emotions and passions
    1a10) as seat of courage man's intellect

When you see how the word is used, you begin to get a feel for the fact that the word "heart" is referring to the true nature of man, his inner being, his mind, and his soul. Jeremiah declares that the heart is deceitful, and desperately wicked. This is teaching a Scriptural doctrine of a sinful nature for man.

In the Book, *You Take Jesus, I'll Take God*, Samuel Levine asks "If the concept of the original sin is correct, why did the entire Bible (Old Testament) ignore it?"[71] Mr. Levine's question includes a statement that is totally incorrect. The doctrine of original sin is not ignored in the Jewish Scriptures, but is taught in the Jewish Scriptures.

Mr. Levine, in order to make his point, selects several passages of Scripture where obedience is both encouraged and expected. Levine mentions both chapters 28 and 30 of the book of Deuteronomy. In both chapters the Lord mentions the blessings that can belong to the nation of Israel if they obey Him. The teaching of national obedience, and of subsequent blessing, does not in any way discount the teaching of personal depravity.

In further discussion Levine quotes from I Samuel 15:22. *And Samuel said, Hath the LORD as great delight in burnt offerings and sacrifices, as in obeying the voice of the LORD? Behold, to obey is better than sacrifice, and to hearken than the fat of rams.* The conclusion that Levine draws from this verse is "that obedience is within the potential of man."[72] The only certain conclusion we can draw from I Samuel 15 is that King Saul disobeyed. The fact that obedience is required says nothing at all about man's potential. However there are examples of men who have obeyed the Lord in the Scriptures. In Genesis 12: 4 we read *So Abram departed, as the LORD had spoken unto him.* On the basis of that verse we must conclude that man is capable of obedience. Abraham, however, in the midst of his obedience, still needed to be declared righteous by faith. As we read in Genesis 15:6 *And he believed in the LORD; and he counted it to him for righteousness.* The more man obeys the Lord, the more blessed his

---

[71] You Take Jesus. I'll Take God Pg. 81

[72] Ibid pg 82

life will become. But no amount of obedience can change the nature of the man. The cleansing that mans needs can only come from God.

The concept of original sin is introduced in the book of Genesis. In Genesis 2:17 we read, *But of the tree of the knowledge of good and evil, thou shalt not eat of it: for in the day that thou eatest thereof thou shalt surely die*. What does it mean to die? What did God mean when he said that to Adam? To the Christian it means that man will become a sinner, will die spiritually, and will reproduce after his own kind.

To Mr. Levine, God meant absolutely nothing. The phrase *thou shalt surely die* is of no particular consequence whatsoever. Levine never mentions it in his discussion of original sin. Why is man kicked out of paradise? How did man become ashamed? Why was man hiding from the Lord? Why is mankind no longer allowed access to the tree of life? What happened in the garden? According to Levine, nothing at all because everything is as it was. Man is still given rules to obey, and if man obeys the rules he will be fine.

Something terrible happened in Genesis chapter three. If Mr. Levine doesn't like our interpretation, he should at least tell us what he thinks the passage is teaching us. Instead, Mr. Levine simply sweeps our view aside and says that the Jewish Scriptures nowhere teach about original sin. Since Levine doesn't give us an alternative position, we are left with our interpretation versus no interpretation.

Jewish people also see an opposition to sexuality in Christianity. Please forgive me, but in order to fully appreciate this objection I need to quote the entire argument. "Isn't the Christian opposition to sex psychologically harmful? In I Corinthians 7:1-9 Paul says *It is good for a man not to touch a woman. Nevertheless, to avoid fornication, let every man have his own wife, and let every woman have her own husband...Defraud ye not one the other, except it be with consent for a time...and come together again, that Satan tempt you not for you incontinency. But I speak this by permission, and not of commandment. For I would that all men were even as myself...I therefore say to the unmarried and widow, It is good for them if they abide even as I. But if they cannot contain, let them marry, for it is better to marry than to burn.* These are powerful words - it is better to marry than to burn. If that doesn't make a Christian feel guilty every time he or she has sexual relations, even with their spouse, nothing will. This Christian attitude goes completely against the basic human sexual drives of man. It does not try to control or guide the sex drive, but rather, it tries to eliminate it altogether. Paul urges the unmarried people never have sex, and those who are married are to try to limit it as much as they both consent to (verse 5). Christianity thus goes against the nature of man. It urges man to repress and destroy one of man's strongest drives, and so, Christianity will inevitably make all Christians reach a stage of neurosis, at least, if not worse. So why become a Christian -won't it make you a psychological mess? If you don't have sex, you will go crazy, and if you do, you will feel guilty -does that sound like something any sane person would want to join?"[73]

I realize that without the guidance of the Holy Spirit the Scriptures cannot be understood by the natural man. So I can understand the misunderstanding of the clear teaching of I Corinthians chapter 7. However, Mr. Levine very nicely omitted some of the text in his quote. The portion he omitted directly contradicts Mr. Levine's conclusion. In verses 3-4 of First Corinthians Paul teaches that regular sexual activity in the marriage is a responsibility that the husband and wife owe to each other. 1 Corinthians 7:3-4 *Let the husband render unto the wife due benevolence: and likewise also the wife unto the husband. The wife hath not power of her own body, but the husband: and likewise also the husband hath not power of his own body, but the wife.* Paul is not telling married couples to limit their sexual activities. He is simply permitting them to abstain from regular sexual activity for brief periods of time.

The Scriptures do speak rather clearly about sexual purity. However, the New Testament teaches that marital sex is not impure. Hebrews 13:4 *Marriage is honourable in all, and the bed*

---

[73] Ibid Pg 84

undefiled: but whoremongers and adulterers God will judge.
Earlier Mr. Levine suggested that if God gave laws then He expected man to obey those laws. Mr. Levine tells us that man has the potential for obedience. Now Mr. Levine protests against Christianity because we expect unmarried people to remain chaste.

There is a religion that is clearly opposed to human sexuality. This religion teaches that married couples should not look at each other's bodies, that they should only have sexual relations for the purpose of reproduction, and that they should never have sex within the same room of a Sefer Torah, showing that this religion expresses that sex is dirty, or at least unholy. The following quote shows clearly that this religion goes against the nature of man; it urges man to repress one of man's strongest drives. "When having intercourse, his intention should not be to satisfy his personal desire, but to fulfill his obligation to perform his marital duty like one paying a debt, and to comply with the command of his Creator and that he may have children."[74] A sane person would not want to join such a religion. However, the religion that teaches against human sexuality is not Biblical Christianity at all. The religion that teaches against human sexuality is Rabbinical Judaism.

Some see Christianity as limiting. "Isn't Christianity psychologically harmful, because of the way it limits man? Christianity is based on a major principle, and that is that man is condemned to sin, and will burn in hell forever, unless he is saved from hell by accepting Jesus in his heart. Thus, as we pointed out before, Christianity rests on the assertion that man is weak, he is a sinner, and he can never achieve saintliness through action. This doctrine will necessarily make man feel weak, it will make a person feel incompetent, insecure, and worst of all, always guilty. This is psychologically harmful, for people thrive the most when they feel positive about themselves. The Jewish teachings have always been that man can overcome evil, man could be holy and wonderful, and that man is precious. In fact, the Talmud states that the reason why God created only one individual human first is in order to teach man how unique and precious he is, so that it is

---

[74] *Code of Jewish Law* Hebrew Publishing Company 1981 New York Chapter 150 pg 15 sec 9

perfectly justified to feel that the entire creation was justified for any one human being. The Jew therefore walks around being aware of the difficulties, aware of his weaknesses, but positive and confident. The Christian walks around thanking Jesus for sparing him from hell. Isn't that unhealthy?"[75]

No, it is not unhealthy to be aware of the true condition. What Levine states as an unhealthy attitude is exactly the heart that David shows in Psalm 51. Christianity does not limit man in sin. Christianity frees man from his sin. There is nothing limiting in standing above reproach in the sight of God. Paul writes that Christ died in order *to present you holy and unblameable and unreproveable in his sight.*[76]

Having cancer is a depressing fact. Would it be better to never test for cancer? That way we could avoid psychological stress. However, if there is a cure, then we must test early, and discover the truth, so that we might apply the remedy. The psychological effects are not very important in a life and death situation.

Eternity in hell is worse than cancer, yet there is a cure. Ignoring the facts might be of some psychological benefit, but I recommend discovering the truth and seeking the cure. The issue is not the ramifications of the religion, but rather, are these truths taught in the Scriptures or not, and indeed the are.

Levine asks a question about responsibility. "If man is condemned to sin, then how can he be responsible for his crimes?"[77] The answer is rather complex. However, this objection could be leveled against the Torah as well. We read of Pharaoh and of Esau. They were both selected for their roles. God hardened Pharaoh's heart. Was pharaoh still not responsible and held accountable for his own actions?

Christianity teaches that man has a will. He chooses to sin. Yes, man is a sinner, but depravity is a condition, not an excuse. An unsaved man is never right with God. But there are degrees of

---

[75] *You Take Jesus, I'll Take God*

[76] Colossians 1:22b KJV

[77] *You Take Jesus, I'll Take God* Pg.89

evil. All sin is sin in God's sight, but on earth men can do human good, if even for the wrong motives.

However, if an unsaved person obeys Biblical principles he can find some blessings in life. A man who is faithful to one wife will have a more abundant life than a man who is immoral and unfaithful. However, his morality will not win him a place in heaven because he will never be without sin. The law of God is written in a man's heart. Men know right from wrong, and can choose a more righteous path. That choice will never make a man holy, and will never make him sinless. The more wicked a man's actions, the more he seeks the darkness because his deeds are evil. The more a man seeks the darkness, the more he abhors the truth that is in the light. The question again is not the ramifications of the belief, but rather is the truth taught in the Jewish Scriptures, and again, indeed it is.

Teaching on Salvation

This question is raised on the basis of Deuteronomy 24:16 where we read *The fathers shall not be put to death for the children, neither shall the children be put to death for the fathers: every man shall be put to death for his own sin.* The question is, how can Jesus die for us, when the Scriptures teach that everyone shall die for their own sins?[78] The context of Deuteronomy 24 seems to be one of fairness and justice in human affairs. The concept of righteousness with God is not being discussed. God's sacrificial system is not a system of fairness. Why should an innocent animal die for the transgressions of a guilty person?

Jesus is the fulfillment of the unfair sacrificial system. Christian theologians didn't invent this idea. It is what we learn from reading the Scriptures. Isaiah 53:5-8 says *But he was wounded for our transgressions, he was bruised for our iniquities: the chastisement of our peace was upon him; and with his stripes we are healed. All we like sheep have gone astray; we have turned every one to his own way; and the LORD hath laid on him the iniquity of us all. He was oppressed, and he was*

---

[78] *The Real Messiah* Pg 56

afflicted, yet he opened not his mouth: he is brought as a lamb to the slaughter, and as a sheep before her shearers is dumb, so he openeth not his mouth. He was taken from prison and from judgment: and who shall declare his generation? for he was cut off out of the land of the living: for the transgression of my people was he stricken.

The question was asked, how can Jesus die for us? The answer is Jesus can die for us because Isaiah 53 says that he was *cut off out of the living, for the transgression of my people was he stricken.* The Scriptures clearly teach the necessity of a sacrifice. Jesus is that sacrifice, and Deuteronomy is not contradicting the concept of sacrificial atonement.

Mr. Levine questions the necessity of human blood He makes the following statement: "Nowhere in the book of Leviticus or anywhere else does the Torah allow any form of human blood as an atonement."[79] First there is no real need to respond to this objection. There are many truths that are not directly addressed in the Scriptures. This truth is mentioned only by inference, but it is no less a fact. Mr. Levine draws our attention to the lack of direct mention of this truth. We read in Leviticus 17:11 *For the life of the flesh is in the blood: and I have given it to you upon the altar to make an atonement for your souls: for it is the blood that maketh an atonement for the soul.* The word translated "life" is nephesh. That word is used 751 times in the Jewish Scriptures. In about 730 times, it is referring to human life. In this Leviticus passage the following verses are about dietary laws. The word "life" is obviously animal life, and the passage is introducing the sacrifice system. According to Leviticus 17:11, blood makes atonement for our souls.

The instructions for the Day of Atonement are in Leviticus chapter 16. The atonement that is being spoken of in chapter 17 is the national, annual sacrificial work of the high priest. The blood that is spoken of is the blood that is used in that atonement. If the blood that is used to make atonement is animal blood, then Leviticus is teaching about animal blood. If, however, the blood

---

[79] *You Take Jesus, I'll Take God* Pg. 43

that makes ultimate atonement is human blood, then Leviticus 17:11 is teaching about human blood.

The Scriptures show that it is extremely important to keep the dignity of the sacrifice. Eating blood, which would detract from the true sacrificial purpose of blood, is forbidden. In fact, to eat blood is one of the capital crimes that is outlined in the Scriptures. We see the punishment for eating blood is to be cut off. This expression "cut off" is used 280 times in the Hebrew Bible. It is often connected to the word "covenant." A scroll would be cut, and in so doing a contract was made. There are only a few crimes for which a person would be cut off, many of which have to do with breaking a law in the Levitical system.

- a person who refuses circumcision was to be cut off (Genesis 17:14)
- an abuse of the Sabbath (Exodus 31:14)
- homosexuality, bestiality, and incest (Leviticus 18:29, and 20:17,18)
- dedicating your children to Moloch (Leviticus 20:3-5)
- dealing with familiar spirits (Leviticus 20:6. Exodus 12:15,19)
- abuse of Passover (Exodus 12:15,19. Numbers 11:13)
- desecration of anointing oil (Exodus 30:32,38)
- defiling the tabernacle (Numbers 19:13,19)
- eating blood (Leviticus 17:10,14 & 19:18)
- sacrificing in the wrong place (Leviticus 17:4,9)

There is only one remaining place where the term "cut off" appears. That is in Daniel 9:26. ***And after threescore and two weeks shall Messiah be cut off, but not for himself.*** All of the remaining places where we see the expression "cut off," there has been a crime committed. Frequently that crime has to do with the sacrifice system itself. This man is cut off, and is cut off through no fault of his own; he is clearly not the perpetrator of one of the previously mentioned crimes. The one (Messiah) who is cut off here is cut off as a sacrifice, to make atonement for the crimes of others. In Leviticus 16 we read about the Day of Atonement. That day needs to be repeated every year. If the day of atonement provided permanent atonement, then we would not need additional atonement on the following year.

The sacrifice on the Day of Atonement is only temporary. There needs to be an eternal sacrifice, a lasting atonement. In Isaiah 53 we see the concept of a substitute making complete atonement for others. This thought is repeated in that chapter several times. In verse 5 we read *But he was wounded for our transgressions*. In verse six we read *the LORD hath laid on him the iniquity of us all*. In verse 8 we read *for he was cut off out of the land of the living: for the transgression of my people*. In verse ten we read, *when thou shalt make his soul an offering for sin*, and again in verse 11 we read *shall my righteous servant justify many; for he shall bear their iniquities*, and finally in verse twelve we read *he hath poured out his soul unto death: and he was numbered with the transgressors; and he bare the sin of many, and made intercession for the transgressors*.

Isaiah 53 is teaching that a person is going to provide atonement for us. Daniel nine describes that person to be the Messiah. The Messiah is a human, and since a human's death is the final atoning sacrifice, the Leviticus 17:11 is referring to the blood of a human. I knew we could get across the highway at the "No U Turn" sign.

The fairly popular objection that blood is not essential is often raised. Judaism has several methods of accomplishing righteousness. They list good works, fasting, prayer, and sacrifice. Within the sacrifice system they see several offerings including grains and coins that do not require blood. One anti-missionary reminds us of Psalm 34:18 *The LORD is nigh unto them that are of a broken heart; and saveth such as be of a contrite spirit*, and Isaiah 66:2 *For all those things hath mine hand made, and all those things have been, saith the LORD: but to this man will I look, even to him that is poor and of a contrite spirit, and trembleth at my word*. In both passages we see that a contrite spirit is acceptable in the sight of the Lord. The anti-missionary asks, "If a person can draw near to God with a contrite spirit, then why is a blood sacrifice required?"

The attitude that is needed to approach the Lord is consistent throughout both Testaments. Attitude, however, says nothing about the method of approach. Before I leave on a trip, I must be

225

inclined to make the journey. If I'm not so inclined, I don't go. However, having the desire to make the trip, I need to select the proper route. Even with a great attitude, if I don't follow the directions, I'm not going to reach the destination.

The contrite spirit is a prerequisite to drawing near to God. However, even with a proper spirit, there is a prescribed method of approach. In type, we see the need for blood established in the animal skins that God provided to clothe Adam and Eve. If it wasn't for the need of blood, Cain's offering would have been just as good as Abel's.

Blood is clearly mentioned in Exodus chapter 12 concerning the Passover; four times we read of the need of the blood. In verse 4, *And they shall take [some] of the blood and put [it] on the two doorposts and on the lintel of the houses where they eat it.* And again in verse 13 we read *Now the blood shall be a sign for you on the houses where you [are.] And when I see the blood, I will pass over you; and the plague shall not be on you to destroy [you] when I strike the land of Egypt.* In Verse 22, *And you shall take a bunch of hyssop, dip [it] in the blood that [is] in the basin, and strike the lintel and the two doorposts with the blood that [is] in the basin. And none of you shall go out of the door of his house until morning,* and verse 23, *For the LORD will pass through to strike the Egyptians; and when He sees the blood on the lintel and on the two doorposts, the LORD will pass over the door and not allow the destroyer to come into your houses to strike [you].*

In verse 13, we read **"when I see the blood, I will pass over you."** The Lord establishes blood as the object of protection. In verse 23 the concept of death is made personal. The destroyer, death, is not allowed to enter into the house when the Lord sees the blood protecting the house. Blood is the agency whereby the nation of Israel is defended from death.

There are sacrifices that are allowed in the Levitical system where blood is not presented. Bloodless offerings are acceptable on some occasions. However, the offerings are brought by a person who has been cleansed by blood, to a priest, who has been ordained by blood, and are offered on an altar sanctified by blood.

The people must be cleansed by blood. Exodus 24:8 *And Moses took the blood, sprinkled [it] on the people, and said, "This is the blood of the covenant which the LORD has made with you according to all these words.*

The priest is ordained by blood Exodus 29:20 *Then you shall kill the ram, and take some of its blood and put [it] on the tip of the right ear of Aaron and on the tip of the right ear of his sons, on the thumb of their right hand and on the big toe of their right foot, and sprinkle the blood all around on the altar.* Exodus 29:21 *And you shall take some of the blood that is on the altar, and some of the anointing oil, and sprinkle [it] on Aaron and on his garments, on his sons and on the garments of his sons with him; and he and his garments shall be hallowed, and his sons and his sons' garments with him.*

The altar is sanctified by blood. Exodus 24:6 *And Moses took half the blood and put [it] in basins, and half the blood he sprinkled on the altar.* Exodus 29:12 *You shall take [some] of the blood of the bull and put [it] on the horns of the altar with your finger, and pour all the blood beside the base of the altar.* Exodus 29:16 *and you shall kill the ram, and you shall take its blood and sprinkle [it] all around on the altar.* Exodus 30:10 *And Aaron shall make atonement upon its horns once a year with the blood of the sin offering of atonemet; once a year he shall make atonement upon it throughout your generations. It [is] most holy to the LORD.* Leviticus 3:2 *And he shall lay his hand on the head of his offering, and kill it [at] the door of the tabernacle of meeting; and Aaron's sons, the priests, shall sprinkle the blood all around on the altar.* Leviticus 3:8 *And he shall lay his hand on the head of his offering, and kill it before the tabernacle of meeting; and Aaron's sons shall sprinkle its blood all around on the altar.*

Without blood, the people would still be in bondage. Without blood, the individual cannot be cleansed. Without blood, the priest can't be ordained, and without blood the altar isn't sanctified. Blood is absolutely necessary for every offering.

Regardless of what works are accomplished, or what offerings are brought, each individual Israelite must take part in the Yom

Kippur services. Each is instructed to afflict his soul on that day. Leviticus 16:30-31 *For on that day shall the priest make an atonement for you, to cleanse you, that ye may be clean from all your sins before the LORD. It shall be a Sabbath of rest unto you, and ye shall afflict your souls, by a statute for ever.* Along with the instruction to afflict the soul, the Scriptures add an awesome warning, Leviticus 23:29. *For whatsoever soul it be that shall not be afflicted in that same day, he shall be cut off from among his people.* The Yom Kippur service takes precedent over all other sacrifices, works or offerings. To not be included in this sacrifice was fatal. This superseding sacrifice was a blood offering. Therefore blood is essential. Regardless of what modern Jewish teaching might be, or what the rabbi might say, the Scriptures teach that blood is absolutely necessary.

One of the most common objections raised against the Christian faith is that if there is faith, then there will be no works.[80] And the raising of this objection shows a sinner's misunderstanding of the character of sinful behavior. One night we were discussing the possibility of sin in the life of the Messiah. As we expert theologians were debating whether or not Jesus could have sinned, my wife quipped, "why would he want to?" I realize that question ignores some of the great doctrines of the faith, but it does show a righteous attitude toward sin.

Sin separates us from God, and therefore separates us from joy and blessing. Why would we want to miss out on blessings? Why would we want to embrace misery? The religious person is laboring under a misconception about sin. Some religions teach that Satan has a cookie jar, and that God has a stick. When we reach out for a cookie, God hits us with the stick. Hell is the final and biggest stick. Most believe that it is the fear of hell that keeps us from eating the cookies. In reality God has the cookies, and Satan has the stick. God has an abundant life fashioned for us. The more we obey the Lord, the more abundant our lives become.

Levine and some other religious people think that sin is profitable and beneficial. Levine does not recognize that good

---

[80] Ibid pg. 88

works produce their own reward. We believe that the Messiah came to provide two kinds of life. He brings us eternal life and abundant life. We inherit eternal life by faith. We obtain the abundant life through works.

If we have faith, it will in no way reduce the amount of good works we produce. By faith we receive the Holy Spirit. The convicting power of the Holy Spirit makes us aware of sins that we were insensitive to as unbelievers. The indwelling Spirit enables us to overcome temptations that we were powerless to stand up to in the past. The gifts of the Spirit empower believers to do the good works of ministry.

There is no contradiction between faith and works. However, even if the faith method of salvation resulted in a lack of good works, that still would not be an argument against faith. The Scriptures teach faith is the way of salvation, as we read in Isaiah 7:9b *If ye will not believe, surely ye shall not be established.* (KJV)

Attacks on the Christian Belief Regarding the Jewish Response

The oral tradition

In Deuteronomy 17:8-13 we read, *If there arise a matter too hard for thee in judgment, between blood and blood, between plea and plea, and between stroke and stroke, being matters of controversy within thy gates: then shalt thou arise, and get thee up into the place which the LORD thy God shall choose; And thou shalt come unto the priests the Levites, and unto the judge that shall be in those days, and enquire; and they shall shew thee the sentence of judgment: And thou shalt do according to the sentence, which they of that place which the LORD shall choose shall shew thee; and thou shalt observe to do according to all that they inform thee: According to the sentence of the law which they shall teach thee, and according to the judgment which they shall tell thee, thou shalt do: thou shalt not decline from the sentence which they shall shew thee, to the right hand, nor to the left. And the man that will do presumptuously, and will not hearken unto the priest that standeth to minister there before the LORD thy God, or unto the judge, even that man shall die: and thou shalt put away the evil from Israel. And all the people shall hear, and fear, and do no more presumptuously.*

Levine uses these verses to establish the authenticity of the oral law. Levine writes, "In Deuteronomy 17:8-13, the Jews were also commanded that if a doubt would arise in any area of Jewish Law, they should go to the Sanhedrin, the high court, and what they interpret the law to be, will become, in fact the will of God. (That is how the Oral Law understands those verses.)"[81] Levine continues to say that because the Scriptures instruct the Jews to submit to the ruling of the Sanhedrin, and because the Sanhedrin rejected Jesus, then the logical conclusion is that Jews are to reject Jesus.

Levine concludes, "If, as history and the New Testament agree, the vast majority of Jews, and the Sanhedrin, rejected Jesus as the real Messiah, and the Sanhedrin thought that Jesus did not fit the qualifications for being a bona-fide Messiah, according to their interpretations of the Bible, then we should follow the opinion of the Sanhedrin. This is merely a matter of interpreting Jeremiah 31 or Isaiah 53, etc., and when it comes to Biblical interpretations, we are commanded by God to follow the Sanhedrin."[82]

This is circular reasoning. The oral tradition says that we must follow the oral tradition, therefore we must follow the oral tradition. Actually, the oral tradition says that Deuteronomy says that we are to follow the Sanhedrin. However, Deuteronomy doesn't mention the Sanhedrin at all. The Sanhedrin trace their origin back to the council of elders created in Numbers chapter 11. Since they were already in existence at the time of the Deuteronomy writing, if the Lord meant that council he could simply have named them.

---

[81] Ibid pg. 22
[82] Ibid. Pg. 22

The Sanhedrin assumed their authority on the basis of this passage, but we can't be certain that it is the Sanhedrin that Deuteronomy refers to. Deuteronomy speaks about the priests, the Levites, and the Judge. However, even if the passage meant the Sanhedrin, when it referred to the priests, the Levites and the Judge, the passage is not talking about interpretation of Scripture. The passage is speaking of Judicial matters only. Historically the Sanhedrin dealt with matters of civil law. According to the Illustrated Bible Dictionary, the jurisdiction of the Sanhedrin extended over civil and criminal areas.[83]

Who, then, is to interpret the Scriptures? According to the oral tradition, the oral tradition. However, the Scriptures seem to teach that the Word is a lamp and a light. The Scriptures interpret the Scriptures. Teachers and councils may help, but the individual must stand before God. In fact the Scriptures teach that the Lord Himself is to be our instructor; Psalm 25:4 *Shew me thy ways, O LORD; teach me thy paths.* Psalm 25:5 *Lead me in thy truth, and teach me: for thou [art] the God of my salvation; on thee do I wait all the day.* Psalm 25:9, Psalm 94:12, Psalm 119:12, 26, 64, 66, 68, 108, 124, 135, 171, and Psalm 143:10 also teach that the Lord is our teacher. A new Jewish believer shared an interesting testimony. She was challenged by a believing friend to simply ask the Lord to guide her into the truth. After that simple prayer she discovered a New Testament among her old college text books. She began reading the New Testament, and many questions arose in her heart. A week later she met a born again believer who was able to answer the questions that she had. Over the years I have heard many similar stories about people whose first step toward discovery was to ask the Lord to guide them into the truth.

The Sanhedrin was designed to serve as a civil and criminal court. It wasn't designed to guide the Jews into spiritual truth. The Scriptures teach that the Lord Himself is the one to guide us, and that He guides through His Word.

---

[83] *The Illustrated Bible Dictionary* Tyndale House publishers vol 3 pg. 1391

Almost all rejected

Many Jewish people make the assumption that most of the Jewish people at the time of Jesus rejected his claim to be the Messiah. If the people of that day rejected Him, then why should we accept Him?[84]

Less than 9% of the Jewish people are Orthodox. Over 91% of the Jewish people are not practicing Orthodox Jews. If we were to use the reasoning that the majority rules, we should reject the Orthodox religion. Of course this kind of logic is ridiculous. 17% of the Jewish people are Reform, so 83% are not Reform, since the majority of the Jewish people are not Reform we should abandon Reform Judaism. That leaves the Conservative movement. 27% of the Jewish people are conservative. That means that 73% of the Jewish people are not Conservative, so we, by the rule of majority, must also reject the Conservative movement. The same logic that would reject Jesus because most of the Jews rejected Him; but this would dictate to us to reject all of Judaism.

The Jewish people of that day had more information available to them. They were closer to the scene, and many of them did believe. It is of no significance whether the majority believed or not. There was enough evidence for some, and we need to examine the evidence for ourselves. The majority of the people can be, and often are, wrong.

We cannot be certain that the majority of Jewish people at the time of Jesus rejected Him. The New Testament in the book of Acts records the number of Jews who were added to the new Church in one day was about three thousand. On another day the number of Jews who believed was listed as five thousand men. On other occasions we see in Acts 14: *And it came to pass in Iconium, that they went both together into the synagogue of the Jews, and so spake, that a great multitude both of the Jews and also of the Greeks believed.* An undefined multitude believed the message.

---

[84] *You take Jesus, I'll Ttake God* Pg. 52

Those who do not believe the New Testament may reject it as a source of valid history. However, would they also reject the Babylonian Talmud? In the discussion of the difficulties that faced those who were attempting to codify the Talmud we read the following statement. "Added to all this, he was forced to clear the Mishnayoth from the insertions incorporated into it by the Messianists; for being many and considerable persons, and in close alliance with their colleagues the Pharisees during two centuries, they could not have failed to introduce into the Mishnayoth their own peculiar opinion and beliefs, many such passages indeed, being found in the Gemara."[85]

So the Talmud and the New Testament both agree. The Jewish people at the time of Jesus who believed in Him were both many and notable. Based on the response of that day, there is every reason for us to consider the credentials of Jesus in our day.

No prominent believers

In the book, "The Real Messiah," we read of the protest that there is not one single prominent Jewish person who believes in Jesus.[86] The conclusion to be drawn is that any intelligent person who is Jewish would never believe something as ludicrous as Christianity. What is ludicrous is the original statement.

The New Testament was written entirely by Jewish people. It has probably changed more lives than any other document. The writers of the New Testament would have to be included in any list of prominent people in world history. The writers of the New Testament are all both prominent and Jewish.

However, Aryeh Kaplan writes that there is not one single prominent Jewish person. His reasoning is rather simple. Once a Jewish person believes in Jesus, two things instantly occur, in the mind of Pinchas Stolper. First the person loses all prominence and second, the person ceases to be Jewish; hence there is not one single prominent Jewish person who believes in Jesus. Even if the statement of Aryeh Kaplan were true, which it isn't, why would it

---

[85] The Babylonian Talmud, Boston Talmud Society 1918 Michael L Rodkinson Vol 10 Pg. 14

[86] *The Real Messiah* Pg. 48

be a legitimate attack on the Christian faith? It is a bit difficult to attack the New Testament when it predicts the very conditions that we find. When it comes to important people, often important people are wealthy. And when it comes to wealthy people the New Testament teaches that is difficult for them to come to faith. Matthew 19:24 *And again I say unto you, It is easier for a camel to go through the eye of a needle, than for a rich man to enter into the kingdom of God.* When it comes to popularity, Jesus taught that we should expect that the multitude of any group is going to remain in unbelief. Matthew 7:14 *Because strait is the gate, and narrow is the way, which leadeth unto life, and few there be that find it.*

However, according to the Talmud, as we quoted above, the Jewish believers in the first two centuries were many, and notable. Large numbers of distinguished Jewish persons have continued to respond to the Gospel throughout the centuries. Rabbis and religious leaders, doctors, and prominent persons from all fields have found life through faith in Jesus.

Doubting disciples

Samuel Levine writes, "Why should anyone believe in the supposed resurrection of Jesus when some of the apostles themselves did not believe it?"[87] He then continues to quote Matthew 28:17, *And when they saw him, they worshipped him: but some doubted.* Once again we have a fallacy. The Scriptures say "some doubted" and Levine translates that to mean that the apostles didn't believe. Even if Levine's statement were true, it still wouldn't be a basis for rejecting the Christian faith. The children of Israel didn't believe Moses in the wilderness. They doubted God's ability to protect them and in the motive for delivering them from bondage. Exodus 14:11-13 *And they said unto Moses, Because there were no graves in Egypt, hast thou taken us away to die in the wilderness? wherefore hast thou dealt thus with us, to carry us forth out of Egypt? Is not this the word that we did tell thee in Egypt, saying, Let us alone, that we may*

---

[87] *You Take Jesus, I'll Take God* Pg 70

serve the Egyptians? For it had been better for us to serve the Egyptians, than that we should die in the wilderness. On the basis of their unbelief, should we disregard the Torah? Or as in Levine's words, why should we believe the Torah when even the Children of Israel at the time of Moses had doubts? Of course not; we don't disregard the Scriptures because of the doubts of past generations.

The Hebrew Scriptures record numerous incidents of unbelief. The times when we see those kinds of doubts in the New testament are much less frequent. That some of the disciples doubted the resurrection should come as no shock. A man who was dead was reported to be alive. After the disciples saw the resurrected Lord, after he spoke with them, there were no doubting disciples. Instead we see men who chose persecution and death rather than deny their faith in the resurrection. Their testimony speaks well and loud. Almost two thousand years later their record of martyrdom, of willing self-sacrifice, compels us to recognize that they had grown to be certain of their faith.

Conclusion

In general the entire category of Christian beliefs has only one determining factor. That factor is the question, what do the Scriptures teach? How well a doctrine is received or doubted is of little importance. If it can be demonstrated that a truth is indeed taught in the Jewish Scriptures nothing else matters. The doctrines that are central to the Gospel were all discovered within the Jewish Scriptures.

TEN

Attacks on Christian Behavior

The Behavior of Jesus

Reconciling His image

Levine asks "How can one reconcile the Christian image of Jesus with the way Jesus is portrayed in the New Testament?"[88] This is an absolutely marvelous question. I am not certain as to what Levine is referring to when he speaks of the "Christian image of Jesus." The Christian image of Jesus ought to be as he is revealed to be in the New testament. Any other supposed, or imagined, picture of Jesus is absolutely invalid.

There should be no need to make any such reconciliation. Many times folks don't believe the Scriptures because they don't know the Scriptures. What they have heard is often unbelievable legends devised by men. The true Jesus is a very real, a very genuine historical person. The human Jesus is unique. He behaves and speaks with the authority of a prophet of God. We must examine His behavior in that light. If the things He does are inconsistent with that of a Prophet, then we need to do

---

[88] Ibid Pg 90

reconciliation. However, if His behavior is inconsistent with some religious notion, or some man-made idea, then there is no difficulty to deal with at all.

Harsh words

In *The Real Messiah* we see the suggestion that Jesus is a hypocrite. Luke 19:27 *But those mine enemies, which would not that I should reign over them, bring hither, and slay them before me.* We see some rather harsh language. How can Jesus instruct us to love our enemies when He takes such a violent stand against those who would oppose Him?[89]

It is difficult to know if these kinds of protests are mistakes, or are deliberate attempts to deceive. In Luke 19 Jesus is relating a parable. He tells a story that includes the words that are quoted in verse 27. These words in no way reflect the attitude that Jesus has towards His enemies. The parable is a warning in regards to the ultimate justice of God. The harsh words were only spoken in a story.

His vindictiveness

The vindictiveness referred to here comes from the story of "the good Samaritan." In the relating of this famous account, Jesus belittles a Levite and a Cohen. At the same time the story exalts the behavior of a Samaritan, the enemy of the Jewish people. Rabbi Kaplan mentions that the Samaritans were the enemies of the Jewish people for over five hundred years.[90]

Kaplan also has taken issue with Jesus for lacking in forgiveness. Rabbi Kaplan is carrying on a 500 year old grudge, some 1900 years later, and he calls Jesus a hypocrite! It is true that Jesus gave us the by-word "the good Samaritan." And it is also true that we will probably never hear anyone say "the good Israeli." Kaplan compares the Samaritan to the Nazi. The difference, however, is striking. The Nazi persecuted the Jew. In Biblical times, it was the Jew who persecuted the Samaritan. Jesus

---

[89] *The Real Messiah*, Pg. 59

[90] Ibid. Pg. 61

relates the famous story in response to the question "who is your neighbor?" The question was asked in relation to the commandment "Thou shalt love thy neighbor." Jesus condemns prejudice in this story. Anyone that we see suffering is entitled to love. The harsh way that he pictures the religious leaders is completely consistent with the language that the prophets use. Using that kind of tone was not the sign of vindictiveness, but rather one of righteousness.

Any animosity that existed between the Jewish people at the time of Jesus and the Samaritans begins with the prejudiced thinking of the Jewish people. When Jesus depicts the Samaritan in a positive light, he is defending the downtrodden. There is no vindictiveness involved, and absolutely no reason to assume any.

Lack of forgiveness

In the sermon on the mount Jesus taught us to turn the other cheek. Luke 6:29 *And unto him that smiteth thee on the one cheek offer also the other; and him that taketh away thy cloke forbid not to take thy coat also.* Matthew 5:39 *But I say unto you, That ye resist not evil: but whosoever shall smite thee on thy right cheek, turn to him the other also.*

However, according to Gerald Sigal, Jesus himself did not follow His own teaching. Sigal writes, "this sublime dictum was not practiced by Jesus himself. According to the Gospels, Jesus preached turning the other cheek, loving one's neighbor and praying for them, and forgiving those who wrong you. The fact is that he himself never turned the other cheek. Jesus responded to his opponents, not with passive resistance, but by answering criticism with criticism, reviling and threatening his adversaries (e.g., Matthew 15:1-20). Jesus never forgave anyone who wronged or criticized him. He only forgave those who wronged others. On the cross, in a verse not found in the earliest New Testament manuscripts, he allegedly offered a general forgiveness of everyone: 'Father, forgive them, for they do not know what they are doing' (Luke 23:34). However when an opportunity to personally forgive others presents itself he always declined."[91]

---

[91]*The Jew and the Christian Missionary.* Pg. 201

Sigal refers to Matthew chapter 15 in his discussion. Matthew 15 simply records a debate between Jesus and the religious leaders. These were not physical enemies. And there was no physical assault in the chapter. There was a verbal disagreement, and Jesus is obligated to speak that which He believes to be the truth. If Jesus did not speak up, he would be labeled by the critics as a false prophet. Sigal continues to give two examples of this lack of personal forgiveness, the first being that of Judas, and Sigal cites Matthew 26:24. The second example is that of John 18:22-23, where Jesus was beaten by a soldier. In the first example, Matthew 26:24 *The Son of man goeth as it is written of him: but woe unto that man by whom the Son of man is betrayed! it had been good for that man if he had not been born,* Jesus is speaking to Judas, but he is speaking to him before the betrayal.

Jesus had the ability to know the future, and apparently Sigal agrees. Sigal thinks that Jesus should forgive Judas for things that Judas has yet to do. The statement that Jesus makes cannot possibly be thought of as a lack of forgiveness. What Jesus said was a warning to Judas, a warning to alert him of the outcome of his planned behavior.

As to the second example we read in John 18:22-23, *And when he had thus spoken, one of the officers which stood by struck Jesus with the palm of his hand, saying, Answerest thou the high priest so? Jesus answered him, If I have spoken evil, bear witness of the evil: but if well, why smitest thou me?* Sigal refers to this as arguing with the officer. Jesus didn't fight back, he didn't employ any resistance. He did exactly as He instructed. The command to turn the other cheek does not imply to do so silently. It implies that we behave without force.

Neither example shows Jesus to behave differently then the way He taught. Sigal mentions the statement of forgiveness on the cross, *"father forgive them,"* but he also dismisses it. He says that the statement is alleged, and apparently thinks that the statement is too general to be considered. Perhaps that verse is spurious. However, from the entire Gospels, Sigal could not find one example that showed Jesus behaving differently than the way He taught. The only examples that he could find show Jesus to possess foreknowledge in the one, and to behave exactly as He taught in the other. If the verse is not spurious, then there is a record that does show Jesus behaving with compassion to all. This general forgiveness is really revealing a heart of great mercy to all His enemies. He forgave them all, but they are each also forgiven individually. The fact that he forgives all in no way detracts from the forgiveness; it does not become impersonal. If Jesus did not forgive them all, then Sigal would have a contradiction to bring to our attention.

The herd of swine

Luke 8:31-33, And they besought him that he would not command them to go out into the deep. And there was there an herd of many swine feeding on the mountain: and they besought him that he would suffer them to enter into them. And he suffered them. Then went the devils out of the man, and entered into the swine: and the herd ran violently down a steep place into the lake, and were choked.

Sigal begins his objection here by stating, "Jesus did not have the supernatural powers to do what is claimed for him in the incident of the drowning of the swine herd. However this is beside the point, since the evangelists contend that he did. In view of this, let us investigate the implications of the tale."[92] If Jesus did not do it, then there is no question as to His character, and there can be no question in regards to His motives. If Jesus did do it, then we have to first recognize His authority. In the Spiritual realm, we must take that authority into consideration as we try to formulate any answers. Sigal attempts to question Jesus, but refuses to recognize the power that Jesus possessed. Sigal concludes with "We must, thus, accept the inescapable conclusion that Jesus was indeed responsible for the violent death of the swine"[93] Jesus is responsible for the death of the herd of swine. Why would a practicing Jewish person be so concerned about the welfare of pigs? These pigs were bred for the purpose of slaughter. They

---

[92] Ibid. Pg. 205
[93] Ibid Pg. 206

might have been scheduled for slaughter that very day. Perhaps the method of extermination that was planned for them was more brutal then the death they suffered due to the demons. We do not know much about the future of the swine herd.

As well we don't know very much about the demonic world. It is suggested by Sigal that the demons were now free to continue to do evil. The likelihood is, that once disembodied the demons would end up in the very pit that they were trying to avoid. The demons probably didn't realize what their presence in the swine would cause the swine to do. Jesus, however, would have known, and thus as Sigal says, the destruction of the swine was Jesus' fault. We serve a God who commanded Saul to destroy Amelek. Along with the destruction of Amelek, God also commanded that the women, the children, and all the livestock be destroyed. Why does God command the destruction of the animals? In warfare the commander and chief is best obeyed and ought not to be questioned.

We believe that Jesus is God. His power over the demons demonstrates His Deity. If you do not believe He has the power, then you can not make Him responsible. If you believe He has the power, then you must accept His authority. Sigal does not find fault with God when he commands the destruction of livestock. Why then would he question our faith? Our God is responsible for the destruction of pigs that were bred for destruction. The activity of Jesus is not inconsistent with that of Deity.

Violence in the Temple

Mark 11:15-17 *And they come to Jerusalem: and Jesus went into the temple, and began to cast out them that sold and bought in the temple, and overthrew the tables of the moneychangers, and the seats of them that sold and bought in the temple, and overthrew the tables of the moneychangers, and the seats of them that sold doves; And would not suffer that nay man should carry any vessel through the temple. And he taught, saying unto them, Is it not written, My house shall be called of all nations the house of prayer? but ye have made it a den of thieves. (KJV)*

In regards to this passage Sigal sees a discrepancy between the synoptic Gospels and the record in John. The difficulty is that John is recording a different incident. Jesus apparently cleansed the Temple on an earlier visit to Jerusalem. The incident that is recorded in the synoptic Gospels occurs during the last week of Jesus' life and ministry. Sigal declares that the Gospel writers "Matthew and Luke attempted to suppress the information concerning the extent of Jesus' actions so as to minimize the impression that Jesus was a man of violence."[94] If Matthew and Luke wanted to suppress the information, then why did they record the incident at all? They obviously were not withholding information to present Jesus in a positive light. Sigal draws our attention to Jesus' cleansing the Temple not being mentioned at the trial of Jesus. Sigal suggests that the reason it was not mentioned is that the Gospel writers omitted it to draw attention away from the violent nature of Jesus. Since it was the Gospel writers who inform us of the cleansing of the Temple, they could not possibly be omitting information. The cleansing of the Temple was not mentioned at the trial possibly because the Sanhedrin themselves recognized the righteousness of the act.

Earlier Sigal mentioned Isaiah 53:9. He suggested that the man who cleansed the Temple could not possibly fulfill Isaiah 53, since the servant of Isaiah 53 does no violence. Isaiah 53:9 *And he made his grave with the wicked, and with the rich in his death; because he had done no violence, neither was any deceit in his mouth*. "Violence" in Isaiah 53:9 is translated חָמָס *hamas*. "The noun and the verb are together used sixty seven times and, mostly translators seem satisfied with 'violence' in some form (kjv, rsv, niv). It may be noted, however, that the word *hamas* in the OT is used almost always in connection with sinful violence. It does not refer to the violence of natural catastrophe or to the violence as pictured in a police chase on modern television."[95] The action of Jesus is very much like a police action. The activity prohibited by

---

[94] Ibid Pg. 216
[95] *The Theological Wordbook of the Old Testament*, Moody Press. R. Laird Harrispg. 297 art. 678a

the Hebrews of Isaiah 53:9 is not the activity of Jesus in the Temple.

Well what do we have left? There is no textual difficulty between the Synoptic Gospels and the Gospel of John. The activity of Jesus does not disqualify Him from fulfilling the passage of Isaiah 53, so what is left is the activity of Jesus, which is inconsistent with Sigal's concept of Jesus. The concept of Jesus should be based on the Scriptural predictions of the Messiah. Sigal referred to Isaiah 53:9, but at no time did he even mentioned the quotation that John references. Psalm 69:9 *For the zeal of thine house hath eaten me up; and the reproaches of them that reproached thee are fallen upon me.* Psalm 119:139 *My zeal hath consumed me, because mine enemies have forgotten thy words.* The Scriptures depict a Messiah who will behave as Jesus did. His behavior is consistent with the Scriptures as a prophet.

The cursed fig tree

Matthew 21:18 -21 *Now in the morning as he returned into the city, he hungered And when he saw a fig tree in the way, he came to it, and found nothing thereon, but leaves only, and said unto it, Let no fruit grow on thee henceforward for ever. And presently the fig tree withered away. And when the disciples saw it, they marvelled, saying, How soon is the fig tree withered away! Jesus answered and said unto them, Verily I say unto you, If ye have faith, and doubt not, ye shall not only do this which is done to the fig tree, but also if ye shall say unto this mountain, Be thou removed, and be thou cast into the sea; it shall be done.* Mark 11:12-14 *And on the morrow, when they were come from Bethany, he was hungry: And seeing a fig tree afar off having leaves, he came, if haply he might find any thing thereon: and when he came to it, he found nothing but leaves; for his disciples heard it.*

In discussion of these passages Sigal writes, "While on the road to Jerusalem, Jesus became hungry... and seeing a fig tree with leaves, he approached it but found no fruit on it... He cursed the fig tree and it withered either instantly (Matthew 21:20) or by the next morning (Mark 11:20-21). It is the nature of the fig tree that even before the tree is covered with leaves, the *paggim* ("green figs") begin to develop and continue to grow during the summer months. The first ripe figs sometimes appear in the early summer (Song of Songs 2:13), many weeks after the leaves have appeared. Therefore, even if there had been figs, as Jesus had expected, it was too early in the season for them to be ripe for eating. Moreover, a tree, lacking a mind and conscience of its own, cannot be treated as deceptive, and certainly cannot be held responsible for not producing fruit. Why then the violent action against the tree? According to the Torah, not even during the exigencies of war is one permitted to chop down a fruit-bearing tree (Deuteronomy 20:19). That Jesus, in violation of the Torah, destroyed a tree he considered capable of bearing fruit is indicated by his statement: 'May no one ever eat fruit from you again!' (Mark 11:14), alternately expressed as: 'No longer shall there ever be any fruit from you' (Matthew 21:19). When questioned by his disciples about his actions, Jesus said he did to show what can be done by faith (Matthew 21:21-21; Mark 11:22-24). But how does wanton destruction demonstrate faith? No moral lesson is clearly stated or even alluded to in this destructive act. If Jesus was all-powerful and all-loving, would it not have been proper for him to command the tree give forth fruit rather than to command it to wither and die?"[96]

First we must deal with the remarks of supposed discrepancy between Matthew's account and that in the Gospel of Mark. If you combine the two passages Mark 11:14 with Matthew 21:19 you read, "And Jesus answered, No man eat fruit of thee hereafter for ever and said unto it Let no fruit grow on thee henceforward for ever. That would be a double curse; no man will ever eat of the fruit, and no fruit will ever be produced by the tree. In Matthew's account the tree began to wither immediately; in Mark 11:20 we read *And in the morning, as they passed by, they saw the fig tree dried up from the roots*. Notice how here we see that the tree had withered from the roots. There again is no difficulty. The effects of the curse could be seen at that very instant that the curse was

---

[96] *The Jew and the Christian Missionary* Pg. 219

pronounced, but the ultimate death was not totally obvious until the following morning.

As we read the various anti-missionary publications, we find two attacks on the character of Jesus in regards to this event. It is good to keep in mind that none of these attacks ever come from a sincere heart. None of those who find a difficulty in this incident believe that Jesus could work the miracle that is attributed to him. They do not believe that he could do it, they do not believe it ever happened, and so there is no problem. Of course we believe it did happen, we believe that he did have the power to work such miracles, and since he does have that kind of power, there is no problem.

The first attack is that Jesus breaks the law by destroying a fruit bearing tree, and the second is that Jesus behaves with anger and not forgiveness towards the tree. In Isaiah 28:4 we read about the early fruit, the fruit that is before summer. There was a certain kind of fig tree that existed in Palestine. "One of the peculiarities of that tree was that the fruit appeared before the foliage. The presence of foliage on the tree before summer ought to have indicated the fact that fruit was there too.[97] In a healthy tree there would have been fruit. The absence of fruit demonstrates an unhealthy tree. The destruction of that tree is not a violation of the Scriptural prohibition in Deuteronomy.

Sigal says that no moral lesson is clearly stated or even alluded to in this destructive act. The disciples did not question the act at all, but the power of the miracle amazed them. At the time of the incident, the disciples questioned the power of the miracle. Twenty centuries later people question the offense on basis of the civil rights of the fig tree. Jesus directed his teaching toward the questions that the disciples had. He spoke about the power of faith.

Jesus does teach us a lesson about the fig tree, however. In Luke 13:6-7 we read, *He spake also this parable; A certain man had a fig tree planted in his vineyard; and he came and sought fruit thereon, and found none. Then said he unto the dresser of his vineyard, Behold, these three years I come seeking fruit on*

---

[97] *The Gospel According to Matthew* By G Campbell Morgan Fleming H Revell Company Pg. 253

this fig tree, and find none: cut it down; why cumbereth it the ground? The vineyard spoken of is a direct reference to the parable told in Isaiah chapter 5. In that chapter the vineyard is Israel. The fig tree then is a symbolic picture of the holy city, Jerusalem. Jerusalem, that earlier had shown flowers by proclaiming hosanna, now shows herself to be unhealthy and fruitless by calling out, "crucify him!" Just like the fig tree, the city begins to whither immediately, and then dries up from the root. Just like the fig tree there is a dual curse. First the veil was rent in the temple, (and no more shall men eat of her fruit), and then forty years later the Temple was in ruins, (and she shall produce no further fruit). The tree was sick, and needed to be destroyed. As much as Sigal wants to defend the rights of trees, we are not speaking of waste and destruction. This need not be an act of anger; this could be seen as an act of mercy. We have no knowledge of what kind of sickness and havoc an unhealthy tree could produce.

Sigal continues to question why the Lord didn't simply make the tree well, and command it to produce fruit. The same question on a grander scale could always be asked of God. Why does the Lord permit suffering? Elijah shut up the heavens, and I'm sure that there were many who suffered at that time. Elisha caused Gehazi to become a leper. In fact the leprosy was not only put on Gehazi but also upon all his offspring.

Sigal cries out for the poor innocent fig tree. The tree didn't know any better, and didn't deserve to be punished. The children of Gehazi are innocent of his crimes, but do they deserve to become lepers? Do we protest against Elisha? No, we respect his power as a prophet. If he was able to perform the miracle, we assume that he is doing so as a prophet of God.

Conclusion

In this section it must be remembered that we believe Jesus to be unique. He is both God and man. As a man he functions as a prophet. His behavior must be shown to be consistent with that of those prophets which were before him. As God, we expect to see justice, mercy, condemnation, and forgiveness. If the behavior of Jesus does not meet up with a religious or man-made image of Him, there is no need of reconciliation. Jesus is the historical person of the Scripture, not the imaginary character invented by folklore.

The Behavior of Christians Historically

Through this entire section the only real answer is that man is depraved. Christianity teaches depravity, and when we see that truth in life, it should not serve as a reason to disbelieve the truth. Many believers are not aware of some of the atrocities that the Jewish people were subjected to throughout history. For that reason we quote a brief description of each category so that we all will be aware.

Perhaps an awareness will help us to be more sensitive and more understanding. Perhaps we might grow more loving and tender in our witness. We can't apologize for, nor can we minimize these events. We must remember that most Jewish people think that all Gentiles are Christians, and these crimes, therefore, were the crimes of Christian. That means we must be that much more loving to show that we are completely different; we have been changed by God.

For the most part the crimes against the Jewish people were perpetrated by the enemies of God. Any who would oppose Israel are opposing the Lord, and they are not Christians; they are our enemies as well.

During the Middle Ages

Many Jewish people are very aware of the atrocities of the middle ages. It should not surprise us to discover that most Gentiles have very little knowledge of the things that occurred during those years. Rachel Zurer, who entitles a chapter in her book "Anti Semitism as Church Theology," writes the following. "I offer here a capsule history for the many uninformed Christians and for the fewer but also uninformed Jews. This brief survey glances at the longest-lasting persecution of one religious group by another in the entire history of mankind.

With imperial power in church (sic) hands at the close of the fourth century, repressive civil and social legislation began. This legislation has been compared, not incorrectly, with the Nuremberg laws of Hitler's Germany. The Church laws were not so efficiently enforced as under Hitler so Jews could move and manage in this unsettled and shifting world of the early Christian era.

Large scale atrocities did not begin until the Crusades which lasted from the 12th to the 14th centuries. These " pilgrimages" were designed by Church and state leaders (kings, nobles, knights) to attack the growing Moslem power, to gather booty and conquer territory and thus also deal with the problem of unrest and excess population among the poor.

Jews early on became victims, losing life and property. The Crusaders themselves were slaughtered or killed off by disease as they attacked the Moslem forces in the East. At least a hundred thousand, probably more Christians died.

Survivors brought back the bubonic plague. The plague killed an estimated one third of the population of Europe.

This Black Death was attributed to a conspiracy of Jews who were accused of poisoning the wells in order to exterminate their Christian oppressors. That Jews died along with Christians did not diminish the accusations. Perhaps Jewish deaths may have been somewhat fewer in proportion, some writer guessed, because of their religious rite of hand washing and ritual cleansing...

Crimes against Jews included, not only the common ones of robbery, looting, extortion and blackmail, but the more serious ones of book and synagogue burning , rape, forced mass conversion and the abduction of children to be brought up as Catholic. Accusations of desecration of the host (regarded as the body of Christ), accusations of ritual murder (killing a Christian child for blood for the Passover) were used to extract " confessions" by torture. These "confessions" justified their being burned at the stake or otherwise put to death.

Expulsion was a popular method in the Middle Ages by means of which nobles and kings could confiscate Jewish property and cancel debts which were owed...There is a letter dated 1349 from Charles IV of Bohemia to his friend the Margrave of Bradenburg promising him three Jewish houses when the next massacre of Jews takes place.

Wherever and whenever Jews had been left in peace, they prospered. Their generally high level of civilization, their education, sobriety, chaste family life and their industrous habits brought them material gain. But their prosperity was also their misfortune.

The peasants, often semi-Christianized, illiterate and barbarous resented them. The lessons of the Church Fathers which had filtered down to them through the priests and monks had taught them that Jews were an accursed deicide people destined to suffer misery and enslavement for not accepting Jesus as Savior. Inflamed often by ignorant and superstitious monks, they would fall upon the defenseless Jews to bring them to the state of misery prescribed for them by the Church Fathers.

During the barbarous Middle Ages-which for Jews lasted until well after Hitler's twentieth century-they were exposed to mob attacks; women were raped; whole communities were slain or burned alive; children were sold into slavery.

The ghetto was another form of persecution which church and state employed. The Church was always uneasy that contact with Jews might unsettle the faith of the still nominal Christians. It was a form of enslavement as well. When Jews did go out of the ghetto gates (which were locked at night) they were forced to wear a distinguishing "Jew Badge," usually yellow, a conical hat and a covering garment which set them apart."[98]

I quoted the entire passage because it is quite possible that many Christians are unaware of the extent of Jewish suffering. What most Jewish people are unaware of is that these crimes were not perpetrated by Christians. The Church that is repeatedly referred to is the Roman Catholic Church. The Roman Catholic

---

[98] *A Jew Examines Christianity* Pages 102-3

Church is in many ways closer theologically to Judaism then it is to Biblical Christianity.

I have met and maintained close relationships with many Roman Catholics. I know a dozen Roman Catholics who are born-again believers. These people have stayed in the Roman Church and continue to worship there. They have come to embrace the truth of God's grace, more in spite of the teachings of the Church than because of the teachings of the Church.

I do not think a week has gone by when I did not meet a believer in a fundamental evangelical church who had a Roman Catholic background. These folks refer to themselves as former Catholics. They will tell you that Catholicism is not Christianity. They became Christians and came out of the Roman church.

Recently I was involved in an impromptu debate with a neighborhood priest. And although there were many areas of agreement between us, the areas of disagreement were clear and distinct. We differed on the role of the Bible as authority. We differed on the sacraments, on Mary, and the saints. However the big area of disagreement was in the subject of soteriology. The priest believed that there were many roads to God. The priest believed in works over faith, and the priest did not believe that a person could be certain of eternal life.

We believe that man is depraved. In his depravity, man is capable of hideous crimes. We believe that upon the confession of faith, the Holy Spirit of the Living God enters into a man. That man becomes a new creature in Christ. The old sin nature continues to exist. However, a community of Spirit-filled believers would be expected to produce the works of God. A thousand years of atrocities do not reflect the work of the Holy Spirit. The aforementioned anti-Semitic actions reflect the work of the old sin nature. It is the product of men who have not made that profession of faith, men who are not Christians.

Martin Luther

The Protestant Reformation in Germany was inaugurated by Martin Luther in 1517. In 1521 Pope Leo X issued a Bill of Excommunication against Luther because he refused to recant his position. Luther had become a born-again Christian. Martin Luther is a subject that is difficult to respond to. He was a man of like precious faith and yet he practiced anti-Semitism. The actual personal crimes he perpetrated, encouraged, or allowed are terrible. But they are not nearly as damaging as the subsequent results of his prolific writings.

This hostility of Luther is what happens when Jewish people do not respond to the Gospel. Rosenburg writes, "Luther...was initially very kind to the Jews. He had his reason. His view of the future foresaw that the Jewish people would convert to Christianity en masse and thus hasten the return of Jesus. Frustrated when they refused to convert in the early years of the Reformation, he turned on them, and by the end of his life wrote the vilest statements against the Jews. Many of Luther's anti-Semitic lines have been quoted by Protestants for over 400 years. They were even used by Julius Streicher as part of his defense in the Nuremberg trials."[99]

Friends of Israel has been involved in a ministry in Northeast Philadelphia that is reaching out to the Russian speaking Jewish people. In response to some of the programs being conducted in the area, the Jewish community brought in a professional "anti-missionary" to address the issues of Jews believing in Jesus. Rather than present any Scriptural evidence, the Rabbi who spoke spent most of the time discussing the motives and the methods of Christian evangelicals. The Rabbi mentioned the same kind of things that Rosenburg wrote of. Both think that evangelicals want to see Jewish people respond to the Gospel to hasten the return of Jesus. And both thought that the Christian's love for the Jewish person is either feigned or superficial. Both state that the love is merely temporary, and if the Jewish person does not respond to the Gospel, then the loving behavior will quickly sour and be replaced by open hostility.

I have never known an evangelical Christian who witnessed to Jewish people to hasten the Lord's return. Instead, they are motivated by true love and obedience. Many believers have maintained their love and their witness to Jewish people in spite of

---

[99] *The Christian Problem* Page. 90-91

years of rejection. Believers do not turn hostile to a Jewish person because of rejection. Yet that is what Martin Luther has apparently done, adding fuel to anti-Semitism. Some people attempt to apologize for Martin Luther, others try to explain his behavior, and still others deny that he was a true believer. Some have pointed out that he repented of his crimes before he died. With all of that we are still left with the glaring results of Martin Luther's actions. Martin Luther is a rare exception. His activity towards the Jewish people is in contradiction to the Scriptures that he believed and taught.

Our lives should always evidence the truth that is within us. Christianity is a faith based on the Scriptures. Christians will and do disobey the Scriptures that they believe. That disobedience will detract from the appearance of the faith. But that disobedience in no way diminishes the reality of the faith. Christianity relies on the prophetic Scriptures. These Scriptures establish and commend a Messiah to us. Christianity relies on the impeccable credentials of Jesus to be that Messiah. Christianity is based solely on the historical Jesus and on His finished work. Christianity is not based on the work of the believers.

The "Protocols"

According to the Compton's encyclopedia, the 'Protocols of the Elders of Zion' was first published in Russia in 1905, and was the secret minutes of the first Zionist Congress, a false document purporting to reveal Jewish plans to dominate the world. It was used in Nazi Germany as anti-Semitic propaganda. According to Rachel Zurer "The protocols forgery began more than a hundred years ago. In 1868, a German post office worker, discredited for his part in a forgery scandal turned to a novel writing under the name of Sir John Retcliffe instead of his own name Hermann Goedsche.

He wrote a fantastic antisemitic (sic) tale in which he had twelve men of the twelve tribes of Israel having their usual centennial meeting in a Jewish cemetery in Prague. Their plan to conquer the world is relayed to the devil who is naturally present.

255

He will spread the news to worldwide Jewry to execute the strategies."

Then Goedsche found a satire called *Dialogue in Hell* published in 1864 written by a French lawyer Maurice Joly who deplored the politics of Napoleon III. He saw that he could plagiarize and use it. These dialogues, purporting to be between the shades of Montesquieu and Machiavelli, has Machiavelli justifying control of the press, repressive measures, financial maneuverings, relations with the Vatican and other presumably unsavory actions which Napoleon III is engaging in Goedsche now reworded the *Dialogue* to pretend that Jews not Napoleon III, were planning these measures...

Goedsche turned his fiction into a presumably factual account in which he has a rabbi make a speech at a convocation of Jews in Lemberg , using all the *Dialogue* material to make it seem like a Jewish plan for world conquest.

Other antisemites (sic) used as a setting the actual meeting of Jews at the 1897 World Jewish Congress of Zionists who sought to find a haven from the pogroms and persecutions they were suffering from the actions of just such antisemites (sic) as Goedsche. By setting the supposed conspiracy meeting at an actual place(Basle, Switzerland) the antisemites (sic) gave the forgery an appearance of verisimilitude...

The material came into the hands of a religious fanatic, a Russian, Serge Nilus, who had written a pamphlet on the Anti-Christ. It was published in Russian was used to foment anti-Jewish riots and pogroms at the time of the Tsar's autocratic rule was crumbling.

The strategy of the *Protocols* was, and still is, a plan to incite hatred and fear of the " all powerful" menacing conspiracy of worldwide Jewry. It was used during the Dreyfus affair at the end of the nineteenth century; it was used in Russia; it was even used in the United States after the disorganization and fears following the first World War, but here there was strong opposition to this shocking hoax.

Hitler made maximum use of this forgery. It was disseminated almost all over the world, translated in every tongue. And in 1967, a new Arabic translation was made in Cairo after the Six Day War...

This conspiracy hoax which was discovered by an English reporter stationed in Constantinople in 1921... has been described as "ridiculous nonsense" by a Swiss judge, has been proved over and over to be utterly false, malicious and stupid, yet has continued to be kept alive like an evil jinni to be evoked wherever there is need to vilify innocent Jews.

In the case of the Protocols the intent was malign. In the case of a missionary who devotedly carries his New Testament with him, the intent is benign. Unfortunately his book contains malign matter in the crucifixion drama and in its vilification of Jews."[100]

Christianity teaches that man is basically evil, and the anti-Semitic behavior we have seen is further evidence of the reality of Christian theology. Rachel Zurer equates the Protocols to the crucifixion account in the New Testament. The glaring difference is that the Protocols are totally fictitious, and the crucifixion is a fact of history.

We love the Jewish people. But that love does not mean that we are going to lie, or change history to defend them. The enemies of the Jews have lied and attempted to change history so that they might attack the character of the Jewish people. The Gentiles who have perpetrated these lies were not Christians.

The Protocols serve as another example of the truth of the doctrine of depravity. The Gentiles who have denied the Gospel are behaving exactly as Christian theology pictures them as behaving. When a person who has denied the Gospel exhibits the truth of the Gospel, that should be a reason to believe the Gospel, not an excuse to deny it.

The Pogroms

Compton's Encyclopedia describes a Pogrom as "a massacre of unarmed civilians, especially of Jews in prewar Russia; in the Russian pogroms of 1903 and 1905 thousands were killed or

---

[100] *A Jew Examines Christianity* Pages 103-105

tortured." Because the last of the Pogroms occurred over 90 years ago, there are not many who can still remember them. However, the Russian-speaking Jewish people who have come to the United States are often children of those who experienced the terror of the Pogroms first hand. These folks believe that by coming to America, they escaped what would have been the Pogroms of the 1990's. Many of these people never had the advantages of a Jewish education. They know very little of the Jewish traditions. Yet they have a grand pride of their heritage. Often they are reluctant to embrace the truth of Christianity because of their fierce pride of being Jews.

The Jewish people are the chosen people of God. Their uniqueness should flow from their relationship with Him. Becoming a Christian fulfills their destiny. They then have the relationship with the Creator that their nation was designed to enjoy. Any appreciation of their heritage or culture is empty if it does not stem from an association with the living God. There is no advantage either from birthright, or from national culture, if they cannot enjoy a closeness with the King.

The pogroms were another example of Satan working his plot to destroy Israel through the hatred of the unbelievers. Those who perpetrated these atrocities were not Christians. The memory of the pogroms might serve to foster Jewish identity; that identity should never be used as a reason to ignore the truth. The awareness of a Jewish identity should drive a Jewish person to seek the truth so that he would draw closer to the Lord.

The Holocaust

Concerning the Holocaust, Compton's Encyclopedia writes the following article:

" 'Death seemed to guard all exits.' This motto defined the fate of millions of Europeans between 1941 and 1945. As Nazi Germany gained control of one country after another in World War II, there was much killing of civilians and maltreatment of soldiers that can be classified as war crimes. These crimes, however, pale in comparison to the massive, deliberate, and well-planned extermination of more than 15 million persons in what is termed the Holocaust. This genocide of staggering proportions was carried out with scrupulous efficiency by a well-coordinated German bureaucracy in which nothing was left to chance."

The tragedy of the Holocaust is both spiritual and physical. The physical loss of millions of lives has caused millions of others to doubt the existence of an all powerful and loving God. That makes the task of calling people to God rather difficult. And because most Jewish people assume that the holocaust is the product of Christianity, they are very reluctant to believe.

In Deuteronomy we read how the Lord will one day remove the Jewish people from Israel to every kingdom of the earth. God chose the Jewish people and made a contract with them. The contract was to give them rules for life, and to give them their own homeland. As long as the people obeyed the rules that God gave them, God agreed to bless them and to protect them in the land. In Deuteronomy the Lord warns the people that in the future if they disobey Him, they will be removed from the land of Israel. Deuteronomy continues to describe the circumstances and the horrors of the Holocaust.

Deuteronomy 28:25-62, *25 The LORD shall cause thee to be smitten before thine enemies: thou shalt go out one way against them, and flee seven ways before them: and shalt be removed into all the kingdoms of the earth. 26 And thy carcase shall be meat unto all fowls of the air, and unto D will smite thee with the botch of Egypt, and with the emerods, and with the scab, and with the itch, whereof thou canst not be healed. 28 The LORD shall smite thee with madness, and blindness, and astonishment of heart: 29 And thou shalt grope at noonday, as the blind gropeth in darkness, and thou shalt not prosper in thy ways: and thou shalt be only oppressed and spoiled evermore, and no man shall save thee. 30 Thou shalt betroth a wife, and another man shall lie with her: thou shalt build an house, and thou shalt not dwell therein: thou shalt plant a vineyard, and shalt not gather the grapes thereof. 31 Thine ox shall be slain before thine eyes, and thou shalt not eat thereof: thine ass shall be violently taken away from before thy face, and shall not be restored to thee: thy sheep shall be given unto thine enemies, and thou shalt have none to rescue them. [32] Thy sons and thy daughters shall be given unto another people, and thine eyes shall look, and fail with longing for them all the day long: and there shall be no might in thine hand. [33] The fruit of thy land, and all thy labours, shall a nation which thou knowest not eat up; and thou shalt be only oppressed and crushed alway: [34] So that thou shalt be mad for the sight of thine eyes which thou shalt see. [35] The LORD shall smite thee in the knees, and in the legs, with a sore botch that cannot be healed, from the sole of thy foot unto the top of thy head. [36] The LORD shall bring thee, and thy king which thou shalt set over thee, unto a nation which neither thou nor thy fathers have known; and there shalt thou serve other gods, wood and stone. [37] And thou shalt become an astonishment, a proverb, and a byword, among all nations whither the LORD shall lead thee. [38] Thou shalt carry much seed out into the field, and shalt gather but little in; for the locust shall consume it. [39] Thou shalt plant vineyards, and dress them, but shalt neither drink of the wine, nor gather the grapes; for the worms shall eat them. [40] Thou shalt have olive trees throughout all thy coasts, but thou shalt not anoint thyself with the oil; for thine olive shall cast his fruit. [41] Thou shalt beget sons and daughters, but thou shalt not enjoy them; for they shall go into captivity. [42] All thy trees and fruit of thy land shall the locust consume. [43] The stranger that is within thee shall get up above thee very high; and thou shalt come down very low. [44] He shall lend to thee, and thou shalt not lend to him: he shall be the head, and thou shalt be the tail.*

[45] Moreover all these curses shall come upon thee, and shall pursue thee, and overtake thee, till thou be destroyed; because thou hearkenedst not unto the voice of the LORD thy God, to keep his commandments and his statutes which he commanded thee: [46] And they shall be upon thee for a sign and for a wonder, and upon thy seed for ever. [47] Because thou servedst not the LORD thy God with joyfulness, and with gladness of heart, for the abundance of all things; [48] Therefore shalt thou serve thine enemies which the LORD shall send against thee, in hunger, and in thirst, and in nakedness, and in want of all things: and he

shall put a yoke of iron upon thy neck, until he have destroyed thee. [49] The LORD shall bring a nation against thee from far, from the end of the earth, as swift as the eagle flieth; a nation whose tongue thou shalt not understand; [50] A nation of fierce countenance, which shall not regard the person of the old, nor shew favour to the young: [51] And he shall eat the fruit of thy cattle, and the fruit of thy land, until thou be destroyed: which also shall not leave thee either corn, wine, or oil, or the increase of thy kine, or flocks of thy sheep, until he have destroyed thee. [52] And he shall besiege thee in all thy gates, until thy high and fenced walls come down, wherein thou trustedst, throughout all thy land: and he shall besiege thee in all thy gates throughout all thy land, which the LORD thy God hath given thy sons and of thy daughters, which the LORD thy God hath given thee, in the siege, and in the straitness, wherewith thine enemies shall distress thee: [54] So that the man that is tender among you, and very delicate, his eye shall be evil toward his brother, and toward the wife of his bosom, and toward the remnant of his children which he shall leave: [55] So that he will not give to any of them of the flesh of his children whom he shall eat: because he hath nothing left him in the siege, and in the straitness, wherewith thine enemies shall distress thee in all thy gates. [56] The tender and delicate woman among you, which would not adventure to set the sole of her foot upon the ground for delicateness and tenderness, her eye shall be evil toward the husband of her bosom, and toward her son, and toward her daughter, [57] And toward her young one that cometh out from between her feet, and toward her children which she shall bear: for she shall eat them for want of all things secretly in the siege and straitness, wherewith thine enemy shall distress thee in thy gates. [58] If thou wilt not observe to do all the words of this law that are written in this book, that thou mayest fear this glorious and fearful name, THE LORD THY GOD; [59] Then the LORD will make thy plagues wonderful, and the plagues of thy seed, even great plagues, and of long continuance, and sore sicknesses, and of long continuance. [60] Moreover he will bring upon thee all the diseases of Egypt, which thou wast afraid of; and they shall *cleave unto thee. [61] Also every sickness, and every plague, which is not written in the book of this law, them will the LORD bring upon thee, until thou be destroyed. [62] And ye shall be left few in number, whereas ye were as the stars of heaven for multitude; because thou wouldest not obey the voice of the LORD thy God.*

There are four facts about the Holocaust. First, the Nazis were not Christians, they did not believe the Scriptures, and they were not following Scriptural instructions. Second, the Lord did show his marvelous grace in that in spite of the attempt at total annihilation of the Jewish people the Lord still preserved them. There is still a nation of Israel to whom He will one day return to establish the Messianic kingdom. Third, out of the horror of the ashes of the Holocaust the modern day nation of Israel has blossomed. The prophecy of the Jewish people returning to their homeland has miraculously come to pass. The prophetic truth of the Scriptures are proving the word to indeed be the word of God. Fourth, the same Scriptures that predicted the restoration of the land of Israel also predict the horrors of the Holocaust. Because God predicted the events of the Holocaust, it is unreasonable to doubt the existence of God on the basis of those same events.

The Holocaust also introduces another issue, and that is the existence of suffering. The fact that there is suffering on the planet is an apologetic problem. It is not necessarily an objection from a strictly Jewish perspective, however. No amount of explaining can ever alleviate the tremendous suffering that took place in the Holocaust, or on the planet.

We can deduce answers to "what," "when," "where," and sometimes "how" from the scriptures, but "why" is in the counsel of the Triune God, and unless clearly stated we are out of our realm. However, in defense of the faith, we must attempt to postulate some of the possible motives of the Creator. Above, under the heading God's righteousness, we discussed some feasible reasons for permitting the existence of evil. Now we will try to explain why God would allow that evil to function in the lives of "good people."

The Bible does predict and show some causes for suffering, if not reasons. The following study outline may be of some help as an apologetic to the suffering problem.

A. The problem

1. Order and goodness in the universe argue for the existence of God.

2. Disorder and suffering argue against God's existence and character.

3. The Scriptural teaching regarding Satan does not remove the philosophical problem God is still in control.

4. The Scriptures, however, do open to us possible reasons for allowing evil to enter the universe.

B. Suffering in Individuals

1. The lost

a. to bring them to God. 2 Peter 3:9 *The Lord is not willing that any should perish, but that all should come to repentance.*

b. to punish unrighteousness. John 3:36 *he that believeth not the Son shall not see life; but the wrath of God abideth on him.*

c. the outworking of Biblical principals. Proverbs 4:19 *The way of the wicked is as darkness: they know not at what they stumble.*

d. to display god's glory and power. John 9:3 *Jesus answered, Neither hath this man sinned, nor his parents: but that the works of God should be made manifest in him.*

2. The saved

a. to make Jesus known 2 Corinthians 4:11 *For we which live are alway delivered unto death for Jesus' sake, that the life also of Jesus might be made manifest in our mortal flesh.*

b. life to others 2 Corinthians 4:12 *So then death worketh in us, but life in you.*

c. to manifest grace 2 Corinthians 4:15 *For all things are for your sakes, that the abundant grace might through the thanksgiving of many redound to the glory of God.*

d. to edify us Romans 8:28 *And we know that all things work together for good to them that love God, to them who are the called according to his purpose.*

C. Suffering in Nations

   1. The גוים (Goyim)

      a. the treatment of Israel Genesis 12:3 *and curse him that curseth thee: and in thee shall all families of the earth be blessed.*

      b. the working of iniquity Jeremiah 48:7 *For because thou hast trusted in thy works and in thy treasures, thou shalt also be taken*

   2. The Nation of Israel

      a. Biblical times (national disobedience)

      b. Times of the Gentiles (rejection of Messiah)

The Behavior of Christians Today

Most Conversions are Psychological

This is a common belief that many Jewish people have. To this day my family believes that I came to Christianity because I suffered a psychological trauma in Vietnam. I was a cook in Vietnam. I saw more combat in Chicago's O'Hare airport on the way home than I did in the thirteen months that I spent in Vietnam. Levine writes that most people who accept Jesus do so for psychological reasons.[101] The assumption is that there are no intellectual or theological reasons for a person to believe in Jesus. Unfortunately this is only Levine's opinion. He offers no surveys and no statistics to back up his statement. He says that Christians are people who have problems and need a "Big Daddy." My question is, even if that were true, how is it that Judaism offers no comfort? Is Judaism the religion for those who have no spiritual needs?

---

[101] *You Take Jesus, I'll Take God.* pg. 11

262

One of the shop keepers I visit often refers to believers as members of the sect. He jokingly points out any problems they exhibit when they are anxious or upset. He does, however, have the same lack of esteem for the religious Jew as he does for the Christian. He sees every religion as a crutch. I agree with him. What he does not recognize is that all men are crippled.

A Messianic congregation having many Yuppie types also had a family with a "special" adolescent son. He was visibly different. This congregation practiced a Davidic style of worship and during the service there was a time for dancing. The circular dancing was always in good taste and because the worship team was concerned about the image of the Congregation the dancing was practiced ahead of time. The "special" young man didn't understand that the dancing was done by the worship team members only. He only knew that it was a way of expressing his joy before the Lord. Many members were concerned about their image. They were afraid that people would get the wrong idea when they saw this "special" youth up front. They thought that he was a poor representation of their faith. I thought that he was a trophy of God's grace. I was thankful for the fact that he felt comfortable in our midst. I didn't care much for the carefully choreographed entertainment / worship. But I rejoiced to see him lift up his holy hands before the Lord. He and his family probably wouldn't be very welcome at most synagogues.

It is interesting that when we speak of the need for blood, the Jewish argument is that the right attitude is all that is needed. When we exhibit the proper attitude it is an evidence of psychological weakness. There are probably many Christians who have psychological problems. We confess that God has chosen the foolish and the weak of the world. However, that in no way detracts from the massive evidence that exists for the certainty of the faith.

Emotionally Depressed Converts

This is similar to the previous attack, only a bit more direct and specific. In this discussion Rachel Zurer actually mentions a few people by name.[102] One person she discusses is Edith Stein. Edith was born Jewish and later in life embraced the Catholic religion. Becoming a Catholic she could have escaped death, but she chose to identify with her people and died at Auschwitz. I don't know enough about Edith to testify to her faith. However, the only evidence of emotional instability is her faith. Once a Jewish person believes in Jesus, he or she is deemed emotionally unstable. Hence only emotionally unstable people believe in Jesus. Edith Stein chose a heroic and selfless act. If she had chosen to survive the Holocaust, she would have been labeled a coward and an anti-Semite. Since she has identified with her heritage, she has been called emotionally unstable because of her faith.

Turn the Other Cheek

In *The Real Messiah* Kaplan complains that the Christian teaching is not practiced, and that Christians are among the most "hawkish" of people. Kaplan has proven repeatedly that he has no idea who a Christian is. Like most Jewish people Kaplan believes that all Gentiles are Christians. Christians might be the most docile people in the community, and Kaplan would not know them because he does not see the real Christians. However, even if it were true, and it could be shown that Christians as a rule do not follow the teachings of Jesus in their personal lives, that fact would not detract from the authenticity of the teachings of Jesus.

Millions of lives have been supernaturally changed by believing the gospel. If some lives and some incidents do not display that supernatural change, that does not mean that the rest of the lives were never changed. The question isn't why the few haven't changed. The question is, how do you explain the power that changed those that did?

With any discussion of Christian testimony, it must always be remembered that Christianity depends upon the historicity of Jesus and not on the testimony of His followers. Our lives can lend evidence to the authenticity of his, but we cannot detract from the truth.

---

[102] *A Jew Examines Christianity*, Pg. 149

No Law

According to Kaplan, Christians do not keep the law.[103] Of course 91% of the Jewish people do not even make an effort to keep the law either. However, Christians believe that the Holy Spirit is guiding them. In Matthew 5:17-18 we read *Think not that I am come to destroy the law, or the prophets: I am not come to destroy, but to fulfil. For verily I say unto you, Till heaven and earth pass, one jot or one tittle shall in no wise pass from the law, till all be fulfilled.* Jesus is referring to the eternality of the Old Testament Scriptures as in the following verses: Exodus 40:15 *And thou shalt anoint them, as thou didst anoint their father, that they may minister unto me in the priest's office: for their anointing shall surely be an everlasting priesthood throughout their generations.* Leviticus 16:34 *And this shall be an everlasting statute unto you, to make an atonement for the children of Israel for all their sins once a year. And he did as the LORD commanded Moses.* Leviticus 24:8 *Every sabbath he shall set it in order before the LORD continually, being taken from the children of Israel by an everlasting covenant.* These verses indicate an eternal Priesthood, and an eternal sacrifice, and an eternal sabbath. However, when we read Hosea 3:4-5 *For the children of Israel shall abide many days without a king, and without a prince, and without a sacrifice, and without an image, and without an ephod, and without teraphim: Afterward shall the children of Israel return, and seek the LORD their God, and David their king; and shall fear the LORD and his goodness in the latter days,* we can plainly see that the Priesthood and the sacrifice are only temporal. The phrase translated everlasting really means "to the end of the age."

The covenant that the Lord made with the Jewish people at Mount Sinai was already broken by the time the book of Jeremiah was written. Jeremiah teaches that there will be a new covenant, where the believers live by the power of the Spirit. In Biblical times the Jewish people were set apart from the nations by the way

---

[103] *The Real Messiah* Pg. 47

they dressed and the foods they ate. Today we must manifest our distinction by they way we live.

Christians rarely live the life they should, but usually there is more evidence of reality in a Christian life than we realize. The Holy Spirit does make a difference. Although the Word of God is eternal, the Mt. Sinai contract was temporal. When it can be shown that Christians are more honest, more sincere, more humble, kinder, etc., it softens the complaint of lawlessness.

Glossary of Terms

Bar Mitzvah -"The literal meaning is 'son of the commandment.' It is a religious ceremony at which time the Jewish lad of thirteen becomes a member of and assumes his inherent responsibilities to the Jewish community."[104]

Bobeh - Grandmother

Chassid -" (pl. Chassidim; adj.. Chassidic) The word itself means " pious" in actual reference it is a follower or a member of the Chassidic movement which was founded by Israel Baal Shem Tov in the 18th century... still practiced by numerous small groups."[105]

Flaishik -pertaining to meat, or meat dishes

Gefilte fish -Filleted fish, chopped fine, stuffed, and seasoned with various spices. Usually served as a separate course for the Sabbath or Seder meal. Takes on the same place as the Chinese egg roll, and can be thought of as a Jewish meatloaf made from white fish.

Goyim -plural of the word Goy, which means Gentile, or non Jew

Haftorah -portion of the Old Testament, but not from one of the first five books. A different Haftorah portion is read each week at the Saturday service.

High holidays -The holiday of Rosh Hashanah, the holiday of Yom Kippur, and the ten days between them.

Kabbalah -from the Hebrew קבל (qbl) to receive. It refers to Jewish mystical writings.

Kipporah -from the Hebrew כפר (kfr) to make an atonement, to cover.

Kosher -"Food prepared according to Jewish ritual law. Relates to the slaughter of animals, preparation of food and dietary regulations."[106]

---

[104] *Encyclopedia of Jewish Humor* Jonathan David Publishers 1969 Henry Spalding p. 448
[105] Ibid. p. 449
[106] Ibid. p. 452

Massoretic text -Old testament Hebrew text standardized by the Massorites, Jewish textual scribes of the fifth through ninth centuries C.E. Refers to a particular translation of the Old Testament

Meshumad -A Yiddish word משומד An apostate Jewish person who has been Baptized

Midrash -"A Hebrew term meaning 'investigation' or 'study,' and applies to a special type of broad interpretation of the biblical text. These are devotional and ethical in character and illustrate the literal text of the Bible and its allegories."[107]

Milchik -"Dairy; pertaining to dairy foods, to the cooking utensils in which they are prepared and to the dishes and cutlery used in serving them.[108]"

Minyon -A quorum of ten Jewish men needed before Torah services can be started. (Women have now been accepted to make up a minyon)

Mishnah -The oral tradition believed to have been given at Sinai.

Mitzvah -a Hebrew word מצוה Literally means commandment, but has come to refer to all good works.

Pesedic -Pertaining to the holiday of Passover, as well as all foods that would be kosher for Passover, foods that contain no leaven, and have been kept free from any possible leaven contamination.

Shabbos -Yiddish for Saturday, the Sabbath

Shiva -Hebrew word for seven. Refers to the seven days of mourning that a Jewish family will keep immediately after the burial of a loved one.

Skull cap -An expression for the religious hat worn by practicing Jewish men.

Tenak -A reference for the Hebrew Bible (Old Testament). Made up by combining the first letters of each of the three words that name the three sections. **Torah** (the law) **Nevihim** (the prophets), and **Kethuvim** (the writings).

---

[107] Ibid. p 453
[108] Ibid.

Teshuva -From the Hebrew word שׁוּב (shuv) to return. It refers to repentance, to return, to turn to God.

Torah -The first five books of the Bible.

Yarmulke -The traditional head cap worn by practicing Jewish men.

Yenteh -"Someone who sticks her nose into everyone else's business, a busybody; a gossip and tattle-tale.[109]"

Yiddin -A term in Yiddish for the Jewish people

Yom Kippur -The day of atonement. Considered by many to be the most sacred day in the Jewish year.

---

[109] Ibid. p 457